The Marine Fish and Invert Reef Aquarium

The Optimum Aquarium for the Reef Hobbyist Series

Albert J. Thiel

Also Author of :

Advanced Reef Keeping Made Simple (1989) 425+ pp
Small Reef Aquarium Basics (1989) 176 pp
The Trickle Filter (1990) 100 pp
Advanced Reef Keeping II : The Lifeforms(1990)
Marine Reef : the Newsletter

Published by :

Aardvark Press
A division of Thiel•Aqua•Tech Inc.

D1625522

0 0909

Published by Aardvark Press
a division of Thiel•Aqua•Tech
575 Broad Street
Bridgeport CT 06604

Telephone : (203) 368 2111
Telefax : (203) 367 5872

Original Title :
© 1988 A. Thiel
The Marine Fish and Invert Reef Aquarium
Printings 1 through 6
XXXXIIM-88.89

**7th completely revised and up-dated printing
1990 Aardvark Press**

The material in this 7th printing of
The Marine Fish and Invert Reef Aquarium
has been completely re-worked
and re-set using a

MacInstosh Portable ®

Aldus Pagemaker ® 3.02
Aldus Freehand ® 2.0
Microsoft Word 4.0 ®
and an
Apple ® Laserwriter Plus

ISBN 0-945777-04-3

Product Number UPC-A   0 09091 70100 1

7th Printing March 1990

To
Roger Paro
Matthew Cammarata
Chuck Burge, Scott and Tim
Tom Giovanetti
Andy Labasch
Stan in Campbell
Paul Groome and Karen
Leo, Jeff and Brenda
Ken Howery, Linda and Junior
Andrew and Chico in Canada
Scott Dyer
John Tullock
Tom Sheley
Bob Boone,
Don Dewey
Robert and Alan in Brooklyn
The Pet Connection in Lavonia
Nancy's Animal House
Bill Damon III
John Brandt
Dick Boyd

and many many others too numerous
to list here.

and to FAMA for its many
outstanding contributions
to the Hobby

Photo Credit : Steve Ciuccoli

Foreword :

Although quite a few books on the subject of keeping marine fish, invertebrates, corals, as well as macro-algae already exist, and even though many articles have appeared in hobby magazines, there still exists a void in the area of the type of equipment to use on reef aquariums, and what the specific purpose of the many products offered for sale really is.

The literature void is even larger where it comes to sophisticated systems that utilize instruments and controllers to automate functions that the hobbyist has been accustomed to perform manually, mostly on fish-only tanks, before the advent of reef aquariums.

For years much of the equipment advocated was imported, until a few U.S. manufacturers decided to offer their own lines of marine reef duplicating systems and products. I am referring to companies such as Coralife, Energy Savers Unlimited, Marine Technical Concepts, Scott's True Reef, Thiel•Aqua•Tech, Lifereef Systems, Nautilus Aquatics (Canada), Summit Aquatics and many more.

A lot of the imported equipment suffered from the typical foreign product's syndrome: either no instructions, or badly translated ones. Such did not help much, of course, especially since the equipment we are talking about is by no means easy to install and use, and is certainly not inexpensive. Then again, it is quite sophisticated stuff.

On the positive side, the introduction of all this equipment, both foreign and U.S. made, allows the implementation of more novel ways of keeping tanks, especially the reef type ones we are concerned with in this book and which are growing in popularity very quickly.

Reef-like systems that are equipped with the right filters and devices allow each and every hobbyist to maintain vibrant looking tanks, providing the equipment is installed correctly, and providing also, that the hobbyist maintains the aquarium by adhering to a strict husbandry program of both the tank itself, and the equipment used.

Marine fish keeping still has a certain mystique attached to it. Why this should be so is not quite clear. Perhaps the reason is that many hobbyists think that the salt water side of the hobby is far more complicated than the fresh water one, or perhaps the perceived expense of getting into salt water aquariums and reefs is such, that hobbyists feel that they cannot afford to get into it.

Fortunately this is slowly changing. Articles published in magazines such as Marine Reef and Freshwater and Marine Aquarium (FAMA) are certainly one of the main reasons for this additional interest in keeping salt water aquariums, especially reef aquariums such as the ones described in this book. Marine Reef, the newsletter published by Aardvark Press, deals exclusively with reef aquariums and is highly recommended reading for any hobbyist wishing to maintain a reef system.

Still, a lot needs to change for the reef hobby to become as popular as it is in Europe. Knowledge on the part of the hobbyist and store owner / manager is, in my mind, where progress needs to be made. Store owners' interest has been growing very rapidly over the last year or so, and more and more reef products are finding their way into wholesalers and onto shelves in stores. Such is a very good sign.

Unfortunately, a lot of conflicting information is still found in magazines and heard at aquarium society meetings and in pet stores. This often leads to the appearance of hybrid systems, systems in which the hobbyist uses some of the technology of one manufacturer and mixes it with different types of technology from other manufacturers. This can only lead to a lot of confusion, especially when things go wrong, since who does one call then to get advice. Too many different approaches are mixed, often making it difficult for anyone to come up with a recommended solution to a problem the hobbyist may have.

It seems as if hobbyists are "buying insurance" against problems by mixing various approaches to keeping reef tanks. Such may seem like a good idea, but it is in reality not. Techniques used in one approach may be detracting from the efficiency of techniques used in another one. Ideally, you should stick with one approach that you find both believable, and can live with in terms of the labor involved, and the finances required to set it up.

Many approaches are designed to be synergistic, meaning all parts together produce more the sum of the individual components. Using only part of such a system is, therefore, not an efficient use of the approach. Mixing several approaches seems even less appropriate and when things go wrong, perhaps as a result of such hybridism, the hobbyist gets frustrated, and he or she may even decide to get out of the hobby altogether. Such is unfortunate and should not be so. Additionally, a lot of animal life and dollars will have been lost and wasted in the process.

Sadly enough, store owners and their personnel cannot always be relied on for sound advice. They too have a lot of catching up to do. Sometimes in their eagerness to make a sale, they may recommend products that the hobbyist does not really need, or substitute others for the ones requested. Such substitutions may not always be appropriate replacements for what the hobbyist intended to buy in the first place, and may in fact not perform the function that was necessary for the tank's water chemistry.

As a hobbyist in need of answers, you should, as a result, get a second opinion, and get more expert advice. As an analogy, when you buy a car, you go to the show room and buy from a car salesperson. When you have a problem with your car, however, you go to a mechanic, not the sales staff.

You should use the same approach when it comes to your tank. Find a knowledgeable person in a pet store, at a manufacturer's, or at an aquarium society, and discuss your problems with that person as well. Then make a decision. You will be a more educated consumer.

As long as you take the time and have the determination, you will find the answers to your questions without having to re-invent the wheel, sometimes at great expense.

This book, then, is an attempt to demystify the equipment and the instrumentation that is being advocated, and show you how it all fits into the holistic, "overall" that is, approach to keeping reef tanks. Knowing that the equipment exists is one thing, understanding how to use it, and what the technology behind it is - basically why does it work - is a different matter altogether, one we will explain to you in this book, where appropriate.

As time goes on, newer techniques and newer instruments will appear on the market. Therefore, even though this book is up-to-date as far as where the hobby stands today is concerned, you may wish to keep yourself informed of new developments by subscribing to the Marine Reef Newsletter, or similar publications, and by reading other books. A. Thiel published two more books in his Reef Series so far : Advanced Reef Keeping Made Simple (I), and Small Reef Aquarium Basics. Advanced Reef Keeping II : The Animals, is planned for June of 1990. Call Aardvark Press for more details if you need them, or if you want to order.

Applying the techniques advocated in this book will not only ensure that your tank looks vibrant, but it will give you much greater joy, while teaching you a lot about the marvelous environment that a reef aquarium is. It will also greatly reduce your fish and invertebrate losses, thus you will be contributing in a small way to the preservation of the natural reefs.

Acquiring all the instrumentation listed, and discussed, in this book at once, is obviously one way to go. More than likely, however, you will be buying it piecemeal, and improve the efficiency and automation of the aquarium, over a period of time. At least that is the experience we had, in the last five years, with people who have been buying Thiel• Aqua•Tech products and instruments. Complete reef aquariums are not inexpensive by any stretch of the imagination. Anyone getting into the hobby at this level, should therefore budget carefully.

We welcome any suggestions for additions and improvements

to this seventh completely revised and up-dated edition of : " The Marine Fish and Invert Reef Aquarium ". Send your letters to Aardvark Press, a division of Thiel•Aqua•Tech Inc. The book was completely rewritten over an 8 months period of time, and includes all information on the latest known requirements of reef aquariums as developped by Albert J. Thiel.

Those scientists, and other chemists, who read this book, will forgive me for having tried to keep the terminology used to the lay level. This book is intended as a guide, not as a text book. Reef keeping is an art, not a science. Not yet, anyway.

Albert J. Thiel

Notes Regarding the Seventh Printing :

The Marine Fish and Invert Reef Aquarium has gone through 6 printings already. Quite a feat for a book that deals with such advanced technology, and obviously a sign of the healthy interest that exists in reef aquariums and the technology needed, or recommended, to run them.

All six initial printings were materially the same, except for some changes in photographs and the correction of some typographical errors. The sixth printing contained a 32 page addendum with up-dates on various subjects, and a long article on marine macro-algae.

The seventh printing is a totally different book. It still incorporates what is to be found in printings one through six, but it is written in a different style, and includes a lot of new material as well. It is hoped that it covers the subject in a still more thorough and better organized fashion. As a result of all the changes and up-dates, we have given the book a new ISBN number. Copies of the original 6 printings are no longer available from the publisher, but may still be available form resellers.

Only 25 hardbound copies of the first printing are in circulation in hobby circles. All are signed and numbered, and are to be considered collector's items. Anyone wishing to sell such a hardbound edition can contact Aardvark Press, who will try to find a buyer for the book. A recent sale fetched $185.00 for a book that cost about $45.00 at the time it was purchased, about 15 months ago, in early 1988. Some hard bound copies of this 7th totally revised printing of the Marine Fish and Invert Reef Aquarium will also be made, and should be available towards July 1990. Call Aardvark Press for more details.

I hope you will enjoy reading this revised edition of the book as much as I enjoyed writing, or should I say re-writing, it. Anyone having questions regarding material contained in this issue may contact Albert J. Thiel, c/o Aardvark Press, 575 Broad Street, Bridgeport CT 06604, Telephone (203) 368 2111.

Information on Marine Reef, the newsletter on reef tanks, can be obtained there as well. We highly recommend it. Subscription pricing for one year, or the equivalent of 17 issues (about one every three weeks) is US $ 40.00. Stores should call for resale store pricing.

Albert Thiel has written two other books on reef tanks : Advanced Reef Keeping Made Simple (I), a 440 page book that describes how to easily set up highly sophisticated reef set-ups, and Small Reef Aquarium Basics, a 175 page book, that details how to run and set up a reef tank without automation. The latter book is a must for anyone who finds the level of this one a little too technical.

A fourth book is being completed : Advanced Reef Keeping II, a book that deals more specifically with the animals kept in the reef tank, and how to care for them. Advanced Reef Keeping II should be out in June 1990. Advance payments for that book are now being taken by Aardvark Press. Call them for more details, as advance orders for the first printing are large. Advanced Reef Keeping II is a hardbound book, with color photography, and its price is tentatively set at $ 34.99.

1. Introduction

In just a short 5 years, keeping fish and invertebrates together in a marine aquarium, has made a significant amount of progress, not only technologically, but also in terms of the number of hobbyists who either already maintain such aquariums, or show a real strong interest in doing so soon. Additionally, the variety of life forms now offered for sale has greatly increased, and because shipping methods have been improved upon as well, survival rates have risen dramatically.

Books by such recognized authors as Stephen Spotte, Martin Moe, Frank de Graaf, Peter Wilkens, Guido Hueckstedt, Albert Thiel, and many others, have, and are greatly contributing to spreading the knowledge required to keep sophisticated reef aquariums that utilize the available technology to its fullest extent. Aquarists everywhere have greatly benefited from the suggestions and techniques outlined, with the overall result that reef aquarium keeping is becoming a much more professional part of the hobby.

Although trial and error methods may still be advocated in certain reef keeping areas, overall, the ground rules are pretty well laid out and can easily be followed by hobbyists, providing they are willing to take the time to do so, and learn, mostly through reading, what kind of care and maintenance is required to run an optimum and vibrant looking reef aquarium.

Thanks to all the literature now available, the hobby has become more a little more of a science and a desire to perfect the tank is becoming more and more apparent at the hobbyist level. This is, of course, a good trend as it will result in animals living for longer in home aquariums, resulting in less depletion of the real reefs.

Manufacturers, noticing this desire to perfect the aquarium are now, more than ever, willing to invest in producing advanced equipment in the U.S.A. and Canada. This results in the prices of many of the required items coming down, which in turn allows more hobbyists to get into the reef keeping hobby, which is of course one of the reasons reef keeping now has become the fastest growing segment of the hobby.

The trend to perfect the aquarium is also helped by more restrictive legislation aimed at reducing reef depletion, or geared at stopping the collection of coral altogether, at least in certain areas. When animals (for example corals and other invertebrates) become more scarce, hobbyists will tend to invest more in their systems in an effort to keep the animals they already have alive for much longer periods of time. When the supply becomes scarcer, the sophistication of the systems increases. This reinforces the perception at the manufacturing level that investing in technology is a wise decision and results in more locally made equipment becoming available. Such is a good trend, as it greatly reduces the dependency on foreign products.

Such restrictive legislation has existed in several European countries for quite some time, and is now finding a larger resonance in this country in States such as Florida, California and Hawaii.. Anytime the availability of animals is restricted, hobbyists have to go to greater lengths to maintain what they have, or the limited supply they can buy. This is a very positive trend for the natural reefs.

Keeping animals alive for longer requires better technology, different equipment, and more dedication and care on the part of the hobbyist. Such is exactly what this book is all about : what equipment should you use, how should you use it, when does it become necessary, and how is it installed. Besides the information found in this book, you may also wish to read " Advanced Reef Keeping Made Simple (I) " A. Thiel (Aardvark Press, 1989), for even more details on really advanced systems.

This book can be read from front to back, or you can read selected passages that are of more interest to you. If, at first, some of the concepts described seem esoteric, keep reading, soon you will grasp the reasons for them, and you will start seeing the holistic picture that I referred to earlier. Reef keeping is not simple, but if you approach your tank as an ecosystem you will have much better long term results.

There is also a large section on macro-algae, completely updated, giving a great amount of detail on what should be done to keep these lovely marine "plants" looking in good shape and growing for the benefit of the water quality. And in reef tanks everything always boils down to the relative quality of the water chemistry. If the latter is good, the tank will look in good shape and you should have no problems. If the latter is not good, disease, parasites, and dying animals are just around the corner.

Obviously no book can be complete. We did not set out to teach you the basics of aquarium keeping. Many books on that subject already exist. You have probably read at least one, if not several already. If you need a refresher, we suggest that you go back to them and up-date your knowledge on the subjects where you feel you may need to do so. This book builds on your existing knowledge, especially to apply it to corals, invertebrates, macro-algae and fish for the reef aquarium.

Lighting is covered in the latter part of the book, and is a subject that is still open to a large amount of controversy. We will try to give you the various approaches that are advocated at the present time, together with our own recommendations, leaving you the option to go in several directions. Light is a most important part of a successful reef tank, and it should be taken very seriously.

Besides familiarizing yourself with what we have to say, you may also wish to read up on lighting some more in other books, for example in Martin Moe's **The Marine Aquarium Reference** : Systems and Invertebrates (Green Turtle Press, Plantation FL, 1989).

Because of the increased interest in redox potential, and the fact that many hobbyists are confronted, at some point, with the decision whether or not to acquire a unit that measure it, we have covered that subject in great detail, including equipment and methods that directly affect its level, for example the use of protein skimmers and ozone.

To keep a reef tank is to enjoy the beauty

of nature in your living room.

2. The Basics :

Setting up a reef tank is exciting. Looking at it will give you many hours of pleasure, no doubt about it. Maintaining a reef tank and taking the time to service both the aquarium and the equipment is, however, a task that cannot, and never should be taken lightly as it is both complex and necessary.

Many areas can become causes for concern if the aquarium is not well taken care of. Many imponderables may enter the picture, and many things can happen to your tank and its inhabitants that you cannot find an explanation for. It may very well be that no one can. Indeed, the seawater environment in your aquarium is an extremely complex system. Many chemical and biological reactions occur at the same time, and continuously, and affect the well being of all the animals in the tank. You may not have control over all of these reactions, but there are a great number over which you do.

We believe that we have covered the latter in this book in enough detail to give you the ability to be in control of your aquarium, and not the opposite. You must re-think your whole approach should the latter happen to you. It is not a good sign, and is likely to bring about problems down the road. "You" must be in charge.

2.1 The Aquarium :

Typically, the aquariums that you will contemplate buying are made of glass or acrylic material, the latter often referred to by one of its trade names : Plexiglass, Lucite, etc.

Whereas acrylic tanks are very popular nowadays, especially on the West Coast, and are gaining popularity in the East, glass tanks still constitute the majority of aquariums sold.

Which exact type that you decide to buy is not really material. You should, nevertheless, know the following about each type :

• Glass tanks are heavy, not as easy to drill, but do not scratch as easily as acrylic ones do. They are usually less expensive. Glass tanks, contrary to what you may think, can withstand quite a bit of abuse. Drilling them may seem like a chore, but it really isn't. Glass places in your area, or even some pet shops, will do so for you at a nominal cost.

Keep in mind that glass is fragile and must be handled with some care. The tank needs to be absolutely flat (level) when it is set up, especially if you are going to drill holes in the bottom plate. This prevents stress in the glass. Stress can lead to the tank rupturing. A most unpleasant experience. You need to ensure that it is level when you set it up. Once it is filled with water it is too late to do so. The tank will be too heavy to be moved, plus, the stress created may make the glass crack.

Glass tanks are held together with silicone glues. These glues have now been so perfected that they will hold for decades. Well made tanks have no air bubbles in the silicone joints. If you see such air bubbles, at least if there are too many of them, do not buy the tank. Look for a better made one if you can. Be fussy, you do not need sloppy work-manship on your aquarium.

Every type of glass, with the exception of tempered glass, can be drilled. If the glass is tempered, it will usually say so. A sticker will have been affixed by the manufacturer. Why you should want to drill holes in the bottom of the tank may not be clear to you now, but it will be, after you progress through a few more chapters of this book.

If you decide to make your own tank, which some hobbyists do, keep the above remarks in mind. Incidentally, silicone glue can be removed with Toluene or Xylene. These can be found in paint shops.

The thickness of the glass used in making the aquarium, is determined more by the top to bottom measurement, than by the length. Long tanks should preferably be braced across the top (front to back), to prevent bowing. Most tanks bow somewhat, but such should be minimal, and no reason for concern. Tanks that bow excessively may require a top brace, or may have to be taken out of service.

Because glass is easy to clean, it is often preferred for tanks where algal growth is expected. You can use razor blades to scrape off the algae from the glass, but if you are not careful, you will soon have scratches. Best is to use one of the many aquarium glass scrapers that are available in pet stores. Alternatively use crinoline, a plastic based fine mesh that is often used in dressmaking. It works very well and removes even the most stubborn algae without too much effort being required.

• Acrylic tanks are lighter, can very easily be drilled, have more complete tops (which may inhibit light going into the tank some-what), and scratch more easily than I personally care for. Because they are light, they are easier to move around and work with when setting them up. A 300 gallon tank, for instance, made out of 1" acrylic such as the ones manufactured by BioZone, can be moved by 4 people without too much difficulty.

Scratches on the outside can be removed rather easily with special compounds that are available (buffing compounds). It is when scratches appear on the inside that problems come about. They can only be removed after the water level has been lowered. Such is not a task that most hobbyists look forward to, or want to have to deal with.

Acrylic warps easily. Tanks must be braced, and usually are. Tall tanks must be made out of thick acrylic, lest they will balloon. Some bonding agents used in constructing these tanks blush over time, making unsightly marks around the edges. Some acrylic, especially the imported brands, are of real poor quality and are not suited for aquarium use. If you decide to build your own, get only US made quality. I prefer Dupont's Lucite®. Ask for it specifically.

Because of the way acrylic aquariums are braced, they may

restrict the light going into the tank. This may not be apparent right from the start, but will become a problem after salt deposits settle on the underside (tank side) of the top braces. You should, therefore, watch for such deposits, and remove them on a regular basis (clean).

• I have used both types, and have no real personal preference at this point. I used to lean towards the glass tank, but have lately seen some real high quality work in the acrylic variety as well. It is therefore a personal judgment call that you must make. Talk to some other hobbyists, or pet stores, and get their opinion as well. BioZone, a relatively new company, in Bridgeport Ct, does some real fine work. So does Summit Aquatics of Fulton, Mo.

Acrylic is easy to drill. All you will need is a set of the right kind of tube drills, and a strong electric power tool to do. When drilling, ease out of the groove that develops, from time to time, to prevent build-up of acrylic chips. Practice on a piece of scrap before actually drilling the tank. This will give you the assurance that you need when actually working on the aquarium.

As time goes on, better types of acrylic will be used in aquarium building, perhaps making them less prone to scratching, and less to bowing as well. On the positive side, the ones available now are already of excellent quality and any improvement is, there-fore, a boon. Acrylic tanks are, probably, the way future tanks will be built in years to come.

2.2 Sizing the Aquarium :

You should go for the largest aquarium that you can afford, both in terms of space, and outlay of funds. Larger aquariums are much easier to care for, and offer more of a water chemistry security buffer. Take, for instance, the impact on the water quality of just one dead fish. Its effect on a 55 gallon tank will be different that its effect on a 29 gallon one, and totally different again than on a 110. Because of dilution factors, larger masses of water attenuate the effects of pollutants better, with less resulting stress on the lifeforms.

Size is of course influenced by many factors, not the least of which is the financial aspect. Larger tanks require larger filters, and perhaps more equipment (lights for example), but they are also more expensive to stock. Keep especially the latter in mind, as filling a large tank with various types of rock and invertebrates can be quite costly.

Reefs can be kept in small aquariums. They can be kept in really small aquariums too. The additional constraints placed on you will be, amongst others, increased care and maintenance, and increasingly more efficient filtration as the size of the tank diminishes. This will allow the system to cope with higher loads of animals per gallon of water actually in the tank. The latter is not necessarily the case in larger tanks.

Larger aquariums, especially the 18 inch deep ones (front to back measurement), give a greater sense of realism, and make the tank look more like a real piece of the reef. You have probably observed such yourself at pet stores you visit, or in public aquariums. Such tanks are also much easier to decorate. Giving them depth of field enhances the overall impression you, and others seeing the tank, will have. It makes the tank look more tangibly real, much more appealing, and truer to nature.

Because you may have decided to drill the tank, and use an overflow corner box to bring the water down to the trickle filter (see later chapters for more details if you are not familiar with this type of a set-up), you must keep in mind that such corner overflows reduce the size of the aquarium. Not much, but probably 4" square in one of the back corners. This may not seem like much, but in a small tank, e.g. 29 gallons or so, it does make a difference.

Because of the remarks already made, we would suggest that you consider 55 gallon tanks as the minimum to use for reef aquariums. You can, unquestionably, set up a reef using a smaller aquarium, but the overall look will be less dramatic, and water quality parameters will be more critical. I have personally seen some really stunning 55 gallon tanks, both drilled and using surface skimming arrangements (see later chapters).

It is a good idea to first decide what type of lifeforms you will keep. Small aquariums fill up rather rapidly, especially if you have decided to use live rock combined with some of the nicer and large corals, e.g. Elegance, sometimes called Elegant (Cataiaphylia jardinei or plicata). If such is the case, you may want to rethink either the stocking plan, or the size of the tank.

Deep tanks, in the top to bottom direction, are nice to look at, but much harder to maintain. It will be difficult for you to reach the lower parts of the glass or acrylic panes to clean them. You will also have trouble removing detritus that is all the way at the bottom of the aquarium. Stick with a size that you can easily service. **Remember : The easier it is to clean a tank, the more often you are likely to do so**. And cleaning the tank is an important part of good husbandry and maintenance. It removes material that can break down, from the water, and prevents that material from putting an undue burden on the filtration system. Overall, this results in better water quality, and better looking fish, corals and invertebrates.

Size may also be determined by the location of the tank. The length of the wall, or the available space in a room is often a constraint you may have to deal with. Remember too that large tanks are heavy, on average you must multiply the gallon content by 10 to have a pound weight estimate of your tank, unless you really place a lot of rock in the aquarium , in which case you may have to multiply by 12. Older houses, and older apartments, may not be able to deal with this high weight. Check it out before you buy the tank! Floors can usually sustain more weigth closer to the wall. Aquariums placed in the middle of a room may need to be smaller.

It is a misconception to assume that custom built tanks are not affordable, or very expensive. The methods for building such aquariums have evolved so much that they are now a viable solution for hobbyists who have serious space constraints. We do not recommend that you build your own aquarium, unless you have experience in handling glass and bonding it with silicone glue (or acrylic), or know someone who does, and can do so for you.

We are often asked where one can call for such tanks. One

supplier we deal with on a regular basis is World Class Aquarium in Brooklyn, New York. They make an excellent product and will discuss your needs with you on the phone. Robert, one of the owners, has been in the business for over 20 years, and has built aquariums for over 14. We have never heard of any problems with any of the tanks they built for hobbyist we referred to them. Bio_2zo_3ne Filtration, a division of TAT also builds custom aquariums, but acrylic ones only.

2.3 The Stand :

Any wooden or metal stand will do, providing it can support the weight of the aquarium and its contents (see earlier in this chapter for ways to estimate that weight). Because we advocate the use of trickle filters to run reef aquariums, it is important that enough space be available underneath the tank, in the cabinet, to place the filter and other accessories that you will be using.

The tank must be absolutely level on the stand, and the stand must be absolutely level on the floor. This serves two purposes :

◆ it protects your aquarium by eliminating stress points in the glass, or acrylic material,
◆ it ensures that the overflow corner box, or surface skimming siphon, will work properly. This is especially so if you install more than one of them.

Since the sump of the trickle filter may need to be cleaned from time to time, it is important that easy access from the front of the cabinet to whatever you place underneath the aquarium is possible. Keep this in mind when looking for a stand. Some have very small doors and are not practical for reef keeping hobbyists. You must have wide doors, and at least two of them.

Some stands are partially open at the back. This may be handy to guide hose, or pipe, through the back and up to the tank, but it is of no use in servicing the components in the cabinet as, in all likelihood, your tank will be against a wall, making the back of the stand inaccessible, or difficult to work through.

Some hobbyists place the trickle filter higher than the tank, for example on a shelf, and let the water flow back in to the aquarium by gravity. In such a case, space underneath the stand is not a consideration. A cabinet can be built around the trickle filter to hide it from view. I used to run a 55 gallon tank set up in such a way for over a year, and found it to be easy to operate and service.

2.4 Aquarium Substrates :

The selection of the right reef tank substrate is an important decision. Then again, you will not need a lot of it. In reef tanks only very thin layers of substrate are used, and recommended. Putting too much substrate down directly on the bottom of the tank, can quickly lead to low oxygen levels in that same substrate, which in turn leads to anaerobic areas, and the appearance of hydrogen sulfide. The latter is a very noxious gas that quickly mixes with the water, lowers the dissolved oxygen level, and stresses the fish and other lifeforms, especially the ones in the lower parts of the tank.

Thick layers of substrate used to be the norm when used in conjunction with an undergravel filter. Since the latter is not part of the reef set-up that we advocate, the amount of substrate used must be adjusted downwards considerably. We suggest that you do not place more than $\frac{1}{4}$ inch on the bottom of the tank, and only in those areas where you need to cover the glass or acrylic. You do not need to place substrate underneath the rocks. My own tank has no substrate at all ! Not even a thin layer.

Undergravel filters, with their thick layers of calcareous rock, for example dolomite, crushed coral or coral rubble, served one main purpose : biological filtration, but they also served an accessory purpose: mechanical filtration. In reef tanks we want to avoid mixing different types of filtration. The reason for this is simple : by segregating the types of filtration, all can be present in their own right, and you can clean, replace, or do whatever needs to be done to them, without disturbing the others. Such is a major advantage, as it disturbs the chemical balance of the water chemistry much less, reduces the stress on the animal life, and results in a much better looking tank.

Dolomite, aragonite (unstable) and crushed or rubble coral, were also used to enhance the carbonate hardness of the water (see later in this book for more details). Carbonate hardness is very important to corals with exoskeletons (hard outside part), as the components of the carbonate hardness allow the corals to thrive, and even grow, providing the water the quality is up to par. Coralline algae require the calcium carbonate part of the carbonate hardness as well.

Both dolomite and crushed and rubble coral will increase the hardness for a short period of time. However, after they cover themselves with slime and other impurities, this beneficial action stops rapidly. Hobbyists then have to resort to the use of additives, e.g. liquids, powders, or tablets (we will cover this more in detail in a later part of the book).

Some hobbyists buy calcareous substrates in outlets other than pet stores. This may sound like a good idea. Often the material is cheaper. Unfortunately, the percentage of impurities in such materials is very high. This makes them unsuitable for use in reef tanks. Crushed oyster shell is an example of such a material.

When selecting a substrate, keep the type of animals that you plan to place in the tank in mind. Some need rocky substrates (live rock for instance, or similar types. They are sold under many different names), others require a smaller type (crushed or rubble coral). Moe (1989) gives a more complete description of the types of substrates that are found around reefs, and also some of the types required by the invertebrates you may keep. Advanced Reef Keeping II, my own book (published by Aardvark Press, late 1 st quarter 1990), also deals with this subject in more detail.

German hobbyists prefer non calcareous substrates, especially since articles written by Preis (1987) advancing the theory that calcareous substrates may precipitate trace elements out of the water. This contradicts earlier statements by Wilkens (1976 and 1979) recommending the addition of lime water (kalkwasser) which increases the amount of dissolved and non-dissolved calcareous matter in the water.

My own experience has been that with regular water changes

(see later) and the addition of trace elements on a routine basis, no such deficiency will occur, even at very high carbonate hardness levels. Since corals do better at these higher levels of carbonate hardness (Calcium and magnesium carbonates and bicarbonates as well as borate components), I recommend the use of live and similar rock in tanks, and the addition of KH generators and especially lime water, either manually, or by means of a dosing pump (explained later in this book).

It is important, when selecting the substrate and other rocks used in the tank, to keep in mind that you must be able to create strong circulation, also called current, throughout the entire tank. Such is important for the invertebrates, for the fish, and also for the quality of the water. Indeed, detritus needs to be moved around and into the mechanical filters; the invertebrates are accustomed to strong currents on the real reef; fish need strong water currents to keep them clean and healthy; and strong water movement inside the tank adds to the realism of the aquarium.

George Smit (1985) advocates the use of calcite and, as already indicated, Albert Thiel (1987) suggests the use of calcite in combination with the use of carbon dioxide, to increase the carbonate hardness of the water (see later chapters). Both, however, suggest that you do not keep thick layers of calcite on the bottom of the aquarium. Keep layers there as thin as you can. Your tank will benefit from it. The water quality will be improved. Levels of dissolved oxygen will be higher too.

Regardless of how much substrate you use, and which exact type you select, you must make it a point to clean it at least once a week, and more often if necessary. Accumulating dirt, dead algae, uneaten food, and so on, all contribute to the lowering of the water quality. As decay starts :

■ undesirable intermediate breakdown compounds are added to the water continuously,
■ oxygen is consumed, lowering dissolved oxygen levels and stressing the animal life.

Those hobbyists presently using undergravel filter plates, who are considering leaving that undergravel in place, and adding a trickle filter to the system (see Converting to a trickle filter, later in this book, and also in my other book Small Reef Aquarium Basics), may want to read more on grain size, flow rates, and thickness of the layer, in Stephen Spotte's : Seawater Aquariums, A Captive Environment, John Wiley Inter Science, NY, 1979.

2.5 Other Basic Equipment Needed :

Besides the tank, a trickle filter, pump, the stand, and other items discussed in this book, other types of equipment will be necessary to keep a well balanced aquarium running successfully for long periods of time. Most of these are not the subject of this book. Moreover you are probably familiar with them anyway. Some of them include, amongst others :

- a heater (or several),
- fish nets,
- scrubbers to clean the glass (or acrylic),
- optional canister filter(s),
- filter(s) using micron cartridges
- and so on.

If you are not familiar with them, refer to one of the many books that deals with basic aquarium keeping. TFH publishes several of them. Martin Moe's Marine Aquarium Handbook is also strongly recommended (Green Turtle Publications). Most of you probably have all that equipment already, especially if you have kept aquariums before.

2.6 Artificial Sea Salts :

Of all the elements present in the water used to run the tank, aquarium salt, in the form bought from pet stores, is the major constituent we rely on to adjust the quality of raw or treated water, to make it suitable for fish, corals and invertebrates.

Seawater is a very complex fluid. It contains not only inorganic elements, but also a great number of organic ones, as well as very small lifeforms (microscopic). In nature around the reefs, the chemistry of seawater changes very very little. All parameters are nearly constant. This is universally so, not just around one reef. The animals are, as a result, not used to deal with changes, or water chemistry that varies from day to day, or hour to hour.

This is also the reason why many authors, including myself, recommend that conditions in the aquarium, especially the reef aquarium, should be kept as stable as possible at all times. Even minor variations can stress the animal life too much, and can result in loss of life or outbreaks of disease, because of the reduced ability of the lifeforms to deal with parasitic attacks. Marine life forms are just not as resilient as their fresh water counterparts, especially if they are stressed to begin with from shipping, being in bags while you transport them home, coming from aquariums with totally different water conditions, and so on. The reasons are too numerous to mention all.

Seawater contains both major and minor elements. The major elements make up 99 percent of the mix. These inorganic elements are: sodium chloride, magnesium chloride, magnesium sulfate, calcium sulfate, potassium sulfate, calcium carbonate, and bromide salts. These elements are always present, and in the same proportion, regardless of where the seawater came from. Where individual differences occur, is in the concentration of the minor elements, also called trace elements, and the organic compounds and microscopic lifeforms. These vary from reef to reef.

It is usually said that seawater contains all known chemical elements, albeit some only in very minute quantities. This obviously makes it very difficult to recreate seawater. Artificial seawater is, therefore, only a distant cousin of the real thing, yet close enough for us to be able to maintain animals in it for extended periods of time, providing we keep it at a level of purity commensurate with the requirements of the animal life present in the tank.

While we know that certain elements are necessary for the survival of fish, corals, invertebrates and algae, a great number of elements may, or may not, be crucial to the survival of the lifeforms kept.

This complicates the manufacturing process of artificial sea salts a great deal. Indeed, which elements should be included, and which ones should be left out ? Typically artificial sea salts will contain around 70 different trace elements, and time has proven that such is enough to maintain reef tanks.

Because many of these elements will not dissolve instantaneously, it is recommended that artificial seawater be prepared several hours before it is actually being used. Twenty four hours is not uncommon. This allows the water to which the salt has been added to stabilize, and be re-oxygenated by means of a small air pump and an air stone. It also makes it less harsh because the chemical reactions that take place when the salt and the water are mixed, have reached the end of their course. You may consider this a minor point. It is not. **Attention to detail is often what makes the difference between a reef tank that runs well, and one that looks vibrant and in super condition.**

Many of the elements present in the artificial seawater that you have prepared function as nutrients for the lifeforms that you keep. As such, they are depleted as time goes on. This is also the reason why many authors recommend that trace elements should be added from time to time, to make up for the deficit. Some nutrients, or should we say trace elements, are known to be of great importance to algae, bacteria and invertebrates. They include, amongst others : iodine, strontium, molybdenum, iron, zinc, cobalt, and others. Because they are all depleted rather rapidly, the discerning hobbyist should replace them on a regular basis. Commercial products are available that allow you to do so. My own company, Thiel•Aqua•Tech, markets an iodine supplement, a strontium-molybdenum one called KSM, and our vitamins contain extra B-12, a major source of cobalt.

Whereas nutrients are depleted, pollutants increase as soon as you place animals in the aquarium. Pollutants reduce the water quality, stress the tank lifeforms, and need to be removed at all cost. This is the reason for the various types of filtration that we will be advocating and discussing in this book. Keeping the water in the aquarium as close as we can to seawater, is what filtration is all about.

Since aquarium salt will, for a large part, determine the quality of the end mixture in which you place the lifeforms, it is important that you select it carefully. Many brands are available. Some are regional, others are sold nationwide. Most are of excellent quality.

When it comes to reef tanks, however, we should place some extra requisites on the salt we use. The reasons are multiple, but the main one is that the corals and invertebrates kept in reef tanks are not as resilient as the fish kept in fish-only tanks. Corals and invertebrates react more markedly to certain compounds that may not affect fish, or affect them to a lesser degree. Two of these compounds are nitrates and phosphates.

Good reef aquarium salt should be extremely low in both nitrates and phosphates. In fact, ideally, it should not contain any of either. How do you determine whether the salt you are using, or plan to use, fits the requirements ? Such is fairly easy. All you will need is a low range nitrate test, and a low range phosphate test. Prepare a small batch of salt water, wait for a few hours while aerating the mixture, then test the sample you have prepared for NO_3 and PO_4. If it contains any of either, look for another salt, and test it to ensure that it is allright to use on a reef tank.

NO_3 and PO_4 can cause several problems in a reef tank, not the least of which is severe and uncontrollable outbreaks of micro-algae. Besides the latter, excessive amounts of NO_3 will affect the appearance of your invertebrates and corals, and may shorten their life span, influence their feeding, and affect how they react and interact with their environment (the water in the tank). Recommended levels are as low as 1 ppm of $N-NO_3$, or a maximum of $4\frac{1}{2}$ to 5 ppm of NO_3. Phosphate, on the other hand, should be present in even lower amounts. I recommend levels of no more than between 0.05 ppm ($\frac{1}{20}$ppm) to 0.1 ppm($\frac{1}{10}$ppm) of PO_4.

The amount of salt you add to the water determines the salinity, or specific gravity. Around natural reefs the salinity is 35 ppt (parts per thousand), or a specific gravity of 1.023 at 76 degrees Fahrenheit. You should try to maintain a similar salinity in your reef tank. Many hobbyists lower the salinity in an effort to stave off parasites and parasitic infestations. The reasoning is that at lower salinities parasites do not thrive as well as at higher ones, while fish are not as stressed, because they have to work less at maintaining their internal salt balance. This sounds good in theory. In actual fact my experience is that it does not make any difference whatsoever, and that most corals, and invertebrates, do better at the higher salinity of 35 ppt. I maintain all my tanks at that salinity. Those who have seem my tanks can attest to the fact that they all do extremely well, and that all corals, anemones, and other lifeforms all open to very large sizes. Besides, your protein skimmer will perform at its most efficient level if the salinity is at 35 ppt.

Stay away from generic salts, shoddily packed material, or varieties sold in bulk quantities and without a name. You have no way of knowing whether, in fact, they are even meant for salt water aquariums. Pure NaCl, sodium chloride, or salt, is of no value for a reef tank. Far too many chemical components are missing. Buffers especially, in the form of carbonates and bicarbonates, are an absolute must. They are the compounds that will result in a pH that is acceptable for a reef tank, and a carbonate hardness that is at least in the right range. Without such buffers the KH (carbonate hardness) and the pH may be totally off kilter. This will seriously damage the lifeforms you keep in the aquarium, especially the corals and the invertebrates.

Check your salinity on a regular basis. Evaporation will result in an increase (since salt does not evaporate, only water). On the other hand, loss of salt occurs in skimmers (see later) and also due to salt creep in various areas of the tank or filters. I check mine just about every day, but I use a salinometer, a modified refractometer that indicates salinity in parts per thousand as well. This is a highly accurate device, and gives instantaneous results. All I have to do is place about 5 drops of aquarium water on the front of the instrument, close the lid, and look through the visor to determine what the salinity actually is. Because these instruments are so easy to use, you are more likely to check your salinity frequently, and make adjustments whenever required. This increases the stability of the aquarium water chemistry. **And in reef tanks, stability is the key to long term success** (Thiel, 1985).

Most hobbyists use hydrometers to measure the specific gravity, rather than measuring the actual salinity. Both are, of course, acceptable ways of going about measuring whether the levels are correct. Keep in mind that you must adjust for temperature if you a hydrometer. Indeed s.g. (specific gravity) is temperature dependent. Martin Moe Jr. and Stephen Spotte have both published charts that allow you to easily make the necessary adjustments in their books The Marine Aquarium Handbook (Green Turtle Press), respectively Seawater Aquariums, A Captive Environment (Wiley InterScience).

As an ancillary to the fact that trace elements are continuously depleted by invertebrates, fish, corals, and algae, it is of utmost importance to siphon out any dead algae that you notice in the tank immediately. Indeed, scientific studies have demonstrated that algae can store trace elements. They can do so in concentrations far greater than what these normally are in the water. When algae die off, they release these large amounts of elements back in to the tank. The larger concentrations can be noxious and can result in stress and damage to the animals you keep in the tank.

In addition to removing the dead or dying algae, I also recommend a 15 percent water change to reduce the concentration of such elements even further. If the amount of algae that died is large, at least two such water changes should be performed within a six hour time span.

Don't let this lead you to believe that keeping macro-algae is dangerous, or not desirable. On the contrary. Macro-algae are beneficial in any tank, as they assist in oxygenating the water during the day, remove certain pollutants by absorbing them, reduce nitrate and phosphate levels, and may leach antibiotic-like substances in the water that reduce parasite and similar problems. A large section on macro-algae is included at the end of this book. It should give those of you who want to culture various species, all the information necessary to do so with success, and with an understanding of what is required to keep them alive. Algae is a very large subject to cover in just one chapter. If you are truly interested in macro-algae you may wish to read some of the excellent books that exist on the subject.

The ones I particularly recommend to anyone who asks me are:

- The Algae, V.J. & D.J. Chapman, The Macmillan Press, 1973
- The Ecology of Algae, F.E. Round, Cambridge University Press, 1981
- Micro-Algal Biotechnology, M.A. & L.J.Borowitzka, Cambridge University Press, 1988
- A Textbook on Algae, H.D. Kumar & H.N. Singh, Macmillan Press, 1979
- Introduction to the Algae, H.C. Bold & M.J. Wynne, Prentice Hall, 1985

and as reference works the two books by Prof. William Randolph Taylor, "Marine Algae", published by The University of Michigan Press, used by scientists worldwide for the identification of micro and macro-algae.

2.7 Raw or treated water :

We have looked at salt, its required qualities, its undesirable components, and we merely stated that such salt is added to the "water" used to fill the aquarium, or make water changes. We now have to take a closer look at the water itself, and what can, or should, be done to such water, before it is actually used. Raw water, whether tap or well, contains, or may contain a number of undesirable compounds, elements, chemicals -call them what you wish- that we do not want to introduce into the aquarium.

Let's face it, you may have spent a considerable amount of money on equipment and instrumentation, or you may be about to do so. All that equipment only has one purpose, it is meant to maintain the water chemistry at very high levels. Does it not make sense, therefore, to make sure that the water you are using is of equally good quality ? We are talking here about removing compounds before you actually add water to the aquarium. This is something you have total control over.

Hobbyists use various freshwater sources (here are a few) :

- tap water
- well water
- river or lake water
- distilled water
- deionized water
- spring water
- rain water

        Some of these sources can be seriously polluted. This is the case
for tap, well, river, and lake water. Only tests will tell you whether or not
the water you are planning to use is of the right quality. Yet that would
only tell you whether certain compounds are present. There are a number
of chemicals that we do not want in the aquarium, that the average
hobbyist cannot test for. Such include, for example, pesticides, organic
phosphate, phenols, etc. Best is, therefore to assume that certain undesirable elements are present, and to set up a method of treating all water
that you will be adding to the tank, unless it is distilled or deionized water
already. Compounds that we can test for, such as nitrate and phosphate,
are often present as well.

        A pretreatment set-up is not complicated to install, neither is it
expensive. My own system consists of the following :

• a micron cartridge canister that contains carbon, and a 5 micron nominal filter cartridge. Do-it-yourself outlets and many hardware stores sell
both the canisters and the replacement cartridges.
• a molecular absorption canister that contains 30 discs (these discs are
made by Poly-Bio Marine Inc., who also make the better known Poly
Filters®).

        The canisters are placed in series, the carbon/micron one first,
then the molecular absorption one. I flow the water slowly through the
assembly. As little as 15-20 gallons per hour. Both are hooked up to the
tap water lines (cold water). The effluent is free of chlorine (because of
the carbon); phosphate and nitrate; other compounds that may be present are removed by the combination of the carbon and the molecular
absorption discs.

        I have tested the effluent many times, and cannot find anything
left in the water, that should have been removed. I replace the carbon
micron cartridge about every 4 to 5 weeks. The molecular absorption
discs last about 18 to 20 weeks (at least in my case, yours may differ
depending on the quality of the tap or well water that you are treating,
and the amount you are actually passing through the canisters).

        Other methods to pretreat the water exist. If you want more

details, you may wish to refer to my other book : Small Reef Aquarium Basics, for more details. Examples of other methods include reverse osmosis and deionization.

When it comes to reef aquariums we often start with the best of intentions, buy the best equipment we can, read books and subscribe to magazines to keep up-to-date on the latest happenings in reef keeping, but then we fail to check the water we use. I would urge you to change that, and test all water used before it is added to the tank, and pretreat it if necessary. My experience tells me that it will be necessary to do so in 99 percent of all cases. You do not even have to perform all the tests yourself. You can obtain a complete water analysis, usually free of charge, from your local water supply company. Just call them up and ask for it. You may be up for some surprises when you see the results.

Once you know that the water you are adding to your tank does not contain, nitrates and phosphates, for example, you will be able to judge much more accurately how well your tank is doing. If the nitrate, or phosphate, found in the tank does not come in with the water, and also not with the salt, then it has obviously been generated in the aquarium. Is such is the case, you will have to look for the reasons why this happened and take remedial action. Maybe you are overfeeding, or you are not removing dying or dead algae, or you are not cleaning your mechanical filters often enough, or your protein skimmer is too small, etc.

Check the carbonate hardness and the pH as well, especially the batches that you use to make top-offs with. You may find that either or both are not acceptable, and need to be adjusted first. The easiest way to affect both is to add a good quality, multiple component, carbonate hardness generator. More on how to do this can be found in later chapters.

Some hobbyists use (buy) distilled or deionized water. Such is of course a good idea, as distilled and deionized water are much purer than tap or well water. The problem is that it can become quite expensive. Treating the water yourself, for instance with the simple set-up described above, will make the process a lot less expensive. Water treated in such a way costs less than 4 cents a gallon. The additional advantage is that it is always available. You can't really run out of it. That may sound trivial, but it is not. Try finding 10 or 15 gallons of distilled water on a Sunday evening, or on a holiday week-end, especially if you absolutely need it to make a water change, because something went wrong in the aquarium. You may have a real hard time !

Keep in mind too, that although your water may be of good quality when you last tested it, its quality changes frequently. Heavy rains, work performed on the city water pipes, and other reasons all affect its make-up. You are never assured of a uniform quality. It pays, therefore, to pretreat it as a routine matter before using it.

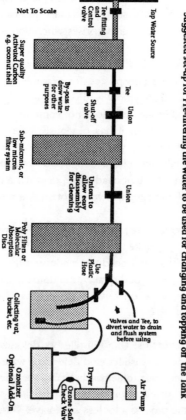

3. Filtration Techniques :

The purpose of all filtration is to remove unwanted compounds from the tank's water, those compounds that when dissolved make the environment less suitable for keeping corals, fish, invertebrates, and any other life forms that you may be planning to add to your aquarium, now or at a later date. As already indicated in the previous chapter, **as soon as animals are added to the aquarium, nutrients are depleted and pollutants are added**. Both these processes occur continuously, 24 hours a day, day in, day out.

We will deal with the replenishment of the depleted nutrients later; at this stage we are concerned with the types of pollutants that are added, and how they can, or should, be removed before they can cause damage to the animal life. Each type will require a special form of filtration, geared to dealing with specific elements and compounds that we wish to remove from the water.

What compounds are we talking about ? There are numerous such compounds, so many that it does not even make sense to list them all. A number of them are, however, well known to you because they are often mentioned in aquarium literature :

• Nitrogen intermediate breakdown products such as ammonia NH_3, ammonium ion NH_4, nitrite NO_2 and nitrate NO_3.
• Organic material, both dissolved and not dissolved. Proteinaceous matter from food, small life forms that died, and so on.
• Yellowing matter, Gilvin, Gelbstoff. Albumin.
• Ortho-phosphate. Organic phosphate. Other forms of phosphate e.g. hexa-meta-phosphate.
• Chemical pollutants : fumes, nicotine, cleaning product vapors, per-

fumes, sprays, polishing products used in the house or appartment, etc.
• Heavy metals that enter the aquarium through water changes, leachings from rocks, etc. Examples include copper, zinc, and others.
• Pesticides that may come in with tap or well water, granted in the parts per billion range, but if they build up over time they will cause problems.
• Amines, nitrosamines, Indoles, scatoles, Phenol, Hydrocarbons, etc.

Most, if not all, of these compounds can be removed rather easily from the aquarium water, providing the hobbyist installs the appropriate type of filtration for each type of pollutant. These forms of filtration may be known to you by the following names :

• Biological filtration,
• Mechanical filtration,
• Chemical filtration,
• Foam fractionation, or protein skimming,
• Ion selective filtration,
• Air scrubbing.

Because the relative success of your aquarium, or said differently, the survival rate and quality of appearance of the animals in the tank, depends for 99 percent on the chemistry of the water, it is most important that reef keeping hobbyists pay very close attention to all of the above types of filtration. All are covered, in detail, in this book.

Installing only part of the required types will result in lowered water quality levels and an aquarium that does not look as good as it could, meaning an aquarium where the animals are not in as good a shape as they could be if more filtration were used.

Anytime you decide to make a trade-off, and forego some form of filtration, or use a process that is less efficient than the one we suggest, you are exposing yourself to problems of many kinds. Usually the first signs of such problems will be the outbreak of parasites on your fish, and a less healthy looking corals and invertebrates. Trade-offs may save money in the short run, they will, however, end up costing you more when you factor in the cost of replacing fish and corals. Be aware of it and think twice before making such decisions.

3.1 Biological Filtration :

Biological filtration is probably the one type of filtration that most hobbyists are familiar with, and have used in some form or fashion if they have kept aquariums before. It is also the one that all hobbyist pay the most attention to, often to the detriment of the other types of filtration mentioned earlier. Such is a dangerous mistake.

Store owners too, tend to put great emphasis on biological filtration, at times perhaps too much. The latter may explain why it has taken on such an important position in the mind of the novice and experienced hobbyist alike. Do not misunderstand me, biological filtration is an important form of filtration. But it can, and should, not be the only one that gets attention, or most of the attention. Especially not in reef tanks. Others types are of as much importance, if not of a greater one in many cases.

To put it simply, biological filtration deals with the removal of nitrogen breakdown by-products from the water. These nitrogen compounds appear in the tank as a result of the animal life that is placed in the aquarium. The food that is added to the tank, the algae that die off, and the respiration and metabolism of the fish and invertebrates, all contribute to the eventual appearance of ammonia/ammonium ion.

There are, basically, three types of bacteria that break down, or decompose, organic matter (de Graaf 1976) in our aquariums : bacterium coli, proteus and subtilis. Decomposition is a multiple stage process, and far more complicated than we usually imagine. Organic matter, for example protein, first breaks down into peptides and subsequently into amino-acids, but the process also includes many intermediate stage chemical compounds such as amines and nitrosamines, some of which can be very toxic.

It has even been suggested that in filters that do not run properly, these intermediate products may be the cause of the dreaded "wipe-out" syndrome (Thiel, 1988), especially when in addition to such pollutants a sudden increase in organic waste occurs, for example as a result of a fish or other animal that died. The chemistry of protein and organic matter breakdown is very complex. I attempted to explain some basics of it in the first edition of this book, published in 1988, but my comments did not meet the expected response. Hobbyists found the explanations too complicated and unnecesarry. As a result, I have left them out of this 7th printing and 2nd edition of The Marine Fish and Invert Reef Aquarium.

Unfortunately, even though the water quality is usually excellent when an aquarium is first started up, as soon as animals are added, that same water quality starts deteriorating quickly. The purpose of all filtration is, therefore, to counter-act these negative effects and remove whatever noxious compounds may have been added to the water as a result of populating the tank, feeding the animals, biochemical activity taking place, etc.

Biological filtration deals with the removal of nitrogen breakdown products which, as indicated earlier, involve, in a first stage, ammonia or ammonium ion, or both. The first and very important goal that we are trying to achieve with proper biological filtration, is ensuring that the breakdown of protein and organic material follows its normal course, and is not interrupted at some intermediate stage. The latter can cause major water quality problems, as some of the intermediate compounds can be extremely toxic.

The second and third very important goals of biological filtration, is ensuring that all ammonia gets converted to nitrite, that all nitrite gets converted to nitrate, and that some of the nitrate gets eliminated from the system, through the presence in the filter, pipes, and generally throughout the aquarium, of bacteria that are referred to as facultatively aerobic-anaerobic, which can reduce nitrates through assimilation, also called nitrate respiration.

Our goal, therefore, must be to build up a very potent and large colony of the bacteria that eliminate ammonia and nitrite on one hand, and also not to interfere with their process under any circumstances, on the other. This is the main reason why I am strongly opposed to the addition of medication, and have said so for the longest of times. Medicine can, in certain cases, interrupt the normal course of the chemical and biological breakdown of organic matter, and can result in the build up of the kind of compounds that can be harmful to all lifeforms we keep in reef tanks, especially to the more delicate invertebrates. It is much better when medication needs to be used, to treat the fish in a separate tank, usually called a hospital tank. We will discuss this in one of the later chapters.

Ammonia present in the water is broken down to nitrite by a form of bacteria called Nitrosomonas. These bacteria appear spontaneously, or their proliferation can be sped up by the addition of a batch of seeded gravel or rock from another tank. Seeded gravel is gravel, or rock, that comes from an aquarium that has been running for a while, and already has a great deal of bacterial life. Transferring some of the gravel (rock, coral pieces) also transfers bacteria.

Alternatively you an add one of the many commercial filter starter products, e.g. Super Zyme from my own company, Cycle, Biozyme, Nitro-Quick, and a few others. They will speed up the cycling of the aquarium, and reduce the stress created on the fish and invertebrates as a result. Such is positive insomuch as it also reduces the risk of parasitic infestations during the first couple of weeks your aquarium is set up.

Ammonia can be present in the aquarium as ammonia gas or as ammonium ion. Whether ammonia gas is present at all, and in what proportion, depends on the pH of the water. For this reason ammonia becomes a more important problem in salt water tanks than it is in freshwater aquariums. More ammonia is formed at higher pH's than at lower ones, and because it mixes so readily with the water, it is extremely dangerous. Ammonia tests should, therefore, always show zero mg/l, or ppm. Even small amounts are unacceptable in reef systems, as they will definitely harm fish and invertebrates alike. Ensuring you do not have residual ammonia in your tank's water, is the same as saying that you must ensure that your biological filter is potent enough to deal with whatever amount of organic material may need to be broken down.

Conversely one can also say that reducing the amount of organic material added to the tank, will create less of a demand on the filters. In simple language this translate to, for instance, do not overfeed.

The biochemical conversion process that ammonia goes through results in the creation of nitrite, a closely related compound, just as noxious to the animals as ammonia gas is when it mixes with water.

Nitrite must also be removed at all costs. Fortunately for the hobbyist, another type of bacterium, Nitrobacter species, appears spontaneously as well, and converts the nitrite to nitrate, a compound that is far less noxious, providing it is present only in small amounts. Nitrobacter species bacteria are present in our biological filters but in numbers far smaller than Nitrosomonas. Nevertheless, a well seeded filter that is not subjected to interference from medications such as antibiotics, or heavy metals such as copper and zinc, will harbor a sufficient amount of these beneficial bacteria to cope efficiently with the nitrite that is formed in the tank.

Should tests of the aquarium water show the presence of merely low amounts of nitrite, such still is an indication that somewhere in the aquarium, or in the filters, the natural breakdown cycle has been, or is being, interfered with. The hobbyist should immediately determine where this interference is coming from and remedy the situation. This may entail cleaning all mechanical filters, ensuring that the gravel or substrate is clean and does not harbor trapped detritus and other organic matter, removing dead or dying algae, checking the cleanliness of corner overflow boxes and/or surface skimming siphons, etc.

It may also suggest that, perhaps, the hobbyist is feeding too much, or in the worst of all cases, that the tank is overloaded to such a degree that the filters can no longer deal efficiently with that biological load. This should prompt the hobbyist to remove lifeforms (unlikely to happen in my experience), or to increase the filter capacity by adding additional biological filtration (more likely to happen). We will discuss how this can be done in a later section.

Nitrates are another problem altogether. Traditionally nitrate, NO_3 has been regarded as a compound that is not harmful. Such may be the case in fish-only tanks, the ones we were used to keep before the advent of reef tanks, but it is not so in today's living reef aquariums. Nitrate is definitely a pollutant, and it does affect the well being and appearance of corals and other invertebrates. I have been able to verify that levels as high as 8 ppm of NO_3 result in both Catalaphylia jardinei and Discosoma species corals not opening as much as they do at lower levels, respectively not lifting themselves as far of the rocks to which they are attached, and not stretching out as much as usual.

The differences were even more obvious, and significant, as the nitrate levels were increased to 15 ppm of NO_3 in the same aquarium. These tests were conducted on a 150 gallon aquarium running at generally accepted levels of pH and specific gravity, temperature, redox, etc. and lasted a total of 9 weeks. Objective opinions were obtained from outside parties, who were not aware of the changes made in nitrates, but were merely asked for their opinion as to the appearance of the aquarium's lifeforms. Two such outsiders are George Bepko and Scott Jerome. Because these were blind tests neither even knew why their opinion was being asked so often.

To confuse the picture somewhat more, many tests available to the hobbyist measure nitrate as nitrogen nitrate, or $N-NO_3$, and not the total nitrate. This is unfortunate because many hobbyists do not realize what a large difference exists between the two. For example, 10 ppm of $N-NO_3$ is equivalent to $\pm$ 44 ppm of NO_3. And such a level is much much too high for a reef tank. Because of the lack of knowledge about the differences between these differences, hobbyists assume that their tank is in good shape, and nitrates are low. After all, is their reasoning, 10 ppm "is" low.

Unfortunately those 10 ppm are not low at all, because they are ppm's of $N-NO_3$, which is really equivalent to $\pm$ 44 ppm of nitrate. As you can well imagine, nitrogen breakdown product removal and conversion from one type of compound to the next one, is a much more complex matter than is usually imagined. Because the process is, for the most part, spontaneous, little attention is paid to the process as such. All the hobbyist does, is provide an appropriate area for these bacteria to grow, colonize in large numbers, and do their "thing". The quality of that environment - the area where the bacteria actually grow - is what differentiates excellent and good filters from mediocre ones.

Making that environment not only adequate, but as close to ideal as possible is, therefore, an important part of maximizing the water quality, and running a successful aquarium.

Besides ammonia, nitrite and nitrate, phosphate can also occur in your tank, sometimes in significant quantities, and pollute the aquarium water. Phosphates have different origins : they result from the mineralization of organic compounds (breakdown) such as food, micro and macro algae, the metabolism of fish and invertebrates; they can be introduced in the tank because they are present in the water you use (whether tap or well), and they can be a part of the salt that you add to make up new salt water.

Phosphates are not removed biologically, but through other means, and will therefore be covered in another chapter. Phosphates can, however, create lots of problems for the hobbyist because they often give rise to large amounts of micro-algae on one hand, and can interfere with coral survival and growth on the other. Indeed, text books report that phosphate interferes with the calcium carbonate up-take, and can, as a result, lead to corals coming loose from their hard exoskeletons.

Then again, Thiel (1989) reports that such can also occur as a result of a lack of strontium and molybdenum in the water, two elements normally present in traces only, but rapidly removed from the water as a result of ozonization and protein skimming, as well as through the normal metabolism of all animals present in the aquarium.

We touched briefly on the presence of bacteria in our filters already. Beneficial bacteria that is. Two species already mentioned are the ones that assist in the conversion of ammonia to nitrite, and nitrite to nitrate : Nitrosomonas and Nitrobacter species. Besides those two species of bacteria, many other varieties are always present in the tank, whether we want it or not. Most of them are harmless, and thus are not a concern. There is, however, another type that can cause a great deal of problems if it occurs in the filters and tank : Shigella species (deGraaf 1976). These bacteria, which by the way also cause food poisoning, could be one cause of the so-called wipe-out syndrome that occurs in fish-only tanks that are not well cared for, when these Shigella bacteria are liberated from the filters and end up in the water. One sure way to prevent their presence, is to clean all filters on a regular basis and ensure that no areas occur in those filters where water does not travel freely through whatever material is used inside the filter itself.

3.1.1 Traditional biological filtration methods :

By traditional filtration methods we refer, in this case, to the undergravel biological filtration method, a method that is still used by thousands upon thousands of hobbyists and has "proven" itself over the years. Just about every book on aquarium keeping you read, advocates this particular type of filtration. Spotte (1979) has written extensively, if not exhaustively, on the subject, and so have many other others.

Undergravel filtration, whether reverse flow or normal flow, obviously works very well. There is no question about that and there never has been in my mind. Our hobby would not be where it is now it it weren't for that filtration method. The point that has to be made, however, is that in reef tanks a still better type of filtration can be used, and should be used : wet-dry filters, also called trickle filtration. We shall discuss this method of filtration in great detail later in this book, as the water quality parameters obtained when using such filters is by far superior to the ones found when using any other form of filter, including undergravel filter plates and canisters.

Undergravel filtration can, of course, be used in conjunction with many other types of biological filtration. Often hobbyists supplement U.G. filters with Eheim® type canister filters, outside box filters, and also with Lifeguard® or PEP® type canister filters. Such is, of course, all to the benefit of the system on which these filters are used, leads to better water quality, and better looking aquariums. Notwithstanding all such filtration, and the excellent levels to which the water chemistry can be brought, it is still possible to improve on those methods. Again, wet-dry or trickle filters are the answer, especially when they are combined with adequate chemical and mechanical filtration means.

Undergravel filters require a lot of maintenance, especially to prevent the detritus and dirt that accumulates in them from becoming a problem. If you are of the opinion that your undergravel filter does not trap dirt, we suggest that you stir up the gravel a little, and see for yourself what we mean.

Although some Authors suggest that a well maintained under-gravel filter will not trap dirt and will not clog, we have never found that to be the case for any length of time. Because the water that is pushed through, or sucked into, the gravel always contains impurities, eventually certain areas clog. As the clogging increases, certain areas become low in oxygen content and may turn anaerobic. This leads to a lowering of the water quality on one hand, and possibly the appearance of hydrogen sulfide on the other. The latter is a gas that mixes very readily with the water and can result in both fish and invertebrate losses.

Even water that is pre-filtered results in the undergravel filter eventually clogging, the only difference being that it will take longer for such to occur, but clogging it will. Not only is clogging a problem, but the flow through an undergravel filter itself can be problematic as well. Indeed, the flow is uneven and greater where the water finds less resistance, for example around the base of rocks or pieces of coral placed on the gravel, mainly because the layer of gravel is much thinner in such places. Such does not promote efficient biological filtration.

To prevent the formation of anaerobics, and to re-establish a better flow through the gravel, hobbyists clean the U.G. filters from time to time. This is fine, insomuch as doing so increases the efficiency of the filter, but hobbyists must realize that such happens at the detriment of the water quality, for a few days to a week, each time the filter is cleaned. Indeed, cleaning the U.G. filter destroys a great number of the bacteria that had settled on the gravel kernels, which destabilizes the filter until those bacteria have re-populated the gravel. Less bacteria provide less as well as less efficient filtration, and the latter will result in stress on the fish and invertebrates.

Such is certainly not conducive to having a vibrant looking tank. Even when only portions of the filter are cleaned at a time, bacteria are still destroyed and the above scenario is still accurate. Additionally, how undergravel filters are run greatly influences their efficiency, for example, some parameters to look at include : the amount of water flowing through the gravel bed (usually dolomite or crushed coral), the thickness of the gravel bed, the size of the kernels, etc. All influence the amount of filtration that actually occurs and the quality of the resulting water. This in turn determines how well the fish and invertebrates in the aquarium will do, how they look (appear), and whether or not they will survive for any length of time in your tank.

Marine Aquariums, and especially marine "reef" aquariums that look at their best, will always show high levels of dissolved oxygen in the water on one hand, and very low levels of pollutants such as nitrates, NO_3, and phosphates PO_4, ammonia, NH_3, and nitrite, NO_2 on the other.

Keeping dissolved oxygen levels high is not all that easy to do in tanks run with undergravel filters, not because the hobbyist does not take the time and care to achieve such levels, but mainly because such filters are not as conducive as others to such high levels of oxygen, O_2, in the water. It has nothing to do with hobbyists' maintenance practices, but with then nature of the filter itself.

Some hobbyists resort to a method called "reverse flow" under-gravel filtration, as opposed to flow through from top to bottom. Reverse flow is a system whereby the water is pushed through the gravel from bottom to top (the reverse of what is normally done). Many hobbyists report excellent results with this form of filtration, better, in fact, than with the regular type of undergravel filtration. What is very important when using this approach, is to fine filter (mechanically filter) the water extremely well, to prevent the material used on top of the filter plates that make up the undergravel filter,from trap-ping dirt, and eventually clogging up.

How such a system is set up is explained in great detail in some of the other aquarium books that you may have read, or in Eheim's® instruction manual, the one that comes with the special equipment they sell to install such a form of filtration.

Many hobbyists too will want to run their aquariums, including reef tanks, while keeping the undergravel filters that are already in place, supplemented with, perhaps, a trickle filter. Such is fine of course. The set up can, however, be greatly improved upon by removing the under-gravel filters altogether. How to do so, and why it is a better way to run the tank, is explained later in this book.

If it is not practical to remove the undergravel, or if doing so requires that the entire tank be taken down and started up all over, then it may make sense to keep the filter in place and add supplemental means of filtration to the existing arrangement, thus improving the overall efficiency and water quality. I am certainly not suggesting that you must remove undergravels to be able to run a decent reef tank. What I am saying, is that you will have better results when you do, and use the even more efficient trickle filtration instead.

3.2 Newer Methods of Filtration :
3.2.1 Canister Filters :

Canister filters, known to you by names such as Eheim, Fluval, Marineland, Atlantis, Lifeguard, Pep, and others, can be used on their own, as stand alone filtration, or in combination with other types of filtra-tion. In fact, hobbyists often do the latter. Canister filters are frequently found in combination with undergravel filters, to supplement the effi-ciency of that filter, and/or to perform some other form of filtration, for example, chemical filtration, using Poly Filters®, or activated carbon.

Canister filters are much more recent than other forms of filtra-tion, having been pioneered in Germany, mainly by the Eheim Company. Nowadays, many brands are available, and in several sizes, for example Marineland's Magnum Series, making it possible to match up the size of the canister with the size of the aquarium on which it will be used. As the canister design was improved over the years, these filters can now be used for a variety of purposes : mechanical, chemical, biological, and (although I do not recommend such) as a combination of all three of those.

Canister filters have many uses, one of the more obvious ones being that canister filter can be used to supplement existing filtration in aquariums that carry a heavy load, where such additional biological and other filtration becomes necessary. Such a tank overload can have several reasons : (a) while going on vacation, a period during which the water quality may deteriorate because no water changes can be done, (b) while additional animals are placed in the tank, for instance because you have removed them from another one that you are working on, and (c) due to plain and simple overload because the hobbyist has placed too many animals in the tank, (d) and other reasons you can think of yourself perhaps.

One very important remark : clean all filters regularly, especially if they are functioning as mechanical filters (100 % or even partially). This is most important because any matter trapped in the filter will slowly decompose and affect the overall water quality. Place the filters in a convenient place. Thiel (1981) observes that the easier it is to get to or reach a filter, the more likely the hobbyist is to clean it. Keep that in mind when you set up your system. Do not place filters in odd places where they are hard to get to. Do things right the first time around. It takes less time, and is simpler than changing the system around at some later point in time, when the tank is already running and when any change you make will affect the appearance and behavior of all tank lifeforms, because any such changes will impact the chemistry of the water negatively.

You may not have all the answers, and you may have questions as to what exactly to do when setting up your filters. That is perfectly normal. Several courses of action are open to you : (a) read more about the subject in other hobby books, (b) get expert advice, ask questions to personnel of a local store, (c) talk to manufacturers, (d) talk to members of a local aquarium society. More than likely you will be using several of these options, which is the approach that I, too, recommend. Talk to people that you trust, either because their knowledge impresses you, or because you feel comfortable with what they have to say. Often the solutions to your problems will be simple.

Canister filters can be filled with a variety of materials. Be extremely careful when selecting these materials, making sure that all are totally salt water safe, and will not leach any noxious compounds into the water. Salt water is a very aggressive medium and far less compounds can be used in such water, than in fresh water. This is most important to keep in mind when selecting anything that will be placed in the tank, not just in the filters. Moreover, materials that may be all right to use in a salt water fish-only tank, may not be suitable for a marine reef aquarium. Invertebrates are much more sensitive, and delicate, and may not be able to tolerate certain compounds that fish can deal with to some degree.

Activated carbon, often placed inside canister filters, can be the source of many troubles. Frequently, activated carbon of lesser quality (and a lot of it gets sold in the aquarium hobby under fancy names), will

not remove as many compounds from the water as you expect, on one hand, and will leach phosphates into the water to boot. Phosphates will cause outbreaks of micro-algae to such an extent, that they will be very hard to control, let alone eradicate, even if one uses products to do so such as the ones sold by Thiel • Aqua • Tech and by Energy Savers Unlimited. Make sure that the activated carbon you buy is dull in appearance and not shiny. Shiny stuff is usually non-activated charcoal, a compound that is far less desirable to use and not nearly as good as superior quality activated carbon. Rinse the activated carbon before using it, and do so in warm water, as this will remove trapped gasses and open up the inner cavities of the activated carbon. Always place the carbon in such a way that water can flow through it freely. Baging activated carbon is not always the best way to use it. Water may flow ove the bag rather than through. Don't forget : water always seeks the path of least resistance.

To determine whether or not the carbon you have leaches phosphates into your tank's water, proceed as follows :

• prepare one half gallon of water in the same manner as you would if you were to add it to the tank,
• add a small amount of activated carbon to this mixture. Two table spoons will do fine,
• let stand overnight (or at least 12 hours),
• now test the water for phosphates. Use a low range test. You are looking for very small amounts. Much lower than you expect. I mean levels of 0.1 ppm (not one part per million, but $\frac{1}{10}$ of a part per million, a real small amount indeed, but enough to cause problems with micro-algae),
• if you find any phosphate at all, change brands.

Note from the Author : at the time of re-writing this book (early 1990) I know of only three carbon brands that will not leach phosphates into your water : Thiel • Aqua • Tech's Reef Carbon, Marineland's Carbon, and the Cora brand from Germany. The latter is available, but not easy to find. More on activated carbon later in this book.

When it comes to canister filters, do not skimp on the quality. Get the best you can afford. Keep in mind that if you are going to rely on such a canister to perform filtration for you, it has to be good enough to do so on a continuous basis, 24 hours a day, day in day out, week after week. A flimsy little filter that you got real cheap won't live up to that requirement. Marineland's Magnum's and Eheim are excellent choices.

Filters, including canister filters, need to be cleaned regularly to prevent the trapped material from breaking down and lowering the water quality. Additionally, filters need to be cleaned to prevent them from getting so clogged that they fail to run properly. Whenever a filter performs a biological function in addition to some other form of filtration, each time you clean the filter you destroy a good part of the bacteria in the biological bed as well. This, too, lowers the water quality, and stresses the fish and other animals in the tank. **This is the reason why I strongly recommend that all forms of filtration be segregated**.

Lately, mixtures of activated carbon and special resins have appeared on the market. Such products combine the effects of the carbon with the de-ionization capability of the resins. Whether such is a product that you want to use shall have to be determined over time. Resins do

not work well in salt water. The reason is the heavy chloride and sodium ions, which interfere with the functioning of the resins, prevent the resins from absorbing the compounds that they should absorb, and do in fresh water. This would make such a product efficient only, if the carbon used is of excellent quality. The resins may not serve a great deal of purpose. However, if the carbon is of excellent quality, the product will certainly remove many noxious elements from the water. Keep in mind that activated carbon does not last for ever. It needs to be changed from time to time. More frequently if your protein skimmer is undersized (Thiel, 1986)

How do you know when? Simple. Take a piece of white plastic. Make a faint yellow line (or several such lines) on the white plastic. Submerse the plastic in the aquarium, and hold on to it. Look at it from about 1, to 1½ feet away. If you can still see the faint yellow line(s), your carbon is still good. If you cannot see the faint yellow line(s), your water has a slight yellow tinge which masks the difference between the white and the yellow of the piece of plastic. If your water is slightly yellow, your carbon needs to be changed. This is a simple and easy to perform test, and one you do not even have to buy. You can easily make it yourself. Any piece of white plastic will do. Permanent markers, found in stationery stores, make the faint yellow lines.

Although stand-alone canister filters can provide a fair amount of biological filtration, the amount of such filtration is small and not sufficient, in my experience, to run a small reef tank. When supplementing a reef set-up with a trickle filter, canisters can serve a number of valuable functions. I use them myself for the following two purposes :

■ Ex-nitrate filter : canister is filled with about 15 pounds of Ex-nitrate from Thiel•Aqua•Tech to keep nitrate levels low in my 135 gallon tank. The water is taken from the sump of the trickle filter, ran through the canister and the Ex-nitrate, and then back to the sump of the trickle filter.

■ Poly Bio Marine® Inc.'s molecular absorption discs : canister is filled with 36 discs (in my case) sandwiched between 2 layers of aquarium filter floss. Again, the water is taken from the sump of the trickle filter, ran through the canister and the discs, and returned to the sump of the trickle filter, where it remixes with the main water mass of the tank.

Note from the Author : These discs, which we will discuss more in detail later, are a proprietary product of Poly Bio Marine® Inc. and are used by Thiel•Aqua•Tech, under special license, in their Platinum Series Trickle Filters, and also in canister filters. Both the Poly Filter and the molecular absorption discs are products that are far superior to activated carbon in 97 percent of the cases I tested. Only in one area is activated carbon still really necessary : the removal of residual ozone from the water coming out of protein skimmers and ozone reactors.

The bacterial beds in canister filters, and in undergravel filters as well for that matter, have a very short life expectancy when a power outage occurs. Within a matter of one to two hours, the filter can go partially or even totally anaerobic, especially if it has not been cleaned regularly, and if a lot of detritus is trapped inside the medium. Should the power come back on, say after 3 or 4 hours, and should this happen while you are absent, a great deal of damage can be done to your tank's lifeforms. Indeed, anaerobic filters produce very noxious by-products, which can create real havoc in the tank.

Special "trip" switches are available that prevent the pumps and canisters from re-starting automatically when the power comes back on. These switches can only be re-set manually. They help when the power has been out for a long time. But when the power outage is only for minutes or seconds, they are of no use, of course, as no damage to the filter beds would occur in such a short period of time. Additionally, your pumps would then stay off until you come back home, or happen to notice that they are not running.

Some hobbyists use canister filters filled with broken up pieces of coral to enhance, or maintain, the carbonate hardness of the water in the tank. This may work for some time, but not for very long, because as soon as the coral covers itself with slime and other detritus, the process stops. Moreover, at the high pH levels of marine tanks, the exchange does not work very well at all anyway (see also Spotte : Seawater Aquariums, A Captive Environment. John Wiley and Sons, Wiley Inter-Science.1979). Similar observations have been reported by Hueckstedt(Kosmos,1967), Thiel(Notes,1986), and others.

Although the use of calcite, or broken pieces of coral, can be used meaningfully to increase, or maintain, the carbonate hardness, such must be done in conjunction with carbon dioxide. This process is explained later in this book under the heading Reactors : carbonate hardness.

Yet another use for canister filters is supplemental biological filtration when the canister is filled with one of the many plastic filtering materials now available: Techs, balls, Pax, cubes, packs, spheres, Super Techs, Plusses etc. This can be very beneficial if the tank is overloaded, or when more biological filtration becomes necessary due to, for instance, overfeeding, a skimmer that does not work properly, and so on.

3.2.2 Box or Outside Filters :

These plastic filters, which can be hung on the side or back of the tank, have been available in the hobby for quite some time. They make excellent additions to other types of filters when such becomes necessary, but they are, in my experience with fish-only tanks, not efficient enough to run a decent reef tank. This makes sense because these filters were developed along time ago, and not with the types of loads in mind that are typically found in reef tanks. Although such bioloads may appear less significant as the ones in fish-only tanks, they are in most cases not.

I have not been able to document any reference material where such filters were used successfully to operate reef tanks, nor do I have personal experience with running them on such tanks either. While we have tried a lot of filters at Thiel•Aqua•Tech, we have not yet ran a reef on a plain box filter. Some hobbyists, however, report that they were succesful in maintaining so-called tiny reefs.

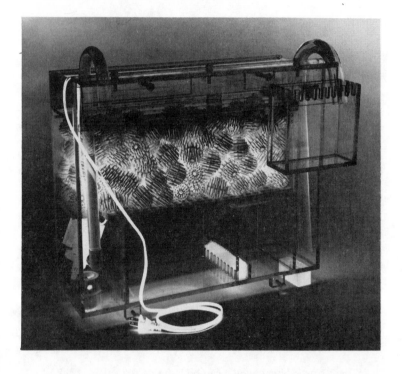

Though very similar to box filters, BioMesh filters differ in one respect : they offer a far greater surface area for bacterial growth. Such is achieved by placing successive mesh filter plates inside the filter, plates through which all the water has to go before it can re-enter the main water stream. The drawing of such a filter shows exactly what is happening in a clearer fashion. Although my company has carried two sizes of such filters for some time (1985 to 1988), we have discontinued doing so in 1989 because of a lack of hobbyist response.

BioMesh filters are extensively used in Germany and hobbyist report excellent results using them, even in large aquaria (Selzle, 1987). What is noteworthy, is that they naturally promote nitrate and phosphate reduction, without the use of any chemicals, fluids, nutrients or denitrators. Because demand was low, we no longer stock these filters, but still make them to order. Call Thiel•Aqua•Tech for details if you are interested. Price-wize these filters are in the same range as the better types of trickle filters, meaning they are not inexpensive, and you may well want to acquire a regular trickle filter instead.

3.2.3 Corner Overflow Filters :

These are, in reality, not really filters, but a means of bringing water down from the tank to the trickle filter, while at the same time pre-filtering that water mechanically. The filter usually consists of two parts, one that sits in the tank, and one that hangs over the lip of the tank and is connected to the top of the trickle filter. The part that sits in the aquarium has edges that are serrated. This prevents the fish from getting in the filter and ending up in the trickle filter on one hand, and ensures that the surface of the tank is strained of accumulated dirt, pieces and tufts of algae, slime, oily matter, etc. on the other.

By filling the larger part of the filter with an appropriate filtering medium, the unit can be made to perform as an excellent mechanical filter, thus preventing dirt and detritus from getting into the biological chamber. Filtering mechanically is especially important if the hobbyist uses DLS, a material that easily traps dirt and is widely used in trickle filters, mainly because it is inexpensive. It is, however, nowhere near as efficient as the plastic filtering media that are now available.

Corner overflow filters, or corner overflow boxes, should be cleaned very regularly. At least once a week is my recommendation. If such is not done, the filter may start restricting the water flow, which will reduce the overall efficiency of the filtration, while also posing a risk of water flowing over the tank and onto the floor, should the overflow box really get totally clogged.

    Many variations on how to set up such filters exist. We will look into some of them later in this book. Overflow boxes are also called surface skimming filters in some literature. This describes their function more accurately, and the credit for coining the name should go to Mike Helton of Summit Aquatics in Fulton, Mo. Look for a unit that has an automatic re-start feature, meaning that it will restart when the pumps come back on after a power outage. If you can find a self-priming overflow filter, such is an even better solution. Look too at the size of the outflow fitting. If you plan to run large amounts of water, make sure that the siphon has an outlet of at least 1 inch, preferably 1¼ inches.

Many materials can be placed in these filters to make them filter the aquarium water mechanically. Here are a few :

■ Biomech, Efimech, EfiGrob (gross), filter floss, small biological balls, coarse foam pads and blocs, foam cartridges, removable foam cartridges, and so on. The choice is yours, as long as you remember that you must clean that filter regularly to prevent it from affecting the water quality by lowering the dissolved oxygen levels, and adding unwanted decay compounds to the tank.

Besides corner overflow siphons, hobbyists use corner overflow boxes, with a hole drilled through the bottom of the tank. Such an arrangement is even better of course, but must be installed when the tank is first set up. Retrofitting is only possible if the tank is taken down completely, which is not practical at all. Additionally, not everyone can have his or her tank drilled, for a variety of reasons. We will discuss this type of arrangement elsewhere in this book.

3.3 Trickle Filtration : General Remarks

If biological filtration is such an important component of a well set up and well maintained aquarium, then surely, we will want the best filter money can buy to run our tank. We will want to maximize filtration efficiency, and we will want to do on a continuous basis. This can only be achieved with a superior filter, and not with some arcane and obscure filter that is inexpensive and is advertised as the latest, or the best, or the newest, the most superior, and other such advertising gobbledygook.

What we want is a superior filter, from a company that has proven itself in the reef business, filled with an advanced biological filtration medium, constructed of the right materials and in a professional manner. To such a filter we can entrust the lives, well-being and growth of the fish, corals and invertebrates that we will be keeping in our tank.

In this case, paying a little more for a filter is certainly better, providing you choose a real advanced unit (and after reading this book, and others by Albert J. Thiel, you will know what to look for).

Several North American companies now offer such filters : Nautilus Aquatics (Canada), Summit Aquatics, Lifereef Systems, Oceanarium, World Class Aquarium, Thiel•Aqua•Tech's Platinum Series filters, and others. German units used to be at the cusp of technology; they no longer are! U.S. made filters now far out perform imported models, especially so since the introduction of the Platinum Series.

Nobody in the "aquarium hobby", however, can lay claim to having invented, or developed, that filter. Trickle filters exist and been used for many many years in the sewage (sewerage) treatment industry (I recently found a 1936 reference to them, in a book called American Sewerage Practices, given to me by Matthew Cammarata, co-owner of Thiel•Aqua•Tech).

We do need to give credit, though, to a German Pet Store owner and manufacturer of advanced aquarium systems : Mr. N. Nollman of Nollman Aquaristik in Sennestadt by Bielefeld, who modified sewage industry ammonia towers (large versions of trickle filters), to make them fit the purpose he intended them for : small freshwater and marine aquariums. He had small units available in the German aquarium trade, in glass, using clear balls with rods as a biological medium, long before anyone in the hobby was using such filters In fact, I imported these filters into the USA in 1985, and sold them through my other company.

Because trickle filters have been around for so long in several other industries, mostly the sewerage industry, they have been improved upon, fine-tuned so to speak, over the years. The filters you see today, are an adaptation of sewerage industry ammonia towers, first downsized, and then tailored and fashioned to better fit the conditions of an aquarium, in particular of a marine reef type aquarium, and freshwater plant tanks. Because of all the improvements made, they are now only distant cousins of the originals ones !

After modifying the filters to better suit aquarium requirements, Nollman, and many others after him, found that these filters performed extremely well : meaning the water quality of the effluent from these filters was superior to what they had obtained, in the past, when using different forms of filtration. This was encouraging of course, and led them to try to perfect these filters even more. As time went on, and as the filters appeared on the U.S. market, manufacturers, here, started producing such filters as well. Summit Aquatics is one such company.

Several years have gone by since the first trickle filters were brought into the country in 1985. Quite a few more modifications have been made since, culminating recently in a filter that includes equipment and many options that are recommended for use on marine reef aquariums, but incorporated in the same filter, meaning in the same space: the **Platinum Series Filters** from Thiel•Aqua•Tech, at this point in time the most advanced and most efficient filters available. It certainly is one you should consider if you are in the market for a trickle filter, not because my company makes them, but because this is the most advanced filter money can buy, and because it is priced very reasonably.

Adding KSM and Tech•Iodine results in a better environment for Corals and Inverts

Trickle filters consist of several parts : a biological chamber, a sump, a drip plate, perhaps a carbon chamber, maybe a built-in protein skimmer, possibly a fine filter placed before the water enters the biological chamber, air inlets into the biological chamber, and so on. The more features the filter has, at least beneficial features, the better off you will be, and the less -overall- you will be spending on your filter. Indeed buying some options that you will probably need anyway, right from the start will save you money in the long run. As an analogy, just think of what it would cost you if you had to buy a car in spare parts !

Whether you buy a good filter, or a better one, depends largely on the features that the filter comes with. The more such features, usually the "better buy" the filter is. We will look at these features, and why you want them and need them, as we progress through this book. Looking through some hobby magazines recently, I counted advertisements for trickle filters, including the ones at the end in the small ads category : 53 different ones to be exact. Just about all of them obviously claim to be the best and the most efficient, and the only filter you will ever need. Caveat emptor. Beware, and study the offerings carefully before investing your good money in a filter that may not be for you, or that may not live up to its advertising claims.

It is unfortunate that, because of the present limitedamount of knowledge that exists in the area of reef tank filtration, the too prevalent gullibility on the part of hobbyists, and the complete lack of verification of advertising claims on the part of hobby magazines, that small manufacturers, frequently not even legitimate ones, are able to make claims that are often misleading if not totally untrue, or unverifiable.

This is unfortunate because it costs the hobbyist money, and gives the trickle filter, in general, a reputation that it certainly does not deserve. Superior filters exist, several of them in fact. Buy your filter from a company that has been around for several years, or has a product line that is so wide in the reef part of the hobby that they obviously know what they are doing, and are serious about supporting the reef hobbyist.

Don't buy from people that sell on the basis of price alone. You are probably getting what you are paying for : meaning a cheap filter, that will not stand up to the task at hand. Look for a manual, and not a short and simple one at that, but a real thorough one (very desirable). The quality of the manual often is an indication of the type of company you are dealing with : is it made using a cheap stencil process, or is it printed ? Telephone support is another feature you will need. Not necessarily an 800- line, but the ability for you to get hold of the manufacturer during

the day time. You would be surprised how many of these small manufacturers actually hold other jobs, and only make filters at night, or on the week-end, making it most unlikely that they will want to talk to you to solve your problems. They want to dedicate the little time they have to building more filters (that they can't service service either). Being able to talk to the manufacturer is an important criterion when selecting a filter. You will probably need to do so when you install the filter. It also comes in very handy to discuss the conditions of your tank, and what is happening in it, as time goes on. Do not under-estimate this ability.

Do not overlook its importance. I hear complaints about not being able to reach such filter manufacturers frequently. We even receive phone calls from people who want information about filters they bought from other companies, but cannot get hold of. To help them, and in the interest of the hobby, we try to answer their questions anyway, even though they do not use our equipment.

3.3.1 The Filter Itself :

The filter can be round or rectangular, or square, or any shape for that matter. As long as you can fill a portion of it with an appropriate biological filtering material, the shape has no bearing whatsoever on the efficiency of the filter, except perhaps for one fact: it should not be too narrow. If such were the case, channeling would occur and the water would not be dispersed properly over the medium. Channeling is a process where the water flows too much along the side walls of the filter and not enough over the biological medium inside the filter chamber.

In the same manner as shape is irrelevant, the material out of which the filter is made is not important either, except for the fact that it must be saltwater resistant, and can not leach any noxious compounds into the water. Trickle filters can, therefore, be made out of glass, acrylic, pvc, cpvc, polycarbonate, polyethylene, polypropylene and so on. You could, conceivably, build a filter out of wood that has been coated with polyurethane (several layers), or 316 SS, or some other saltwater resistant metal. The one constraint that results in most filters being built out of glass, or acrylic, is price. Indeed, most of the the other materials mentioned would price the filter out of the market. Just think of 316 SS, nylon, Teflon, and titanium, for instance.

Practically speaking filters are made out of glass and some type of acrylic, and are, usually anyway, rectangular and upright L-shaped. The size of the filter is entirely a matter of the size of the aquarium on which the filter will be used and how much biological filtering material it must hold as a result. Suggestions on how to evaluate both the type of material and the quantity needed for various size of aquariums, at various levels of biological load, are given elsewhere in this book. You should compare the suggestions to what you are doing now, or intend to do on the aquarium you are setting up, or planning to set up.

Water flows though the filter from top to bottom, and collects there before it is returned into the main water stream back to the aquarium. We call the bottom of the filter, the sump. A large sump is a benefit, as it increases the total amount of water in the system, and allows for the addition of optional equipment.

To disperse the water over the biological medium, a spray bar, or a drip plate, is used. Both have their merits, although I personally prefer the drip plate. It allows for a more even and continuous distribution of the water, and is not subject to stopping, a problem spray bars have had ever since they were introduced, and still have today, even though some manufacturers keep claiming theirs won't.

Even if they do not stop, they will often slow down significantly, and diminish the efficiency of the water distribution over the medium, as a result. Remember, the better the water distribution over the medium, the better the filtration. Additionally, the better the distribution over the medium you use, the less of it you will need. The latter should be pretty obvious - if you use a medium more efficiently, you need less of it- and good enough a reason to make sure that such efficient water distribution exists at all times.

The biological filtration that takes place in a trickle filter is an "aerobic" process, meaning it requires oxygen. In fact, it requires a great deal of oxygen (Hueckstedt, 1968,1976). Providing a supplemental source of oxygen is, therefore, an excellent idea. This is done by equipping the filter with air inlets that allow the hobbyist to blow air (a mixture of a number of gasses, and amongst others, oxygen) into the biological chamber. This results in two positive, beneficial, actions :

◆ Oxygen is present in greater quantities in the area where the bacteria are performing their biological task of converting nitrogen breakdown products, a plus,
◆ The oxygen in the air that is blown into the chamber also transfers, to some extent, to the water that is dripping and running down the biological filtering medium that is used, thus increasing the dissolved oxygen levels of the water in the aquarium, another plus.

Both these actions are beneficial to the overall water chemistry and the well being of the lifeforms you keep in the aquarium. Higher dissolved oxygen levels reduce stress on animal life, and more oxygen in the biological chamber, results in a stronger and more potent colony of bacteria. This, in turn, improves the quality of the water and reduces stress as well. Better water quality = a more vibrant looking aquarium.

Basically that is all there is to a trickle filter : (a) water enters at the top, (b) is dispersed over (c) an adequate medium, (d) bacteria grow on that medium and (e) convert ammonia to nitrite, and (f) nitrite to nitrate. (g) The water collects in the sump of the filter, and (h) is returned to the tank by means of a pump. The process is continuous and automatic, insomuch as water is continuously brought down to the top of the filter, and returned to the aquarium after it has passed through the trickle filter's biological chamber.

Because it is critical that this process not be interrupted, the pump(s) used on the system must be of superior quality. Indeed, they have to run 24 hours a day, day in day out, for weeks, months and years in a row. Skimping on the cost of the pump is, therefore, a big mistake, but one that is often made in an effort ot reduce the cost of running the reef. The life of your tank, and what's in it, depends on it. Interrupting the process results in :

◆ the bacteria in the filter dying off after a few hours. It is believed that the half life of the bacteria in a filter is around 6 to 8 hours depending on temperature and amount of air injected,
◆ the animal life is affected, because levels of dissolved oxygen will start falling soon and quickly after the pumps stop.

Spend a little more on the pump than you intended to. Buy the best pump you can afford. It will pay for itself in the short run because the quality of the water will remain where you need it, resulting in less fish and invertebrate losses, which can quickly eat up the savings you would have made if you had bought a cheaper pump. I speak from experience talking to many hobbyists who have made the mistake.

Some hobbyists want to build their own filters. There is, theo-

retically, nothing wrong with that, except that, in my experience, practically 9 times out of 10 such filter do not perform as required. Only after
you have had a good quality commercial unit for some time, and have
studied it, and figured out why it is performing the way it is, taking all
the small detail in to account, will you be able to build a unit yourself that
works satisfactorily.

Unless you already have this experience, we suggest that you
stick with commercially available filters. Many make the mistake of just
copying filter components, without really paying attention to detail, and
often the latter makes the difference. Copying components of a filter does
not necessarily mean that you have copied the principles, and added the
necessary detail to make the unit efficient. Proportions of various components, small features that may not be transparently obvious to you,
exact sizes of holes and their positioning, are all important, and differen-
tiate a basic filter from a real efficient one.

Additionally, building a unit on a trial and error basis will cost
a lot of money in the long run, and may not make it any less expensive
that a good quality commercial one to begin with. An error that is frequently made by hobbyists who build their own filters, is mixing parts
and portions of different filtration systems, ending up with a hybrid system that may not be all that efficient anymore. Often existing components
of a system are meant to work together, sometimes synergistically. Using
only parts of such systems, and/or combining parts of several systems
may do more damage than good, and often results in a filter that controls
you, rather than the opposite. Moreover, if something goes wrong, who
do you call? And what will the company you call say after they find out
that you have, in fact, mixed several approaches to filtration? Think about
it. How would you react if you were in their position?

We mentioned pumps briefly, and suggested that you should
buy the best pump available for the size system you run. Because such
pumps can cost a fair amount of money, it is a good idea, and suggested,
to protect it with a good quality float switch to prevent it from running
dry and burning out. Float switches serve a second purpose : they even
out the amount of water that goes up and the amount that comes back
down to the filter. For example, if the amount of water going up to the

tank is rather high, and the method used to bring water back down to the filter (the siphon, or overflow corner arrangement, etc. as we shall explain somewhat later), is somewhat slower, the water level in the sump will have a tendency to lower itself (more water is going up than coming down). Without a float switch this can lead to :

◉ the tank overflowing if the pump keeps running and pushes a great deal of water up to the aquarium,
◉ the sump running low in water and the pump sucking in air and blowing millions of little bubbles into the tank,
◉ the pump running dry, heating up and stopping, or burning out altogether if this happens for too long.

All these can be prevented by using a float switch. Several such switches are now on the market : a German unit made by ELB, orange in color, cigar-shaped and about 4 to 4½ inches long, Rule-O-matic switches that can be found in marine supply shops, stainless steel ones that are advertised in catalogues such as McMaster Carr and W.W. Graingers, and a switch sold by Thiel•Aqua•Tech, the Super Float, able to handle loads of up to 6 amps. Many Reed switches are advertised in catalogues but do not usually fit the hobbyist's requirements because they cannot handle the amperage developed by the pump(s) used. Always check that the switch you buy is rated for both 115 volt and the amperage your pump develops. If not, you will ruin the switch.

As systems get more sophisticated they require more intricate piping. This may mean that you will have to use flow and check valves, fittings to divert water to certain optional equipment you are using, flow meters, solenoids, and so on. The more intricate the piping, the more expensive the system will obviously get. Although ball and check valves can be ordered at fairly reasonable prices from mail order companies such as U.S. Plastics and Savco, solenoids, flow meters and other such equipment can be fairly expensive. Later on we will review some of this equipment, but you can find a detailed look at such advanced aquariums in Advanced Reef Keeping Made Simple(I), Thiel 1989, and Small Reef Aquarium Basics, Thiel 1989, both published by Aardvark Press.

Many filters you will see on the market have a space provided for a foam block.   The reason for this, we assume, is that early pictures and drawings of such filters always showed such a compartment. The idea was to fine filter the water on one hand, and provide an area for some amount of controlled assimilation/denitrification on the other (reduction of nitrates in the water). As time went on, I have found that these compartments are a good feature, but can be improved upon by using a better way of filtering the water : a foam cartridge, hooked up to the pump intake, on the inside of the sump of the trickle filter. In this manner, all the water in the sump must first go through that foam cartridge before it can re-enter the main water stream. Such foam cartridges are standard in both the Platinum series, and the Summit Aquatics trickle filters.

The problem with the foam blocks is that water having a tendency to seek the path of least resistance, the water will flow by the foam block and not through it, greatly reducing the efficiency of the set-up. Some filters have the foam installed in such a way that all water *must* pass through it. Such is an improvement, but requires that the hobbyist pay careful attention to its cleanliness, as the foam will plug up rather quickly, creating an uneven water level between the back and the front of the

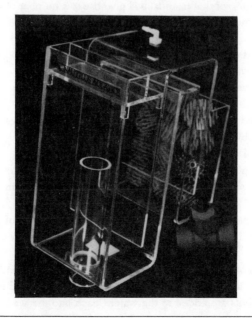

Tech• Coconut Shell Pelleted activated carbon does not leach phosphates in your water

sump, which. Those of you who have such a set-up may have experienced this already, and know what I am describing. Foam cartridges in which the water is "sucked" through, because they are attached to the pump intake side work better, and need less attention. Cleaning them once a week is usually fine, and easy to include in the weekly maintenance schedule of the tank.

Alternatively, the pre-filtering should be done in the main water line, between the trickle filter and the aquarium, by using some form of canister filter, for example : Lifeguard, PEP, etc. Special purpose filters designed to fine filter are also available, for instance the Fin-L-Filter® from Poly Bio Marine Inc. (pronounced : final filter). Of course, the siphon bringing water down to the trickle filter, or the corner overflow box arrangement, should also contain some pre-filtering material to prevent dirt from getting into the biological chamber of the trickle filter.

This is especially so if you are using a material in the biological chamber that easily traps dirt, such as, for example, D.L.S. (Double Layered Spiral) or Biopaks, or shotgun wadding, plastic hair curlers and so on. Plugging of that material will give rise to a number of problems that are detrimental to the water quality. The scenario is as follows :

■ trapped material will plug the filter medium more and more,
■ water will by-pass that area,
■ other areas of the filter will have to handle more flow and more dirt,
■ this will plug those areas up sooner,
■ plugged areas will start containing less and less oxygen,
■ anaerobic activity may start,
■ harmful compounds will be added to the water,
■ decomposition of the trapped material lowers D.O. levels,
■ low dissolved oxygen levels are detrimental to the tank life.

Not a very positive scenario. Cleaning any of the materials mentioned above is difficult and brings about other problems :

■ by removing and cleaning the material, many bacteria are killed off,
■ by moving the filtering material, trapped detritus and its breakdown components are added to the water (leach into the water),

■ this pollutes the water considerably and causes stress for all tank life.
■ stress brings about disease, usually parasitic, which may kill fish.
■ dead and decaying fish pollute the water even more, and so on.

It should be fairly obvious, in light of all of this, that you will need to use a filtering material in the trickle filter that does not trap dirt, or at least lets it get through easily and end up in the sump where you can remove it later on, for instance during your next scheduled maintenance session. More on this in the next few pages when we talk about the required minimum amount of biological surface area.

3.4 Advanced Trickle Filters
3.4.1 General Remarks

Advanced trickle filters are nothing more than basic trickle filters -the ones we talked about so far- that they have been considerably improved, for example :

◆ Better aeration of the biological filtering medium, e.g. several air inlets,
◆ Addition of a skimmer (foam fractionator), preferably a venturi type, as such skimmers are far more efficient than columnar ones,
◆ Drip plate with tapered holes, for better water distribution,
◆ Space for carbon, for example a built-in cmpartment,
◆ Fine filter to prevent detritus from entering the biological chamber,
◆ Fine filter on the suction side of the pump, inside the sump,
◆ Perhaps even space for other pieces of equipment such as oxygen reactors, molecular absorption reactors, carbon dioxide diffusion equipment, salinity measurement cups, and so on,
◆ Equipped with the fittings you will need to hoop up the pump(s), etc.
◆ And others still.

Advanced trickle filters, such as the ones just described, may not cost much more money than regular trickle filters, because the companies that make them usually sell enough of these filters to be able to keep the price down to a reasonable figure. It is really incumbent upon the hobbyist to shop around, and select such a filter from the many offerings that are now advertised in hobby magazines, keeping the remarks made earlier about advertising claims in mind.

Tech●Coconut Shell Pelleted activated carbon does not leach phosphates in your water

The choice is large and yours. Don't buy the first filter you look at, ask lots of questions about the one you are interested in, try to get a copy of the manual in advance (even if you have to pay for it. Ask if the cost will be refunded if you end up buying the filter), get exact measurements so you can make sure it will fit underneath your tank, in short, get as much information as you can before you actually buy. The more you know, the more educated a consumer you are, and the better a decision you are likely to make. This is a crucial buying decision, take your time. Do not buy impulsively, but check several filters out systematically and in detail. Make sure as well that the filter comes with a warrantee.

3.4.2 Trickle Filter Biological Media :

At about the same time as you decide on which filter to buy, you will have to select a medium for biological filtration. Many such media are now offered for sale. Here are just a few (some of these names are trademarks of their respective companies):

>BioMech by Kordon
>Bio Spheres
>Pall Rings
>Flex Rings
>Matrix II
>Super•Techs
>Shotgun wadding
>BioBale
>DLS material
>Broken up dead coral
>Bio Blocs
>Mini Balls
>Impacs
>Jaeger Tri-Packs
>Norton Rings
>Raschig Rings
>Matrix I
>Bio•Techs
>Cut PVC pipe
>Plastic Haircurlers
>Balls
>Crushed Coral pieces
>Biopax
>Bio Cubes
>Lampacs
>Plastic netting
>and still others. The choice is very large and also very confusing to many hobbyists.

All are touted as the one you should use. All claim to have very large amounts of surface area, larger in fact than the original balls that were introduced in 1985. How these companies arrived at the surface area claimed is a mystery. It is so to me, and to many people knowledgeable with how such a surface area is calculated. Rather than write on the relative merits of the claimed surface areas, however, lets look at what the medium that you select should have as qualities and features :

> **(1) it should offer as large a surface area as possible**
> **for beneficial bacteria to grow on**
> **and**
> **(2) it should not easily trap dirt, detritus, algal debris, etc.**
> **and**
> **(3) it should allow for good gas exchanges, especially oxygen.**

What does this all mean? Let's look at each of these feature one at a time, and explain why they are required and what their relative benefits are :

(1) large surface area : the larger the surface area, the more Nitrosomonas and Nitrobacter bacteria can grow in the filter. Within reason though. Only as many bacteria will be present in the filter, as there are food & nutrients for them to survive on. If, for arguments sake, only enough nutrients are available for 10^8 bacteria to survive on, that's all there will be in terms of numbers of bacteria. There cannot be more, because there are no nutrients for them to survive on. Providing space for twice that amount of bacteria does, therefore, not make sense.

Some margin is necessary because the amount of by-products that the bacteria need to process varies over time and can increase, for instance when you add another fish or invertebrate. More space needs to be available, therefore, to accommodate the additional amount of Nitrosomonas and Nitrobacter that will populate the filter from time to time.

How much space do the bacteria really need? Because of their micronic size, very little. It is usually an accepted rule, in my circles anyway, that the following surface areas suffice per gallon of water in a system, of the type mentioned below (I mean true surface area, which is not necessarily what the advertising claims state) :

• Low load : 1.00 to 1.50 square feet per gallon of water in the system

- Medium load : 1.50 to 2.00 square feet per gallon of water in the system
- High load : 2.00 to 2.50 square feet per gallon of water in the system.

These numbers are a guideline and should be used only as such. Before applying them to any material that you plan to use, you must first make sure that you **know the true surface area of the medium**.

For example : blue hedgehog-like balls (also available in clear natural color from several other companies) have a surface area of 80.000 square centimeters per 20 liters of balls (figures taken from the brochure of the distributor). Converted to square feet this is somewhat slightly higher than 16 square feet per gallon volume (which itself is somewhere between 75 and 80 of the balls, depending on the container used).

If you were to use these balls on a 100 gallon tank with a medium to heavy load, using an average of the guidelines above for heavy load, you would need $100 \times 2\frac{1}{4}$ = 225 square feet of surface area for bacteria to grow on. 225 : 16 = ± 14.00 gallons of the balls, or slightly more than 14 percent of the water content of the tank.

Because I have seen claims for those balls' surface area as large as 23 square feet per gallon, you could also conclude that you only need 225 : 23 = ± 10.00 gallons of the balls, or about 10 percent of the water content of the tank. "You" must be the judge, and decide what the true surface area is, and then select how much volume you will need.

The example given here is not meant to place these balls in a negative light, to the contrary, but is used as an illustration of how confusing the decision of how much material you really need can be. You should make these calculations for any of the materials you decide on, but only after you have understood the total picture. Indeed, surface area is only one of the qualities that a good trickle filter biological filtering material should have.

Looking at another example, using Super•Techs, on the same 100 gallon aquarium, gives the following figures : 225 square feet of surface area needed, divided by 29 (surface area of one gallon of Super•Techs) = 7.75 gallons, or roughly 8 percent of the water content of the system.

If one now multiplies the number of gallons needed by the cost of the media looked at, one gets a total cost for the media that will go in the filter. Such is, in my opinion, the right way to look at the media that are available. How much of it do you need? How much does it cost per gallon? What is your best buy?

(2) Does not trap dirt : the reason for this, is not to prevent the space available for bacteria from being reduced, because it is now taken up by dirt. The reason this is mentioned, is because several hobbyists had brought it up as a question during phone conversations I have had with them at Thiel•Aqua•Tech. The real reason is much subtler : dirt that gets trapped in the medium (a) prevents water from flowing through the medium evenly, and (b) results in decay.

Decay occurs because the debris, dirt, detritus (call it what you want), will start decomposing in the presence of oxygen. Decomposition brings about two undesirable results: (a) it reduces the amount of oxygen in the water, the so-called dissolved oxygen level, and (b) it adds noxious decomposition by-products to the water. Both these actions result in a lowered water quality, which in turn increases the stress on the animals and may lead to outbreaks of disease. Even if no disease breaks out, lowered water quality and increased stress lead to a tank that does not look as good at it could, and should.

For a medium not to trap dirt, it must be made in such a way, that whatever dirt flows through the chamber in which the medium is placed, such dirt will gradually pass through the medium and end up in the bottom of the filter : the so-called sump. Media that are tight in their structure, for example DLS, Haircurlers, shotgun wadding, cut up PVC, and like materials, do not fit this criterion, and should be avoided.

They may perform well for a while, but they will invariably cause problems after a short amount of time. The latter will vary depending on how well the water that goes into the biological chamber is pre-filtered. The better it is, the longer the medium will perform. After 8 to 10 months, however, even the best pre-filtered water will have created several areas that are full of accumulated small debris in all these materials. Many hobbyists report problems with DLS after only 6 months.

Surface area and not trapping dirt (having enough void space) must, therefore, be combined when looking at media for trickle filters. They both are important and they both need to have your attention during the selection process. Of course they are somewhat contradictory, because the more void space the less surface, and vice-versa. The right balance between the two, combined with the third criterion, will narrow your choice of biological filtering media down even further.

(3) Gaseous exchanges : since we already know that the biological filter is a very aerobic filter, one where oxygen is needed in large quantities, it should be obvious that the medium that you will use in that filter, needs to allow for efficient and maximum transfer of the oxygen in the air that we are blowing into the biological chamber, into the water that passes through that same chamber in streams and drops. This is important both for the activity level of the bacteria, and for the dissolved

oxygen levels in the water. More oxygen in the water is beneficial because it reduces stress on the fish. Reduced stress is paramount in avoiding disease, especially parasitic disease, and having a tank that looks at its best. Newer media, developed with increase gaseous exchanges in mind will be the media of the future; second generation media so to speak.

3.4.3 Aeration of the biological chamber :

We have alluded to the need to aerate the biological chamber several times already. We have done so because it is an important factor that all hobbyists who run trickle filters must deal with and understand. The bacteria that grow in the biological chamber are aerobic bacteria. Aerobic bacteria need oxygen. Providing large amounts of oxygen to these bacteria enhances the efficiency of your filter. Not providing oxygen means that you are running your filter at a lower level of efficiency. This is somewhat similar to always driving a car in third gear as the highest gear when, in fact, that car has five. Such would not be a very efficient use of that car, would it not? The same applies to your filter.

You cannot blow too much air into the chamber. Use a good quality strong air pump. I personally use and have used Wisa 200 and Wisa 300 pumps for many years, and I highly recommend them. The air must be blown inside the biological chamber itself. Not in the water right underneath that chamber. Some pictures that I have seen, and some drawings in other books, may lead you to believe that you should blow the air in the water underneath the biological chamber. Such is not correct. You must blow the air directly into the chamber where the media is. That is where the best gaseous exchanges will take place.

It has even been demonstrated that varying the amount of air that is blown into the filter can alter your redox potential (more on the latter later in this book). G. Bepko (1988) in tests on a 100 gallon marine reef system equipped with a 10 gallon trickle filter filled with blue biological balls, demonstrated that when he cut off the air his redox potential, as measured with a Sanders controller and electrode, went down significantly after about 40 minutes, and stayed depressed until about 30 minutes after the air had been switched on again. I personally verified this on my own tank and found results close to his.

Super•Techs allow for better gas exchanges

An even distribution of the air throughout the biological chamber may require more than one inlet, especially on larger filters. All Platinum Series filters that we build have 2 such inlets standard, regardless of size. This ensures that the air is distributed all over the biological chamber, for maximum efficiency. If your filter, or the one you are contemplating, does not have such an air inlet, you should either add it yourself, or look for another filter.

It is not unusual for certain kinds of resellers to downtalk products they do not carry, and try to sell you something they do have on the shelves. You should be aware of this. It may not be as common as certain sources suggest, but it does happen. Again, beware, and know exactly what you want and why you need it. The more educated a consumer you are, the better a buyer you will be, and the less likely you are to end up with merchandise that you do not need, or that does not serve the purpose you intended it for.

3.4.4 Drip Plate Fabrication :

Drip plates should do just that : drip. Or better, make the water coming down from the aquarium drip evenly over the biological medium, spreading it out as much as possible, breaking it up in small streams, and wetting as much of the medium used as possible. Any medium that is not wetted is not used, and is, basically, a waste of your money. Although spray bars break up the water very efficiently, they have the unfortunate quirk of slowing down and stopping.

The reason is simple : dirt, detritus, algal debris, and so on, slowly move into the area that assures the rotation and hinder the free spinning of the bar that distributes the water. When this happens water is distributed very unevenly and only on a small portion on the biological medium. This is a very inefficient use of the medium, and reduces the overall efficiency of the filter greatly. Look at it in this fashion : if you used the medium more efficiently you would need less of it because more of its surface area would be populated with Nitrobacter and Nitrosomonas bacteria.

Many different designs have been tried to make spray bars more efficient, and many different materials have been used to make them rotate more smoothly and for longer times. Rulon, Viton, polypropylene, polyethylene and other such noble materials have all been given the test. No one has convinced me, yet, that their model using a specific material will work as long and as well as drip plates do.

Drip plates are relatively easy to make yourself, or to modify if need be. Whether or not this needs to be done depends on the kind of filter you own, or plan to acquire. Several features need to be examined:

- the size of the holes,
- whether they are tapered or not,
- the spacing of the holes,
- how far from the edges they start,
- whether they are staggered or in-line.

Here is a simple procedure to make an efficient drip plate, or modify the one you have :

- carefully measure the inside of the filter's biological chamber.
- buy a piece of $\frac{1}{4}$ inch acrylic of the exact above dimensions.
- scribe lines in one direction, using a sharp tool or a plastics scriber, and make them 1 inch apart.
- now draw lines 1 inch apart, at a 90 degree angle with the first set of lines.
- do not draw lines within approximately $1\frac{1}{2}$ inches of the edges of the plate. This will prevent water from channeling along the sides of the chamber.
- where the two sets of lines intersect drill a $\frac{3}{16}$ inch hole (this could be quite a few holes especially in larger filters.
- after you have drilled the holes, use a taper bit and taper the holes to ensure a better downward flow.

Note : it is not necessary to groove the lines that you draw in both directions. The reason that you use a scribe (that makes a fine scratch in the plastic), is to determine the intersection points and make it easier for you to know where to drill the holes. The drawing shows both the initial step, and the end result. For more flow, space the lines $\frac{3}{4}$" apart.

Step 1   Step 2

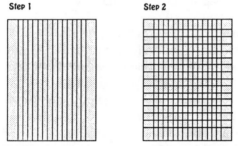

Holes should be spaced equidistant in both directions. Half inch is suggested

3.4.5 Space for Other Media :

Because of the nature of the filtering that an aquarium requires -especially reef aquariums-, other media besides just biological types
need to be relied on to purify the water in the tank. Specifically, activated
carbon and polymer-type media are the more commonly used ones.
Both are quite popular nowadays, especially in fish-only tanks.

In reef aquariums, however, the story is slightly different and
hobbyists should be very careful as to what type of carbon, for instance,
is actually used. We will be dealing with these media, and their relative
merits, benefits and drawbacks, more in detail in a later chapter. Suffice
it to say, at this stage, that if you are planning on using either of them,
you will need space in the tank, or in the trickle filter, or its sump, to place
these media so you can use them properly and make them work
efficiently for you.

Activated carbon definitely needs to be used if you are also injecting ozone into a protein skimmer, or an ozone reaction chamber (see later for more details). Polymer type filters, such as the Poly Filters®, or Molecular absorption discs from Poly Bio Marine Inc.®, are definitely needed in a a reef tank to remove many of the undesirable compounds that other forms of filtration do not remove. By other forms of filtration we mean biological, mechanical, and foam fractionation also called protein skimming. Having spaces, or compartments, already built into the filter where such media can be placed will save you a lot of time later on, and will make it easier for you to add them to your system without having to improvise.

Remember it is not just important that you use such media, it is also as important that you use them in the right manner : **meaning the water must flow through the medium evenly and thoroughly**, not just over the medium, or by the medium.

If the filter that you now own does not have such chambers, or compartments, you may wish to add them yourself by cementing two or more acrylic plates inside the sump between which you can wedge activated carbon or Poly Filters®. Alternatively, you can place the media in a canister filter, for example a strong Marineland, or similar filter, taking water to run it from the sump of the trickle filter and returning it there. In this manner the operation of the canister will not interfere with the functioning of the trickle filter, and will not affect the water level of the sump either. I have used both the Magnum 330 and the Eheim 2217 canisters to this effect. Both work very well.

3.4.6 Built-In Protein Skimmer :

Built-in protein skimmers, or foam fractionators, are not a common feature included in the trickle filters that are nowadays on the market. Most of the skimmers offered for sale are, in fact, not even venturi operated, but columnar. Venturi valves are a special valve, built in such a way, that as water passes through it, forcefully, the valve sucks in outside air because of a differential pressure created inside the valve (right after the air inlet hole).

It is not important that you understand why they work, just be

---

Super•Techs allow for better gas exchanges

aware of the fact that venturi operated skimmers are more efficient that columnar skimmers (Guido Hueckstedt 1967, Aquarien Chemie, Kosmos). More on protein skimmers, both columnar and venturi, themselves in a later chapter.

Owning a trickle filter that is equipped with a built-in venturi skimmer is a definite advantage. Not only will you have a very efficient skimmer, but you will also save yourself a substantial amount of money by not having to buy the skimmer as a separate item. Indeed, good skimmers can be quite pricey, especially if you research available skimmers somewhat, and buy a real good unit properly sized for your aquarium. In a later chapter you will find an checklist that you can fill out to select the right skimmer for your tank. It is simple and straight forward and will let you end up with the properly configured unit that your tank requires based on the load, type of filtration, type of aquarium, whether you use ozone or not, and many other such variables.

A word of caution : if you use ozone in conjunction with a skimmer that is part of your trickle filter, you must make sure that no ozone can find its way to the back chamber of the filter. Indeed, should this happen, some ozone may get into the biological chamber and kill off some of the bacteria. Such would of course greatly reduce the efficiency of your filter. Normally, to prevent any ozone from getting in that chamber, the skimmer should be placed towards the front of the filter's sump, and water from the skimmer should be flowed over activated carbon before it re-enters the main water stream, to allow the activated carbon to remove residual ozone that may still be present in the water.

Until recently, in-filter skimmers could not compete at all with dedicated outside units. Most skimmers built into the trickle filter's sump were air stone operated, and really small. This made them most inefficient and hard to operate because, on one hand, adjusting them correctly was very difficult, and on the other, the scum produced would often leak back into the sump when the collection cup for the scum became overfilled.

Besides, some could not even be operated with ozone at all because several of their parts were not ozone resistant. (Note : make sure that any skimmer you buy can be operated with ozone! Ask the question specifically to the manufacturer, or main importer. Ask them for how long they will guarantee their skimmer against breakdown due to ozone.

Totally ozone resistant skimmers can be built as well, meaning skimmers that can resist ozone for greater lengths of time, e.g. several years. The price of such a skimmer would however be about three to four as much as the price of a regular skimmer.

All Platinum Series filters contain a venturi operated and correctly sized protein skimmer that can be further improved upon by ordering a molded, rather than manual, venturi, for a nominal supplement. These skimmers are built right into the sump of the filter, and do not require extra space since they are part of the footprint of the filter itself. Right after the skimmer chamber, in the area where the water exits, another chamber is already built that can be filled with activated carbon, to allow those hobbyists using ozone to remove residual O_3, or to allow for the addition of Poly Filters® or molecular absorption discs from Poly Bio Marine Inc.® for the much required chemical filtration (for more on chemical filtration see later chapters) that your reef aquarium needs.

3.4.7 Minimum Needed Biological Surface Area :

When looking at trickle filters, the first step in the decision process should not be which filter to buy, but what quantity of medium does the filter need to contain. To be able to determine that number you must first know how much biological surface area will be required to run your tank successfully. Each and every tank is different in this respect. The amount of surface area needed is directly and highly related to the type of tank, how much the biological load is, what type of filtration you will be using, whether or not you will install a protein skimmer, whether or not you will be using ozone, whether you use activated carbon, chemical filtration methods etc.

It certainly is not as simple as some would like you to believe when making recommendation such as : use 10, or some similar number, percent of the water content of your tank, in equivalent gallons of biological filtering medium.

For example : for a 100 gallon tank such recommendations often state that you must use 10 gallons of medium. Now I ask you : what medium? Why 10 percent? Why does this percentage apply to all aquariums uniformly?

What about aquarium loads, types of filtration used, skimmers, ozone, etc. I can honestly not accept such generalized recommendations because they are much too all-encompassing and comprehensive. Moreover, my long experience in running salt water and reef tanks tells me that such recommendations are inaccurate, and always results in filters that hold much more material than is necessary, or hold the wrong type of material, because hobbyists have not paid attention to the suggestions made earlier in chapter 3.4.2 in this book, specifically with regard to the qualities that such media should demonstrate to be efficient in the long run.

This is, unfortunately, compounded by the lack of knowledge regarding trickle filters in general and their required features in particular, and results in hobbyists often ending up with not only the wrong filter, but the wrong filter with the wrong biological filtering medium inside. Not a rosy picture of course.

The more the hobbyist "knows", therefore, the better off he or she will be. Buying as an educated consumer in a market place that, for the time being, is still full of hearsay recommendations rather than true empiric evidence and real requirements is, as a result, a must. At least for a while to come, until such time as acceptable practices for keeping reef tanks become better and better known and acknowledged by pet store owners and personnel.

Reading a lot, and asking many questions is the only way for the hobbyist to protect him, or herself. In this still very much evolving environment, where a lot of untruths circulate in pet stores, articles in magazines and in aquarium society circles the hobbyist must be aware that his or her own knowledge is paramount to getting the right product for the job at hand. But such is the fate of any new method or practice. It is, fortunately, not something unique to the aquarium hobby. It is also not something that we should commiserate about but simply be aware of and take into account when making purchase decisions. As time goes on, and as successive printings of this book come to the market, we will, hopefully, be able to remove this section entirely soon.

Having said all this, what type of surface area should the hobbyist then be looking for, especially since this is the first thing one needs to know before being able to decide on the actual medium and the size of the filter? As is so often the case in matters relating to aquariums, there is not one single answer. This is so for a very good reason : aquariums differ in the amount of livestock that hobbyists place in them, in the type of other equipment that is used, in how they are cared for, fed, what additives are added and so on. All of these variables influence the amount of organic material that is present in the tank, and all those variables need to be taken into account when establishing filtration criteria.

In an effort to simplify the picture somewhat, tanks can in essence be divided into 3 main groups : low, medium and heavy loads, and each of these types sets its own filtration requirements :

◉ Low load tanks are defined as aquariums that are visibly low in life forms, for example less than 1 small to medium fish per 10 gallons of water. A small fish is defined here as the size of e.g. a 3 stripe damsel of the size usually found in pet shops : ± 1 to 1.5 inches in length. Medium is defined is defined as the size of an average sized Centropyge Angelfish, e.g. usually 2.5 to 3.0 inches in length. Alternatively, low is defined as an aquarium that has no more than 1 invertebrate, e.g. Atlantic Pink tip anemone of size normally found in pet shops, per 10 gallons of water. Most tanks do not conform to this picture because, although they may start up that way, hobbyists keep adding and adding lifeforms as time goes on, never or hardly ever changing anything to the filtration.

◉ Medium load is defined here as the above type of fish and invertebrates per 5 gallons of water in the aquarium, or a mix of fish and invertebrates mentioned above, again per 5 gallons of water. Quite a number of hobbyist tanks fit in this category. This is especially so for tanks owned by hobbyists who are aware that loading up the tank cannot go on for ever when the basic filtration, the one that was installed when the tank was originally set up, is not changed.

Super•Techs allow for better gas exchanges

◉ Heavy, or high, load is defined here as anything that is higher than the two categories described already. This definition probably places most hobbyists' tanks in the heavy load category. This is so because most hobbyist tend to keep on buying and buying fish and invertebrates, and eventually their tank ends up in the heavy load category.

If the latter is so, and if the hobbyist is realistic and willing to recognize that this is probably what he or she will end up doing, then such hobbyists should plan for this scenario. Perhaps not consciously so, but because each time the hobbyist goes to the pet store, and sees an animal that he or she likes, it gets brought home and added to the tank. Progressively the tank houses more and more lifeforms, and the system, the filtration that is, gets taxed more and more. Because, in my experience, this scenario is so typical, it makes sense to plan for it at the time the filtration is selected and purchased.

Experience is about all one can rely on to suggest adequate levels of surface area for biological filtration for each of these categories. There are no formulas one can work with, and there is no real scientific way (yet anyway) to determine such numbers. But experience is an excellent teacher and has demonstrated over the years that certain levels of surface area can cope with certain levels of biological load and certain aquarium practices.

Different authors may suggest more generalized numbers. Others may go into more detail. You may wish to refer, for example, to Martin Moe's The Marine Aquarium Reference - Systems and Invertebrates, for some additional insights. My suggestions for surface area in trickle filters **using a plastic medium** that fits the norms and criteria outlined before, are as follows :

◉ Low load : 0.95 to 1.50 square feet of surface area per gallon of water in the system (capacity of tank minus displacement by rocks, plus water in the sump.
◉ Medium load : 1.50 to 2.00 square feet of surface area per gallon of water in the system.
◉ High load : 2.00 to 2.50 square feet of surface area per gallon of water in the system.

Let's look at a few examples using the high load recommendations, as those are the ones that I feel most hobbyists need to provide for :

■ Tank size 55 gallons : 55 times 2.00 = 110 and 55 times 2.5 = 138 square feet of surface area. Using, for example, Bio•Techs you would need between 5.00 and 6.27 gallons of Techs to run an efficient system. A filter holding 5 gallons of Bio•Techs would be the right filter for you. An additional gallon to gallon and a quarter could be placed elsewhere in the system, e.g. in the overflow siphon or in a similar place.

■ Tank size 70 gallons : 70 x 2.00 = 140 and 70 x 2.5 = 175. Again, using Bio•Techs you would need 140 : 22 or ± 6.36 gallons to 175 : 22 or ± 8 gallons. In this particular case you may want to buy a 10 gallon capacity unit, even if you only place 7 or 8 gallons of plastic filtering material in it. You will have space and area to spare.

In the above examples we used Bio•Techs. Using a different medium will, of course, yield different results. Using Super•Techs, which have a larger surface area than Bio•Techs, you would need less material, and you would end up needing a smaller filter in certain cases (numbers are averaged) :

Tank Size	Bio•Techs	Super•Techs	Filter size
55	5.5	4.25	5 gals/5 gals
70	7.0	5.25	10 gals/5 gals
110	10.8	8.25	10 gals/10 gals
150	14.75	11.25	15 gals/10 gals

Use these numbers and examples only **as guidelines only**. You must do a similar calculation for the type and size of tank that you plan to run yourself. The key, when calculating, is to use the exact surface area of the medium which, as already indicated, is not necessarily the one that you may see in advertising. If you overestimate the surface area you will not be using enough material. For the above calculations we have used the figures of 22 square feet for Bio•Techs and 29 square feet for Super•Techs. These are realistic linear surface area numbers, and are based on an as accurate as possible a calculation of surface as could be arrived at using mathematical modeling included in "Mathematica", a mathematics computer software program that is available for both IBM and Macintosh type computers.

The previous six printings of The Marine Fish and Invert Reef Aquarium listed different required surface areas. These numbers have been revised to take the most recent media surfaces into account, as well as more recent information on actual surface area needed to run an efficient system. The changes made are not very significant in nature however, at least not in the domain of gallons of media needed as a percent of the total amount of water in the system.

For illustrative purposes we are including the required surface area numbers chart as it appeared in the sixth printing. We suggest, nevertheless, that you now use the numbers that are part of the 7 th printing as the guideline in deciding the surface areas needed for your particular system, and not the ones of the sixth printing.

Martin Moe, in his new book mentioned earlier, lists recommended surface areas of 3 to 5 square feet per gallon of water, depending on load. Because that number is not qualified with what type of material they apply to, and because of Martin's large knowledge about marine tanks, his recommendations must be taken into consideration as well, particularly if you are using media that are different from the ones mentioned earlier in this chapter : Bio•Techs and Super•Techs. Incidentally, if you have not yet read his book, you must. His latest is also his greatest. Additionally he addresses a number of filtration techniques that are not included in this book, that are also to be considered.

You must keep in mind too, that after a short period of time anything in the aquarium acts as a settling place for bacteria. Rocks, dead coral, decorative pieces, crevices in rocks and decorations, the inside of pipes, the inside of ball and check valves, the siphon or overflow box that brings water down to the filter, glass or acrylic panes of the tank, etc. Bacteria do not know the difference and settle on any appropriate medium. What we are trying to do with a trickle filter, is not only to provide these bacteria with a large amount of surface area to settle on, but influence the area where this surface is in such a way, that it is more propitious for them to colonize, by increasing the amount of oxygen in that area, and keeping the settling medium out of the water. These two factors, combined, result in both a more powerful and more potent colony of Nitrobacter and Nitrosomonas bacteria, which in turn bring about better water quality in the tank. Because the area is favorable to their growth, large amounts of bacteria will colonize it.

■ To recap : First determine the amount of surface area that you will need for the type of tank you are installing, then select a medium, using the remarks made in this chapter as a guideline, and find out its exact surface area per gallon/volume, now calculate how may gallons you will need of that material, and then decide what capacity your filter should have. Take the recommendations made with regard to desirable options and features into account.

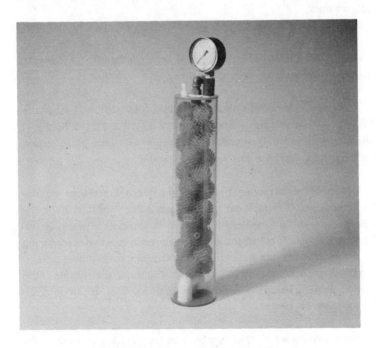

Modular Oxygen Reactor with Pressure Gauge
Fits in Platinum Series Filter

Super▪Techs allow for better gas exchanges

3.4.7 Calculating the size of a trickle filter chamber :

Calculating the size of the biological chamber of a trickle filter is not a complicated task. We will use an example top illustrate this point. Substitute your own numbers and recalculate the results if you are planning on building your own filter, or if you would like to calculate the exact content of a filter you see in a magazine or store.

The premise is the following : for any rectangular or square box that houses a medium for biological filtration, the gallon content can easily and quickly be calculated in two fashions :

◉ take the measurements in inches and multiply length by height by width. Divide that number by 231, and the result is the gallon content of that container.

◉ or, take the measurement in feet, multiply length by width by height, and then by 7.5. This particular method comes in handy, for example, when calculating the content of an aquarium.

A box that is 14 x 18 x 16 can hold 4032 : 231 = 17.45 gallons of media. A filter that has a chamber that is 12 x 4 x 15, can hold 3.11 gallons of media. An aquarium that is 5 feet by 18 inches by 24 inches, holds 5 x 1.5 x 2 x 7.5 = 112.5 gallons of water.

Underneath an aquarium two of a filter's dimensions are usually determined, (for the most part), by the space available inside the cabinet : the width and the height. The third dimension, the length, is usually more flexible. To calculate the space needed use the two constraining measurements to calculate the third. For example : your cabinet is 5 feet long, by 20 inches wide, by 26 inches tall. The inside dimensions of the cabinet, meaning space available to place a trickle filter, are 48" long, by 16" wide, by 24" height.

◉ Your aquarium is a 100 gallon tank. You are planning to install a filter capable of handling a heavy load of fish and invertebrates. You are building your own filter and need to determine the dimensions.

◉ Based on the recommendations made with regard to surface area required for biological filtration, we first need to determine how much of such surface we need for this aquarium. Using the numbers suggested earlier : 100 x 2.25 (average) = 225.00 square feet. You have decided to use small Tri-Packs as the medium. These small round plastic media have a surface area of 14.7 square feet per gallon equivalent. 225 divided by 14.7 or ±15.3 gallons of Tri-Packs. This would require a rather large filter (15 gallon capacity).

◉ Because you do not want to build such a large filter, you look around some more, and decide to use some other media, in this case Bio Blocks from World Class, with a surface area of approximately 20 square feet per gallon equivalent. 225 divided by 20 = 11.25 gallons needed.

◉ This seems acceptable size- and cost-wise to you, and you now set out to calculate the dimensions of the filter's biological box.

◉ Given the cabinet's constraints in terms of width and height, you know that you cannot use more than 16 inches in width, so you settle for 15. Height-wize you have 24, but you need to leave some space for fittings on the top of the filter, so you settle for 21 total height.

◉ Because this total height also includes the sump space underneath the biological box, you must first deduct that height from the 21 inches. 5 inches is a good height for the water level in the sump. 21 - 5 leaves 16 inches.

◉ What we have determined so far, is that the width of the box will be 16, and that the height of the biological box will be 16 as well.

◉ From these numbers we must deduct the thickness of the material used (¼ inch in our case), times 2 (once for each side), as the 16 inches is an outside dimension, and to calculate volume, we need inside dimensions.

◉ This leaves 15.5 inches for the width. The height is only affected on one side (the top) because the bottom is open and in the sump. The two dimensions we thus have are 15.5 and 15.75.

Reef Aquarims require very strong daylight type 5500K light

◉ The following equation represents the third dimension (Y) that we are looking for :

$$15.5 \ x \ 15.75 \ x \ Y \ = 11.25 \ x \ 231$$

◉ Let me explain. Earlier we determined that volume is equal to length times width times height (in our case 15.5 times 15.75 times Y the as yet unknown length). We also saw that to go from volume to gallons we divide by 231. This means that 11.25 times 231 = the volume = length times height times width.

◉ Transforming the above equation gives us :

$Y = (11.25 \ x \ 231)$ divided by $(15.5 \ x \ 15.75)$
or
$Y = 2598.75$ divided by $244.125 = 10.645$ inches long for the box.

◉ To verify that our box indeed holds the number of gallons of media needed, all we now do, as a double checking procedure, is to multiply length by width by height : $10.645 \ x \ 15.5 \ x \ 15.75$ and divide that number by 231. Doing so generates : 2598.71 divided by 231, or $11.2498 \ (\pm 11.25)$ gallons.

◉ The dimensions of the biological box are : Width 15.5" plus 2 times 0.25" or 16 inches, height 15.75" plus 0.25" for the top plate, or 16 inches, and 10.65 plus 2 times 0.25 or 11.15 inches.

◉ This biological filtering box now needs to be fitted in an appropriate sump. The sump needs to be 16.5 inches wide. 10 to 12 inches is a good height for a sump. The total length of the sump (filter) is a matter of personal decision and preference.

Usually you will want enough space in the front part of the filter, to be able to place additional compartments in the sump, and maybe even a protein skimmer. A sump that is 16 inches long (plus 16.65 from the biological chamber, in our case anyway) will allow you to do so, but you can select any number of inches you feel comfortable with. In our case the sump would be around 32.5 inches long. The only constraint on the total length of the filter, is that you have to leave enough space available underneath the cabinet for your pump(s), and valves, and any other equipment that must be installed there. This is most important.

Whatever the size of your tank, you can use the above example to calculate the size of the filter you will need. All you need to do is substitute your numbers for the ones we used. Does it pay to build your own filter? It greatly depends on how handy you are, and whether or not you can work with plastics and know the bonding techniques and tricks. You can order the cut pieces of plastic easily from a local dealer and assemble them in your house, or garage, as long as it is well vented, not too cold, and not humid at the time you will be bonding.

Always use high strength bonding agents. Let the filter dry for at least several hours, better still, let it sit overnight before putting any water in it. Do not try to bond in high humidity areas, or in areas where the temperature is lower than 70 degrees. Before you bond pieces together, make sure that they all fit.

Use masking tape, or something similar, to put the filter together to double-check that all pieces are of the proper size. Once glued you cannot get them apart. All edges need to be checked. They should be smooth, especially if you are using liquid bonding agents that dry rather quickly. No gaps are allowed, the pieces must fit tightly all around. Gaps cannot be filled with liquid bonding agents. To do so you must use a paste-like like acrylic cement. They are available from companies such as Weldon, Cadillac Plastics, and C.R. Laurence. They need much longer to set than other types of bonding agents. If you have never glued plastics such as acrylic before, you must try first on some pieces of scrap.

The filter will require several holes for water inlets and outlets, and also for air inlets. Drilling acrylic is not difficult. Again, practice on some pieces of scrap first, this will give you the feel for it. Use special acrylic drill bits if you can. They make for a smoother hole. Although carbon drill bits are probably the best bits around, they are difficult to use on acrylics if you are not used to working with them, especially in hand held drills. Using a drill press is recommended for drilling holes, but hand held units will work too, providing you practice a little first.

An article on how to build trickle filters was published in the January 1988 issue of FAMA (Freshwater and Marine Aquarium). If you are planning on doing so you may wish to review that article.

3.5 Denitrifying Filters :

Although not the same type of filter as the biological filter we just discussed at length, another filter that operates on the premise that bacteria do all the work is used when filtering reef tanks : the denitrifying filter, also called denitrator (denitrification filter is yet another name, but assimilation filter would be the most correct one).

Introduced to the U.S. hobby by George Smit in 1986, as part of his Minreef System, this filter has gained quite a bit in popularity since, but is still not very widely used. This is so because it is a filter that is not easy to operate, and not easy to keep operating at an efficient level.

Denitrification is a process whereby NO_3, nitrate, is built down, removed from the water that is, by means of bacteria that are facultatively aerobic and anaerobic (also called nitrate respirators); usually in the presence of a carbon source. Unfortunately, some manufacturers and stores still persist to sell such units without a nutrient supplement.

The principle is real simple : flow water slowly through a container, or compartment, in which a medium on which these bacteria can grow is placed, and the latter will slowly, but surely break down the nitrate and remove it from the system. The problem lies in the "flow slowly". Usually this means that the water must be flowed drip wise through a container that houses a medium such as filter floss, or balls, or sponge. Because of impurities in the water itself, the drip rate has a tendency to vary greatly. It usually slows down and may stop altogether, before the hobbyist notices.

When no water flows through the medium for a while, the filter goes completely anaerobic, producing hydrogen sulfide, and possibly methane, as a by-product. The same can happen when the water flows too slowly. The filter can go anaerobic in a matter of hours and such is a very dangerous situation, insomuch as hydrogen sulfide, besides smelling like rotten eggs, is very toxic, even in low amounts, to both fish and invertebrates and can ruin a tank in a very short period of time.

Because nitrates are a cause of problems, especially so in reef aquariums, they should be kept low, which often means removing them in some fashion. Nitrates both affect the well being and appearance of corals and invertebrates, and give rise to the appearance of micro-algae. As a result hobbyists must do something about them.

My recommendation is that you keep nitrates below 1 ppm as measured by tests that read in N-NO_3, or 5 ppm in tests that read NO_3. At those levels problems are unlikely. Lower levels are even better. My own tank, at my house, has no measurable nitrate, even when using low range testing kits. The only way to determine the levels is to use photometry and tests that measure in the $\frac{1}{100}$ of a part per million range.

If levels are to be kept that low, hobbyists have to resort to some method to do so. There are in essence only two ways that seem to give any acceptable result :

◉ using a denitrator, to keep nitrates close to zero ppm.
◉ using a compound that absorbs or adsorbs nitrates.

3.5.1 Denitrators :

A device that is run separately from other equipment attached to the tank, meant to biologically reduce the nitrates that are present and constantly generated in the aquarium, as a result of feeding, metabolism, life, and other process taking place in the aquarium.

Denitrators are, usually, boxes or devices with multiple compartments that are all interconnected, and through which water is made to flow very slowly. The compartments are filled with a medium that offers surface area for bacteria to grow on. Filter floss, plastic filter media, and some coarse sponges make excellent fillers for these chambers and for bacteria to populate.

Because the water flows through the denitrator very slowly, it

is in contact for a long time with that bacterial bed, and is cleansed in the process of nitrates and some other compounds. To keep the bed active, and to make the chemical and biological processes that occur in the denitrator complete, a carbon source needs to be added to the filter as well. Lactose, mixes of lactose and other sugars, for example fructose, are used to achieve the desired result.

In certain filters alcohol is used instead of sugars, and is placed in bags with micron pores to make it migrate very slowly into the water. The need to add a high quality nutrient is not to be underestimated. Indeed, it will make the difference between a filter that is rather easy to operate and regulate, and one that is giving you constant problems.

Theoretically, if the denitrator is operated correctly the effluent should not have any testable nitrates whatsoever (using an aquarium test kit). Practically, however, most denitrators do not function at their optimal level, but at a rather high level of efficiency, yet not 100 %. This is, in most cases, enough to keep nitrate levels very low, or low enough for them not to be a problem. Because different denitrators require different operational instructions, it is not possible to generalize here and give you one way that will cover all instances. Most do require about the same care though.

I have used units manufactured by Energy Savers Unlimited, Summit Aquatics, Marine Technical Concepts, Thiel•Aqua•Tech and Sera from Germany, and find that they all perform as expected from them, providing the hobbyist takes the time, and makes the effort to regulate the units as required. That in itself can be a rather time consuming task. Let's look at a typical unit, and what needs to be done to get it running properly

■ Hook up the denitrator using the instructions you receive from the manufacturer.

■ Typically, this will involve running a water input line to one end of the unit, and attaching hose to the other end to return the water to the sump of the trickle filter, or to the tank.

■ Water will now flow into the denitrator at one end, go through all the compartments slowly, and exit at the other end, after having been in contact with the bacteria that have settled in the filter material.

■ Because the process is of biological nature, the filter needs to run in, very much like the biological filter that removes ammonia and nitrite from the water. The biochemical process that takes place is the reason that an additive, or nutrient, needs to be added to the filter.

■ Before starting up the unit, you should fill it with water and let it rest for about 24-36 hours. This will greatly reduce the amount of oxygen present in that water. This is a necessary step.

■ After such time, start up the drip system, based on the rate recommended by the manufacturer, but not faster.

■ Add nutrient as indicated in the instructions.

■ Be patient.

■ It may take as much as 4 to 5 weeks before the denitrator is actually denitrifying the water, as nitrate tests done on the effluent will show.

　　　To determine exactly what is happening inside your filter, all you need to do is test the effluent for nitrate and nitrite, and smell the water to determine whether any hydrogen sulfide is present. If you want to be real accurate, you can buy a hydrogen sulfide test kit from La Motte

Chemicals, or from some aquarium companies. The following scenarios can occur :

■ The effluent contains no nitrite. Nitrate levels are at about the same level as in the tank itself. The reason is that you are flowing the water through the filter too quickly, or your filter has not started functioning yet. You must slow the drip, or flow, rate down.

■ The effluent contains less nitrate than the tank's water, but nitrite is also present in levels greater than 0.1 ppm. Although you are on the right track, you are still flowing the water too rapidly through the filter. You may also need to add more nutrient. Slow the water flow down a smidgen and re-test about 12 hours later. Slow the water down further if necessary.

■ The water does not show any nitrate content, no more than 0.1 ppm of nitrite, but it has a definite smell that is not normal. You must add more nutrient.

■ The water has lower nitrate levels than the tank's water, nitrite is very low, <0.1 ppm. Slow the filter down just a tad.

■ No nitrate is present, and nitrite levels are lower than 0.1 ppm : the filter is running close to high efficiency. Do not slow the flow down, but use a small amount of nutrient more than you were before.

■ No nitrate is found in the effluent. No nitrite is found either. The filter is running as it should, and at 100 percent efficiency. This is the ideal situation, but the one that only occurs for shorter periods of time, reverting to the previous scenario where the filter is running at very high efficiency levels.

Why is the denitrating filter so often a problem ? There are a number of main reasons :

■ The hobbyist is flowing the water through the denitrator too rapidly and no biochemical reaction is taking place. The water is highly oxygenated. The denitrator has become a regular biological filter.

■ The hobbyist is flowing the water too slowly and the filter is operating partially anaerobically, with all the dangers that such presents.

■ The hobbyist is not adding any, or not enough, nutrients. The process takes place partially but not completely. The filter is not as efficient as it could be. Nitrites will always be present in the the effluent.

■ The drip rate is hard to regulate. The water stops dripping on a regular basis. Because the water coming from the tank to the denitrating filter contains impurities, the restriction made to adjust the drip, gets blocked by small particulate matter. You must clean that piece of hose regularly or more frequently to prevent the drip rate from falling to zero and the filter going anaerobic.

■ The filter is too small; there are not enough compartments in the filter; you have bought the wrong type of filter and may have to look for a better one.

■ Or you may have to run two units in series. This will allow you to speed up the flow rate quite some, because the path the water now has to travel is now much longer.

With some care, and a little patience, you will be able to get your denitrator to do what it is supposed to: lower the nitrate levels in your reef. The key is not to get discouraged if at first you are not succeeding. Many many hobbyists before you have had the same problems. Persevere and try again. Follow the instructions more accurately, or call someone in the hobby who can help you understand where you may have gone wrong. Denitrators can be very effective but you must take the time to regulate them properly.

3.5.2 Compounds to lower Nitrates

Besides using denitrating filters to lower nitrates, hobbyists also resort to a method that is both simpler and more practical for most : a compound, resin, or special filter material is placed in line with the water filtration, or in a canister filter, or in an area with good water circulation. As water flows through the material, nitrates are removed slowly and reduced to within acceptable levels, usually in the 5 to 7 ppm of NO_3, or in the 1 to 1½ ppm of $N-NO_3$. Note that I mentioned "through" and not over. It is important that a good throughflow is achieved. If water does not come in contact with the compound that is used, the latter will not perform as efficiently, and perhaps even not at all, depending on exactly how the flow occurs.

There are several such compounds on the market : Ex-Nitrate, HyperSorb, and Poly-Filters®. Some work better than others, and some have a longer life than others, depending on tank conditions. You may want to experiment with a few until you find one that performs well for you. All are widely available. Some perform more than just the removal of nitrates, e.g. Poly-Filters® from Poly Bio Marine Inc. remove a slew of other noxious compounds as well (see section on chemical filtration for more details on Poly Filters and molecular absorption discs).

I have a lot of experience with both Ex-nitrate and Poly Filters® and can recommend both very highly. Ex-nitrate, a product sold by my own company, is highly selective and lowers nitrate levels. Poly Filters (a polymer based sheet-like medium) on the other hand are much wider in their beneficial effect, and remove phosphates also, for example. Such is a boon, because phosphates are a problem compound as well, leading to the appearance of large amounts of undesirable micro-algae. As already indicated they remove a great deal more as we shall see in a later section.

Ex-nitrate is a granular compound that can easily be placed between filter floss in a canister filter. For example, Fluval, Marineland, Lifeguard and other canisters all can easily be filled with this material. Water is then flowed continuously through the canister, and as it comes in contact with the Ex-nitrate, nitrates are slowly removed. The hobbyist tests for nitrate levels from time to time, and when nitrate levels go up again, the compound is simply replaced. About 3.5 pounds of this material are recommended per 50 gallons of water. In an average tank this amount will last for about 2 to 3 months. More of the compound can be used if the hobbyist wants to lower the levels even further. We have never been able, howe-ver, to bring them down completely to zero with this method, but to levels around 1 ppm of $N-NO_3$ with is totally acceptable even in a reef aquarium.

Thiel•Aqua•Tech, the company that markets the compound, recommends that you do not use Ex-nitrate if your nitrate levels are higher than 40 ppm of NO_3. Not because Ex-nitrate does not work (it does), but because it will be less expensive for you to first bring NO_3 levels down to about 10 to 15 ppm by performing water changes, and then using Ex-nitrate to lower the level somewhat more and maintain it there. Indeed Ex-nitrate is not an inexpensive product.

When sandwiching Ex-nitrate between filter floss in a canister, check the floss from time to time to know when it is necessary to clean it. Once a week is recommended. You may also rinse the Ex-nitrate and then place it back in the canister.

Special canisters for this compound can be made, and placed in-line with the main water pumps. Such canisters, usually fabricated out of acrylic tube, can be made to any size you require, either by yourself, or by other companies in the hobby, including my own. Standard canisters holding two and four 50 gallon treatments are available from Thiel•-Aqua•Tech. Marine Technical Concepts is another company that constructs excellent equipment for this and other products.

Because the marine reef segment of the tropical fish hobby is in a time of rapid evolution right now, and because many new products are being introduced all the time, it behoves every hobbyist to keep on the look out for progress made in this, and other areas. Read the hobby magazines, talk to other hobbyists if you can, call manufacturers, and ask what new products they have available. You would be surprised what you can sometimes find that way.

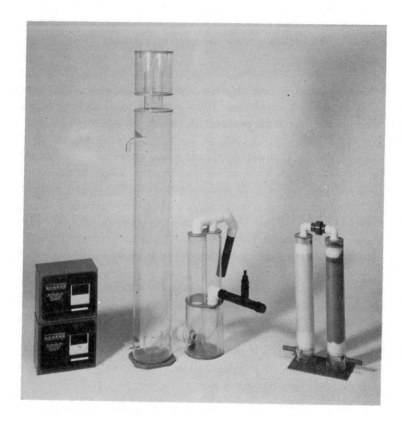

Shown are a double deionizer, a venturi
and columnar protein skimmer and 2 controllers,
one for pH andone for redox potential

Regular Husbandry is one of the most important tasks the hobbyist needs to perform

4. Instrumentation for the Reef Tank :

Lately, much has been said and written about instrumentation to equip the reef tank and control the environment in which our fish and invertebrates live, in an automated fashion. Articles have appeared in magazines such as FAMA, TFH and Marine Reef, hobbyists talk about them at aquarium society meetings, and advertisements for such equipment now abound. Prices are, finally, starting to come down somewhat, making the acquisition of such instruments within the reach and means of a far greater number of hobbyists than was the case only 2 years ago.

Meters and controllers that determine pH, redox potential, temperature, conductivity and oxygen levels -to name the 5 popular ones- are now being offered for sale at somewhat more affordable prices . Ion specific meters, controllers and electrodes, for example to measure ammonia, nitrate, etc. are now also being made available, but are difficult to use in reef tank water, because of the many interfering ions present in salt water. By this we mean other compounds, present in the water being tested , that hinder and distort the reading we are trying to make for one specific compound. To give just a few examples : carbonates, bicarbonates and sulfates all interfere with an ion selective nitrate electrode's accuracy; sodium, potassium and iron interfere with an ion selective electrode for hardness' reading.

Besides meters, which just read a specific water quality feature that the hobbyist is interested in, and controllers, which allow the hobbyist to initiate a reaction to such a measurement by powering up a device that can influence that particular water quality parameter, hobbyists now resort, more and more, to the use of so-called reactors. These are usually nothing more than a large cylinder made out of acrylic material, configured in a specific fashion allowing it to perform in certain way. For example, an oxygen reactor is a device inside of which air and water are mixed under a small amount of over pressure, thus forcing the oxygen contained in the air into the water, and raising the dissolved oxygen level of that water in the process. Other reactors are used to increase the carbonate hardness, or to inject carbon dioxide into the water, or lately even ozone.

Although the technology underlying these reactors is fairly straight forward and easy to understand, the hobbyist is not, yet anyway, accustomed to have to involve himself or herself in special piping arrangements to install this equipment. Traditionally, everything used around an aquarium did not require sophisticated installation procedures. More often than not, all that was necessary was plugging the device into a wall outlet, and that was that as far as the installation went. Such is no longer the case. Some of the devices and equipment now used can be fairly complex to install, often requiring piping, gluing, bonding, using PVC fittings and valves, and understanding more than just a little about fluid mechanics, and how they are and can be controlled safely.

Whether new technology or not, easy to install or difficult, inexpensive or pricey, all these new "tools", are now at the disposal of the hobbyist, make for a much higher level of professionalism in the hobby, and in the manner aquariums are, and will be, kept from now on. We have to thank our German fellow hobbyists for having pioneered a majority of this equipment, and a few Europeans for having brought this technology to the United States, or better, to North America.

George Smit (1986) described a system that was so new to North American hobbyists, that many that I have an opportunity to deal with would stare in disbelief at his articles. Many store owners in those days needed more than a little arm twisting to stock this merchandise. Selling them on this new technology was difficult and very protracted, especially since the prices asked for such merchandise were far above what they had been accustomed to pay.

Thiel (mid-1985) started importing a full line of advanced German aquarium products and equipment, mostly for freshwater plant aquariums, and exposed North American hobbyists to instruments such

---

Add Kalkwasser on a very regular basis

as pH controllers, CO_2 diffusion systems, multiple types of fertilizers for freshwater plants, mercury vapor and metal halide lighting, float switches, dosing pumps, and so on, for the first time. Byerly's Aquarium of Columbus, Ohio, was the first store to fully equip itself with several very large trickle filters, each holding several hundred gallons worth of plastic filtering media. Thiel and Shearer (1985) built and installed these systems on the premises, because they were too large to be moved easily and economically. Two show tanks, fully equipped with advanced instruments, controllers, CO_2 diffusion, and high intensity discharge lighting were also installed in that store, and were up and running by mid-1985. A first in the United States.

That was the start. It took more than 2 years for hobbyists to really begin to look at these new methods seriously, accept the fact that they worked and greatly improved both freshwater and marine tank water quality, and start installing them on their own systems. For months on end, the only ads for this type of equipment were ran by just one company, in FAMA and MFM, until finally a few American manufacturers picked up on it and decided to get in on the act as well.

Around the same time, Scott Dyer, President of the Marine Aquarium Society of Toronto, contacted me, and asked me to come up and speak at their annual meeting. This resulted in Albert Thiel and Peter Schachtschneider (1986) setting up large displays tanks, featuring this technology, at Aquarium Toronto, in Woodbine Center by the Airport.

George Smit's articles had now ran for nearly 8 months in a row in FAMA, and had stimulated a great deal of interest in sophisticated systems. The rest is history.

The technology is nowadays fully accepted, and is here to stay, to the point where large American manufacturers are now even offering molded trickle filters, a choice of metal halide lighting fixtures in just about any configuration you can think of, and a choice of instruments and reactors that is beyond what one would have expected just a few years back. Trickle filters are being advertised so widely now that confusion reigns, and that the hobbyist has a hard time differentiating between the professionals and another group of small time go-along-for-the-ride-type outfits, that produce look-alike equipment that may not really be what the hobbyist wants and needs. We have already touched on that earlier in this book. Hopefully, by the time you are through with reading The Marine Fish and Invert Reef Aquarium, you will be in a position to make that distinction, because you will know what features and qualities to look for in filters and other equipment.

Some readers will already be familiar with the equipment described in this section. Others will not, or will want to learn more about them than what they already know. This chapter is intended for the latter group. Often too, hobbyists would like to acquire one of these instruments, but are afraid that they will not know how to use it, install it, interpret its results, and maintain it. Those readers will, I hope, find the answers that they need here.

Do not let the technical aspect of this part of the book refrain you from reading on. Rest assured that by the time you have read this chapter once, or perhaps twice, you will be a far better educated hobbyist than you were before. And that is what it is all about. The more educated you are about the equipment, the less likely you are to buy something you do not need, and the greater your chances of using the technology to its fullest, which is only what you should since you probably paid real good money for the products discussed in this section.

4.1 Digital pH Meters and Controllers :

We all know that we must maintain the pH of a marine aquarium, and especially the pH of a reef aquarium, within rather narrow bounds : 7.9 to 8.4 is the range usually given, and also indicates the extremes that the lifeforms kept in such tanks, can deal with for some time. Short periods of pH levels outside of these bounds may be all right, but will result in problems if maintained for too long.

For example, although you may not notice any detrimental effect on fish, invertebrates, etc. while keeping your tank at a pH of 8.6 for a short period, a couple of hours maybe, maintaining that pH for days on end will result in excessive amounts of stress on the fish, with the usual appearance of parasitic infestations. And in reef tanks the latter are very

Add Kalkwasser on a very regular basis

hard to deal with, because many medications that can safely be used in fish-only tanks, cannot in a reef tank because they are toxic to invertebrates, corals, crustaceans, etc. Compounds such as copper and formalin, normally added to the tank to control parasites cannot be used in reef aquariums. They are extremely toxic to all corals and invertebrates and will decimate your reef tank in a very short period of time.

In order to maintain the pH within those bounds we often test our tank's water, to determine the pH level, and we may even add compounds to adjust that pH if necessary. This is tedious, laborious, and becomes quickly a chore because of the repetitiveness of the procedure. As a result we have a tendency to neglect testing and let the pH drift to levels where it should not. This is plain and simply human nature, and many hobbyists do so or have done so for periods of time. **We all also have the propensity to judge the tank, and its inhabitants, by what we visually observe, rather than by what we find by means of testing.** Such is very dangerous, because many of the animals kept in aquariums are rather resilient, and can take a fair amount of "abuse" -meaning water quality of a lesser level- for quite some time. Unfortunately, when things then go downhill, they go downhill fast. The hobbyist is then left to wonder what happened, as a few hours earlier everything seemed just fine and the tank looked in good shape.

Fortunately, technology comes to the rescue by offering the hobbyist the choice of several meters, and even controllers, that can monitor and adjust the pH continuously, with little or no intervention on the part of the hobbyist. Technology, good technology, does not come cheap! Keep that in mind. Do not expect to get highly accurate equipment if you only paid $ 80.00 to $ 150.00. **With instrumentation you get what you pay for.** You may have heard it before, but it applies particularly to instruments. A cheap pH controller is just that, cheap, and inaccurate, or expressed more exactly, less precise. Less expensive equipment is meant to give a general idea of what pH, in this case, the water is at, more so than a precise number. To get a real accurate reading, which is what we need, you may have to spend several hundred dollars, especially if you are in the market for a controller rather than just a meter.

Meters can be bought with different types of so-called "resolution". What this means is simply how many significant digits past the decimal point the meter will indicate. For instance : 8, or 8.1, or 8.09, or in very sophisticated laboratory equipment, even 8.093, a range that goes from no significant digit at all, to three. As the resolution increases, so does the price of the meter (controller) and also the price of the electrode, or probe, necessary to read the pH.

It is usually recommended that a meter, or controller, with one, or better with two significant digits past the decimal point, is the the type you should buy. Such units will run you $ 300.00, and upwards, plus the cost of the electrode, which can add another $ 150.00 to the price.

Besides the ones advertised in the hobby, you should check with companies such as Markson's in Phoenix (Az), Cole Parmer in Chicago (Il), Extech in Waltham (Mass.), Omega in Stamford (Ct), Hach, Fisher, LaMotte, and other such scientific instrument resellers who make extensive catalogues available to whomever asks for them and qualifies based

on the standard they use. Be aware too, of the difference between an industrial unit and a laboratory unit. Around your aquarium you want one of the latter. Not the top of the line laboratory quality types such as Beckman, Hach, or WTW, but a good quality unit from the lower to middle end of the price range.

Industrial units are less accurate, often giving a rougher measurement, and are frequently so-called "panel mount" types. Such units do not have a totally enclosed outside case. Additional wiring must often still be done in the back of the unit, and such wiring will be in plain view and subject to moisture and salting up, which besides being dangerous, will falsify your readings or short out the meter.

On the other hand, such instruments are less expensive than totally enclosed ones, and certainly less expensive than laboratory quality units. As already stated, with instrumentation you get what you pay for. Keep it in mind. My contention is that if you are going to spend a few hundred dollars on instrumentation, you may as well spend a $ 100.00 or so more to get a better one, e.g. a laboratory quality controller or meter of the type indicated earlier.

The same applies to the difference between a meter and a controller. The price difference is usually only around $ 100.00 to maybe $ 150.00. Because of the added advantage of being able to control the pH, rather than just reading the value, such is a worthwhile investment, and will allow you to increase the degree of control you have over the conditions in your aquarium.

Place the meter, or the controller, in such a way that it cannot fall into the water. Make sure that no water can drip on it either. Keep in mind as well that the humidity in the cabinet underneath the aquarium is close to 90 percent. That is high. you may wish to place the meter/controller elsewhere, and thus extend its life. Calibrate your meter/controller exactly in the manner that the instructions state. This usually entails using two calibrating solutions, often pH 7.00 and pH 9.00, or pH 10.0. See 4.3 for more details.

If yours is a controller, you can use the unit to control an outside device that will influence the pH. Usually this is done by means of adding carbon dioxide to the water. CO_2 and water combine to form carbonic acid. The latter lowers the pH, and over time the carbonate hardness as well. To mix the carbon dioxide and the water efficiently you will

need a CO_2 reactor. Several companies now sell such units. You can find more details on this equipment in my other two books : Small Reef Aquarium Basics, and Advanced Reef Keeping Made Simple (I).

Besides the units already described, so-called pen-type equipment is now offered for sale as well. Most of these inexpensive units are good for rough measurements, but are not more accurate than good quality powdered reagents. As long as you keep that in mind when you buy them, you should have no problems. Their accuracy can be off by as much 0.2 pH, or the difference between 8.0 and 8.2 for example. There are, however, there are exceptions, and pen-type meters that measure with greater accuracy, e.g. 0.01, or the difference between for example 8.11 and 8.12, certinly exist. Such units are, as you would expect, more expensive : in the range of $100.00 to $150.00. One source for such units is Energy Savers Unlimited, or try Cole Parmer in Chicago. The Energy Savers/Coralife units are of excellent quality and are a recommended purchase for those hobbyists who do not own controllers.

Cleaning electrodes is an important step in prolonging the useful life of any probe, whether it is a pH or redox potential one. It not only extends the electrode's life, but it also ensures that the readings you are getting are accurate, and not distorted by foreign material covering the tip and semi-permeable membrane. Cleaning is a process whereby the organic material that has accumulated on the tip, and the algae that may grow there, so small that you can actually not see them, are removed by means of an appropriate liquid or compound (you will need a different compound for pH and for redox potential electrodes).

Organic material prevents an accurate reading because it forms an additional layer between the water in which the probe is submersed, and the sensing part of the probe, thus reducing accuracy. Algae that grow on the tip will, in all likely hood affect the redox potential more than the pH (which they will slightly lower). During the day, when such algae give off small amounts of oxygen, especially when strong lighting is used over the tank, the redox electrode will sense this oxygen and show a higher redox potential than what the water really is. Indeed, oxygen has a redox potential of around 1300 mv.

A properly manufactured cleaning solution contains more than one chemical. The better ones are based on formulas that are recommended by national bodies such as the American Water Works Association (Washington, D.C,), or the ASTM, the American Society for Testing and Materials (Philadelphia, Pa). Other associations that publish recommended procedures for testing include the American Public Health Association (APHA), and the Water Pollution Control Federation (WPCF).

4.2 Electrodes : A few important words :

You may have noticed that I have insisted particularly that you do not remove the electrode from the water while the meter/controller is in the on position. This is very important. It will prevent the electrode from becoming polarized. An electrode can become polarized in as little as 15 seconds if taken out of the water and held up in the air while the unit is plugged in. Should such happen, your electrode will become sluggish, and read inaccurately. You may even have to buy a new one. And at the price they are, you certainly want to avoid having to do so. Polarized electrodes can sometimes be regenerated. The procedure is not simple and success is not guaranteed. Always unplug the meter/controller before removing an electrode from the water. Always place the electrode in the water before plugging in the meter/controller, or switching it on.

You must also clean your electrode regularly. More so if it is in an area where strong light is present. Algae will grow on the tip and on the semi-permeable membrane around the tip. They must be cleaned using a special pH electrode cleaning solution. Do not use home brews, or generic stuff, even if someone you know tells you over and over that they are safe and do the job. I have seen a lot of ruined electrodes that way. Buy the special cleaning solutions that are offered for sale by scientific supply houses, Route 4 Marine Technology, Thiel•Aqua•Tech and others. Make it part of your regular maintenance schedule. About every 3 to 4 weeks is average.

Never let the tip of the electrode become dry. This will affect the accuracy of the probe and result in increased drift and an inaccurate reading. Drift is defined as an electrode that does not remain stable, even though the liquid in which it is immersed does.

For example, if you immerse an electrode in a pH 8.0 calibrating solution, after a short while, if your electrode is accurate, the meter or controller will indicate a pH of 8.0. If, however, that reading does not remain stable, even though you have added nothing to the solution, your electrode is said to be drifting. Small drifting is unavoidable, e.g. 0.05 pH over 24 hours is not uncommon. If the drift is greater, your electrode is damaged and may need replacing. Mishandling the probe will exacerbate this drift.

Never remove an electrode that is attached to a plugged-in meter or controller from the water. Never switch on a meter or controller before the electrode is already submersed. Doing so will greatly shorten the lifespan of an electrode. This is true for any kind of electrode : pH, redox, oxygen, ion elective and so on. Electrodes are highly sensitive. Protect your investment by cleaning them regularly. About $ 25.00 should get you the two cleaning solutions you will need.

The placement, positioning that is, of an electrode is an important criterion in deciding the set points that will be used when installing a controller for pH or redox potential. It is also important in terms of how often the electrode may need to be cleaned. Electrode must always be in a location where good water flow exists over the sensing part of the probe. Such will ensure a more accurate reading. Here are some suggested locations and their relative merits :

• Inside the overflow siphon - surface skimmer : good water flow, more frequent cleaning needed, position the electrode in such a way that the tip is always submersed, but that the top is always out of the water. Some overflow siphons have a fluctuating level because they are used to pre-filter the water at the same time. When the pre-filter is clean, the water level is low. When the pre-filter gets dirtier, the water level in the box rises. Keep that in mind when installing your probe.
• Inside the tank, close to the overflow siphon or overflow corner box: good water flow, more frequent cleaning required, especially if electrode is in direct light, since algae will grow on the electrode and its tip.
• Inside the trickle filter sump : excellent spot as long as it is in an area of the sump where good water flow exists.
• In-line : my recommended place for both the pH and the redox electrode. Cleaning as suggested already.
• In the top of the filter : not recommended.

4.3 Calibrating Electrodes :

The usual procedure to be followed to calibrate a pH meter or controller is as follows :

• attach the electrode to the meter / controller.
• make sure the unit is not plugged in.
• if the meter has an on/off switch, place it in the off position.
• if such was the case, plug the meter in.
• if the meter/controller does not have a switch do not plug it in.

• pour a little of the pH 7.00 solution in a small cylinder.

• if the electrode has a protective cap, take it off now.

• place the electrode in that solution.

• now switch on the meter.

• let the electrode sit in the calibrating solution for ± 10 minutes.

• check the pH by looking at the read-out display.

• if it not exactly 7.00 adjust the reading with the calibration control knob, or wheel (follow the instructions the came with the unit).

• after this has been done, switch off the meter/controller, either by unplugging it or by flipping the on/off switch.

• prepare a little pH 9.00 or pH 10.00 solution in a test cylinder.

• place the electrode in that solution.

• now switch on the unit, or plug it in again.

• wait about 10 minutes.

• check the read-out and adjust to pH 9.00 or 10.00 depending on which calibrating solution you are using. Use the slope button, or wheel, to do this (follow the instructions that came with the meter).

• After this has been done, your meter/controller is ready and adjusted properly.

• Before removing the electrode from the last solution you used, make sure that you first switch off the meter/controller.

• Now place the electrode in the spot you have selected in the sump, or in the filter, or in the tank, in an area where good water flow exists. Do not submerse the top of the electrode. Submerse about 2 to 3 inches. That is all that is necessary.

• Never contaminate your reference solutions (calibrating solutions).

• never re-use the small amount of calibrating solution you used to perform a calibration. Throw it away.

• Never place the electrode in the bottle that holds your calibrating solution. This will contaminate the solution and make it useless.

Electrodes should be recalibrated after they have been cleaned with a pH or redox electrode cleaning solution. Always be careful not to damage the BNC jack at the end of the wire attached to the electrode. Do not get any water or salt on the BNC jack, this will short out the electrode, give a zero reading on the meter/controller, and may damage both. Be extremely careful not to nick the electrode cable. Do not run this same cable too close to an electric wire, interference may occur that will make

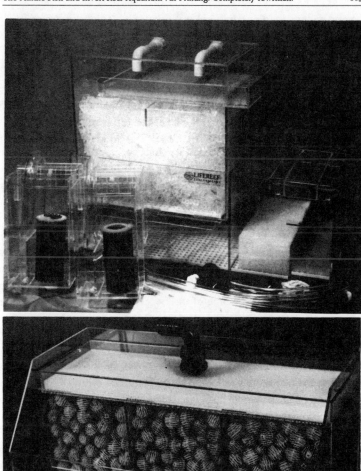

Trickle Filters by LifeReef Systems and Nautilus Aquatics

your meter's reading jump around erratically. If your meter/controller acts in this manner, look first for electric wire that are either touching the electrode cable, or are very close to it.

Do not touch your meter and/or electrode if you suspect that you are carrying static electricity. Touch a metal object first. Transferring static electricity to the meter can damage the circuits and other electronic parts, ruining the instrument. Because the glass tip of the electrode is extremely fragile, take great care not to hit it against the filter or aquarium. If it breaks your electrode needs to be replaced. Never clean your electrode with boiling or very hot water, except if the electrode you own has been certified for use at such high temperatures.

Many types of electrodes for pH, redox potential and specific ion measurements are available through scientific supply houses. That is, too, where you will find the widest choice and the greatest variety of length, thickness, body materials, junctions, and so on. We have already indicated the names of some of the better known ones : Cole Parmer, Markson's, Extech, Omega, and so on.

Brand names of electrodes can vary greatly, mainly because electrode manufacturers will let other companies re-label the electrode in their own names. Buy enough electrodes and companies such as Sensorex will put your own name on them, or let you affix the stickers yourself. Many electrodes sold in the hobby fit into this class.

One can classify electrodes in 3 broad categories : general purpose inexpensive electrodes, medium quality more accurate electrodes, laboratory quality expensive to very expensive electrodes. A pH electrode, for instance, can cost as little as $ 39.00 to as much as $ 475.00 for a specialized Orion, Beckman or Hach brand one.

Most of the ones sold in the hobby are in the lower price category, but because of intermediate mark-ups, they will end up costing you from $ 100.00 to $ 150.00 anyway. You may, however, still be getting an electrode that you can buy elsewhere for $50.00 or so (through the channels already mentioned). There are exceptions of course, some excellent ones are sold by at least two aquarium manufacturers. One electrode is German in origin (Tunze), the other one is English (TAT). The same applies to redox potential electrodes, both quality and cost price wise.

To get a truly excellent electrode you will have to spend upwards of $175.00 when buying from a scientific supply house. Spending that amount when buying from a dealer in the hobby, does not guarantee that you will get excellent quality, except with the two exceptions mentioned. The main reason for this is that all products that are not intended for the hobby, e.g. electrodes, that are sold in pet stores, or through ads in the magazines (especially mail order), are offered to you at greatly marked-up prices. You could buy a better electrode, for less money, if you took the time to buy it from a scientific supply house.

These remarks are not meant to discredit mail order places or pet stores, to the contrary, they are meant to explain the real facts of life. Because the market for electrodes, for example, is small in the hobby, those who buy them from manufacturers to resell them to you, only buy small quantities and cannot obtain large discounts. Not much more, usually, than 20 to 25 percent, if that. When such an item now goes through 2, or sometimes 3, intermediaries, you can be sure that after its has been market up once or twice, it will cost more than what it originally was listed for as a retail price in the manufacturer's catalog.

To give you an idea of the prices of some pH electrodes that you may want to consider here is a sampling taken from the 1989 catalog of Cole Parmer, page 510 and onwards :

• Low cost, with Teflon junctions: General purpose, Sealed and gel filled $45.00, Aggressive environment electrode $ 96.00,
• Low Cost : General purpose $39.50, General purpose $45.50,
• Medium Cost : Ross from $125.00 to $195.00, Ross Sure-Flow $ 195.00.
• High cost : Hach, Beckman, WTW and other such companies make electrode available for measurements to 3 digits past the significant one, e.g. 8.237. Such electrodes cost in excess of $500.00, and are too sensitive for use in a salt water environment, in water loaded with organic and other materials.

As already indicated a good electrode for use in reef tanks should be selected from the lower range of the medium cost type electrodes. Get either a really inexpensive electrode and replace it often, or buy a real good quality one, but not the top of the line.

4.4 Redox Potential Meters and Controllers :

Most of the remarks already outlined in the pH meter and controller section apply to these instruments as well. In fact perhaps more so, because redox potential is a more difficult to measure parameter of the water quality. It is certainly a more misunderstood one, and one that is only recently beginning to find a good following amongst hobbyist maintaining reef aquariums.

Thiel (1985) was perhaps the first one to point out its usefulness in judging the water quality of aquariums, in the United States, in articles written for magazines, and lectures given to aquarium societies. Obviously others in the hobby, in the more professional end of it, have suggested the use of redox potential at earlier dates. Thiel (1986) introduced the redox potential concept to the hobbyist market, and offered the first redox controllers for sale in the hobby in the United States on a large scale, the ATK model from Klaes Aquaristik. In all fairness, Sanders of Germany had had such a meter/controller available for some time before that, but had not been promoting its use very widely, even though their ozonizers had been around the United States for some time, and were being used in Germany in conjunction with those controllers.

As more literature that explained redox potential in greater detail became available, its measurement became more widespread and hobbyists started installing meters and controllers on their aquariums, especially on reef tanks. Little by little more brand names appeared on the market, to the point where the choice offered to the hobbyist is now rather large. Prices have started to come down as well, and excellent controllers can be bought for less than $ 500.00.

A separate chapter of this book deals with redox potential at length, and even includes the results of an experiment in redox potential control. Martin Moe in "The Marine Aquarium Reference" is an excellent source for more information on redox potential as well. In the literature you will sometimes find references to ORP, or oxidation reduction potential, rather than redox potential. They are both the same concepts, just different names. Redox is used mostly in Europe, and ORP more so in North America.

Because redox potential is such an accurate gauge of the water quality, hobbyists should take the time to familiarize themselves with its concept and meaning, as well as how it can be used to effectively improve the living environment that a reef aquarium is. A good deal of information on redox potential can also be found in Advanced Reef Keeping Made Simple (I) and in Reef Aquarium Basics, both by A. Thiel as well (Aardvark Press).

4.5. Conductivity Meters and Controllers :

Conductivity is used by a number of more advanced hobbyists as an indication of the salinity of the water. Even though such is a much more accurate way to monitor salinity or specific gravity, we only recommend it in systems that are very automated. For example, conductivity controllers with two, rather than one, relay can be used to automatically dispense fresh water when the salinity is too high, and brine when the salinity is too low.

Such systems are very easy to set up, and were it not for their high price, they should be part of every good marine reef set-ups. More details on installing such an automated salinity control can be found in my other book : Advanced Reef Keeping Made Simple (I), available from Aardvark Press (published 1988, 440 pages).

Because of the type of equipment needed, the typical price of such a set up is around $ 900.00 to $ 1,000.00. If, however, you want full control, that is the way to go. All is relative, and if you have a system that houses several thousand dollars worth of fish, corals and invertebrates, such an expense can be very justified. Alternatively, if you travel a lot, and cannot rely, or do not want to rely, on someone else to take care of your system, a conductivity controller in addition to a similar unit for pH and redox, will take all the guess work out of running the tank, and will greatly increase the stability of the system. And stability is the one factor that is very important, and common to all successful reef set-ups that I have ever seen.

4.6 Combination pH and Redox Controllers :

Although I used to favor such a double function instrument, and offered some for sale through my own company, I have recently changed my recommendation. I now strongly suggest the use of two totally independent controllers. One for pH and one for redox potential. The main reason for this is simple : when two units are housed in one and the same enclosure, and when something goes wrong with one of them, you must send in the whole unit for servicing. In the process you loose the use of **both** controllers, not just one. This can have dire consequences for an aquarium that is running well, and may contain very valuable livestock, especially if the servicing takes weeks, which is often the case, as some may have found out.

Moreover, it has been reported that interference between the two circuits boards can also be a problem in such units, even in microprocessor based ones. As a result I have switched my own system to independent controllers, and recommend that you do the same, especially if you are in the market for instrumentation.

4.7 Temperature Meters and Controllers :

Meters are used to obtain information about many parameters associated with the water quality in the tank. Controllers are used to both measure, and take action, if the tested values requires such action. Stability in the reef tank has always been one of my main concerns, especially since time has proven that the more stable the environment is kept, the more successful the aquarium will be, providing, of course, water quality is at generally recommended levels.

Temperature is one of the many parameters that must be controlled, primarily because the animals kept in the reef are not accustomed to great variations in temperature, and will only do well in a very narrow range to boot.

There are few temperature controllers available in the hobby. The ones that you want to consider are, however, advertised in the magazines. Select a unit with a high degree of accuracy. Call the manufacturer is the value is not advertised. Check the literature that comes with the unit before you buy it, to make sure that you are getting an instrument that is highly accurate, preferably within 0.5 degrees Fahrenheit, either way. Less accurate equipment is not worth considering because it presents too many dangers for the lifeforms in the aquarium.

Many types of heaters are available. From the very inexpensive and highly inaccurate bayonet heater (usually imported and not intended for the reef tank), to the more expensive bayonet heaters from Germany (for example Ebo-Jaeger brand). Other types include flexible silicone cable heaters (dangerous in reef tanks because the cable can easily be ripped by rocks and some fish) and excellent quality American made bayonet heaters made, for instance, by Aquarium Systems.

Most hobbyists will require some form of heating, some time of the year. If possible use more than one heater. Let me clarify : if you need 100 watts of heat, use either four 25 watt units, or two 50 watt units. If you need 250 watt, use one 100 and three 50 watt heater. The reason for this recommendation is simple : because bayonet heaters can "stick" and possibly boil the tank if they do, more heaters protect you from a dangerous overheating of the aquarium. Small wattage units are less likely to heat the water to the point where it becomes dangerous, even if they stick.

Keep the temperature stable around 75-76 degrees. This will probably require some form of heating during the night, and maybe some form of cooling during the day, especially in areas where the daytime temperature runs very high, or if you are using lighting that is transmitting a lot of heat to the water and/or pumps that put of a lot of heat and transfer it to the water in the process of keeping cooler.

You must, of course, get the right kind of light for the reef aquarium (see a later chapter), but you must also make sure that only a minimal amount of heat is transmitted to the tank by such lights. Use either pendant type lighting, or make sure that the hood housing the lights is equipped with one or more fans that remove the hot air from inside the fixture, and thus reduce heat transfer to the water (companies such as Energy Savers offer a very wide choice of lighting sure to satisfy your needs). If yours does not have such a fun, muffin fans sold in electronics stores and often used for computers, can be used and retrofitted rather easily.

Pumps, too, can also be a great source of heat transfer, especially submersible pumps. Indeed, the latter use the surrounding water to cool down and protect their internal parts. Some brands of motors are notorious for transferring heat, even though they may be advertised as cool running. You should talk to other hobbyists to determine what their experience has been with individual brands.We tried an Iwaki 55RLT motor on one of our skimmers recently and, using a thermometer equipped with a special probe, measured a temperature that varied between 106 and 111 degrees Fahrenheit. Much too high of course. This does not mean that all such pumps will run that hot, but it is certainly food for thought, and reason for getting more information.

4.8 Dissolved Oxygen Meters :

Although it is difficult, and probably not appropriate, to select one water quality parameter as being more important than any other one, dissolved oxygen levels certainly qualify as one of the most crucial ones for the survival of all lifeforms in the tank. Indeed, its level conditions the ability of all fish, invertebrates, corals, bacteria, etc. to survive and thrive. Its level reduces the stress on the fish etc., and its level ensures that a sufficient amount of oxygen is available for proper biological filtration.

Oxygen levels are measured using standard tests sold by several companies. Most of these tests are based on the Winkler test, dating back to the 1880's, and small modifications of that test (for example the LaMotte Chemicals test). One can, however, use a sophisticated instrument to do so as well. Dissolved oxygen meters are expensive instruments and really not something the average hobbyist is really in need of, especially now that at least four aquarium product manufacturers offer a chemical test that is reasonable in price, easy to use, as well as highly accurate.

Should you, nevertheless, decide to acquire such a meter, you should buy a unit that is fully calibrateable, and preferably adjustable for measurements in salt water (higher chlorinity level). Such a unit, and the necessary electrode, may well cost over $ 800.00. Because the level of dissolved oxygen saturation is different in salt water than it is in fresh water, the ability to adjust for chlorinity is important. It will ensure a more accurate reading and prevent you from having to refer to charts to calculate the true D.O. level.

Often when dissolved oxygen levels are low, the tank will be in less than perfect shape, and all animals will be stressed. You must always determine the cause for this oxygen deficit, and remedy the situation by correcting whatever problem was causing the oxygen to drop. Not doing so will lead to more problems and probably outbreaks of parasitic disease, and invertebrates that do not open to their fullest. When your tank does not look all that good, suspect lower dissolved oxygen levels and do what is required to bring them back up.

4.9 Carbon Dioxide Diffusion Equipment :

CO_2 is a very common gas that is used for two main purposes in both freshwater and marine aquaria : fertilization of plants and macro-algae, and balancing the pH of the water. Not all hobbyists who maintain reef tanks maintain macro-algae in their tanks as well, but most hobbyists who maintain a reef tank and run it with a trickle filter, may need to add CO_2, especially if they maintain the water at a high degree of carbonate hardness. Such high levels are advocated for the benefit of corals (Thiel 1986).

The merits of adding carbonate hardness generators and how such is to be done are discussed elsewhere in this book, in Advanced Reef Keeping Made Simple (I) and in Small Reef Aquarium Basics. Several of the reasons are described in great detail in Martin Moe's The Marine Aquarium Reference : Systems and Invertebrates, in the section where he goes into detail regarding the carbonate hardness, CO_2, and pH equilibrium. If the theory interests you, it is recommended that you refer to that book for further details. Suffice it here to say that CO_2 and KH (carbonate hardness) are very closely related and form a 3 way equilibrium with pH.

Change one, and at least one of the other two will be affected as well. This is important, as by influencing this equilibrium, one can also influence the amount of carbon dioxide that is dissolved in the water. Because CO_2 is important for the formation of calcium carbonate in the artificial seawater in our tanks, we must ensure that sufficient quantities of it are available. Indeed, calcium carbonate is important to all corals kept in our tanks. In fact, adding supplemental calcium carbonates, in the form of Kalkwasser is highly recommended.

Carbon dioxide can be added in two ways : manually and in automated fashion. Both are viable solutions for the reef hobbyist. Manual systems are, of course, far more affordable than automated ones that cost a goodly more. Often hobbyists will start with a manual set-up, and up-grade the latter to an automated one as time goes on. Indeed, all parts bought for a manual set-up can be re-used and are not redundant when up-grading. Manual systems are easy to set up, affordable, and can

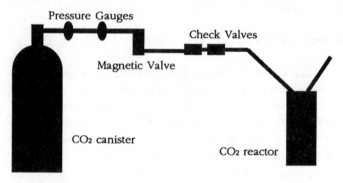

Pressure Gauges

Check Valves

Magnetic Valve

CO₂ canister

CO₂ reactor

deliver the same benefits as the automated ones, providing they are set up correctly.

4.9.1 Manual Addition of CO_2 :

To install a manual carbon dioxide set-up you will require the following items (minimum suggested configuration, Thiel 1985) :

• a canister filled with CO2. Can be bought in $2\frac{1}{2}$, 5, 10 and 20 pound canisters, and larger sizes if you acquire an industrial 55 pound or greater unit. Make sure that the canister you buy carries a DOT stamp or you will have great difficulty in having it refilled. It is often illegal to refill bottles that do not carry such a stamp.

• a set of CO_2 gauges, preferably coupled with a pressure reducing valve. These are highly recommended because the pressure in a CO_2 bottle is over 800 PSI. If you do not reduce the pressure first, you will have great difficulty in adjusting the output going to the diffusion system. It is a good idea to get gauges that are U.L. listed, and American made, to ensure that the threads on the bottle and the threads on the gauges match properly.

• CO_2 resistant hose (should be silicone hose or flexible PVC hose, sometimes called Tygon, one of its brand names). Regular airline tubing type hose hardens quickly when put in contact with carbon dioxide and will crack, causing you to loose CO_2 and resulting in your canister being empty frequently for no apparent reason, making you wonder why it only lasts a few days.

• one or more check valves that are CO_2 resistant. One is the minimum. Two is better. They prevent water from backing up in the CO_2 line and entering your gauges, shortening their life, or ruining them altogether.

• a CO_2 diffusion system (reactor, or other device to mix the carbon dioxide and the water efficiently). The more efficient the diffusion set-up, the less CO_2 you will be using, and the longer your canister will last.

And a highly recommended option :

• a solenoid (magnetic valve) to shut off the CO_2 supply at night.

The hook-up procedure is as follows :

• Measure the pH and the carbonate hardness of the tank that you are planning to add carbon dioxide to. If the pH is too low already, you cannot add CO_2 now. A pH below 8.1 is too low for the purpose of adding carbon dioxide. You must first adjust it. In all likelihood, if the pH is low, the carbonate hardness will be low too.

• Adjusting the KH (carbonate hardness) is necessary because it protects the tank from acid fall. When CO_2 is added to the tank's water, a weak acid called carbonic acid is formed. This acid will lower the pH of the water quickly, unless the KH is high. Levels of dKH 12 and higher are re-commended (4.3 meq/l and higher). To adjust the KH level, use a liquid or powdered buffering compound. Make sure it does not contain binders, or your protein skimmer will overflow after you add it to the water. Make sure, too, that it does not contain phosphate based compounds, or you will have problems with micro-algae soon after using the compound.

• Raise the KH level slowly. Do not increase it by more than 1 dKH degree per 12-24 hour period (dKH stands for German degrees of hardness). Although formulas for home-made hardness generators are described in several books, be careful when using them. Most hobbyists do not have access to the carbonate part and, as a result, only use the bicarbonate part usually in the form of baking soda. Such is very dangerous as it will raise the pH of the tank to dangerous levels and make it very difficult for you to bring it back down to the correct range. Additionally, adding too much sodium bicarbonate (baking soda) will quickly raise your pH to a level that cannot be sustained safely in the aquarium for long periods of time.

• Make sure the canister of CO_2 bottle is full and closed. Attach the gauges to the CO_2 bottle (canister). Do not open the bottle yet. If you are using one, hook the solenoid up to the gauges. Run a short length of CO_2 resistant hose from the gauges, respectively solenoid, and insert a check valve. Run another foot of hose and install the second check valve (if you are using two). Now run hose from the output side of the check valve to the input of the diffusion system that you are using.

• The solenoid (magnetic valve) must be plugged in to a 110 volt power source. If you are using a timer (which is strongly suggested), plug the solenoid into the timer, and the timer into an outlet. Run the magnetic valve (normally closed type) for the same number of hours as the lights. Alternatively, plug the solenoid into the same timer as the one that controls the lights, if such can be done. The reason for this is simple : during the night, when metabolism is low, and when photosynthesis is not taking place because the lights are off, algae add CO_2 to the water themselves, rather than removing it. Moreover, during the night less carbon dioxide is required to begin with. Such a hook-up will also prolong the useful life of your CO_2 canister refills.

• Start by opening the bottle completely, making sure first that the solenoid is not plugged into an electrical outlet (or into a timer thatis energized). Since it is not plugged in, it will be closed, and will not let any carbon dioxide go through.

• Adjust the pressure reducer to a pressure of around 1 to 2 psi. If you are not using a pressure reducing gauge you cannot follow these directions because you will not be able to adjust the pressure of the CO_2 coming out of the canister.

• Let the CO_2 go into the diffusion system, together with the water with which it will mix. Follow the directions for setting up your diffuser carefully. If you are unsure, call the store you bought it from, or the manufacturer to get an explanation over the phone.

• Because of the back pressure exerted by the water going into the diffuser, 1 to 2 psi may not be enough pressure for the CO_2 to get through, and mix with the water. If such is the case, increase the pressure gently until CO_2 does get into the diffuser and mixes with the water.

• Optional : use a bubble counter to determine how much CO_2 is actually going into the diffuser. This is a small device that is hooked up in-line with the CO_2 line and allows you to actually see how much is going into the diffusing device.

• You should only let very little CO_2 get into the diffuser when you first start the system up. The reason is that you do not know yet what its effect is on the water. As a result you want only little CO_2 to mix with the water until you can actually test what is happening. If you can determine how much is actually entering the diffusing device, for example because you are using a bubble counter (a small device that lets you see how many bubbles of CO_2 past through the lines), adjust the system to push about 45 bubbles per minute through the CO_2 line. If you are not using such a device, adjust CO_2 output for its minimum.

• In a 55 gallon aquarium let the system run for about 4 to 5 minutes, on average, (less in smaller tanks, more in larger tanks).

• Now stop the output by closing the CO_2 canister shut off valve. Do not adjust the pressure gauge, such is not necessary. Moreover, you probably spent quite some time to adjust it to the correct level.

• Now test the pH of the water again and compare it with the first reading you obtained, the one from the test before you started adding carbon dioxide.

The following three scenarios can now occur :

• If the pH has not varied increase the output of the CO_2 line a little, for example to 60 bubbles a minute, or slightly more than before if you are not using a bubble counter. Wait a few minutes and test again. Keep doing so until the pH has fallen by a minimum of 0.1 pH to a maximum of 0.2 pH. Once that is achieved leave the system as it is.
• the pH has gone down. The drop is between 0.1 and 0.2 pH. Leave the settings as they are. This is the correct level of diffusion.
• the pH has dropped more than 0.2 pH, for example from 8.2 to 7.9 pH. You are adding too much CO_2 and you must reduce the CO_2 amount that you are dispensing even further. In all likelihood your carbonate hardness is still low, probably below 12 dKH. Check it and adjust it, if necessary.

The key when using carbon dioxide is to understand right from the beginning that it is a process that you need to understand and have control over. Carbon dioxide lowers the pH and if you dispense too much of it, especially if your carbonate hardness is below dKH 12, the pH will drop drastically, quickly, and perhaps to a dangerous level if that too strong diffusion goes on for too long.

Carbon dioxide diffusion is not a dangerous process at all, as long as you know what you are doing, and take the time to make the adjustments. Do not walk away from your system while you are setting up a carbon dioxide system. Stay around until the diffusion procedure is completed. Does not kill fish, as you sometimes will hear. You must, however, take care that both the dKH are correct and that the amount dispensed is not lowering the pH by more than 0.2 pH.

After the CO_2 system is up and running, two water quality checks need to made from time to time :

• the pH drop should never be more than 0.2 pH from the first reading you took.
• the dKH needs to be checked at least once a week, preferably twice, and needs to be adjusted upwards whenever necessary, using a KH generating liquid or powder. Keep the remarks made earlier about such compounds in mind.

Once you start using CO_2, you must ensure that you have a continuous supply available. Check your bottle (canister) regularly and locate a source for refilling it, in advance. Do not wait to do so until it is empty. If you own a bottle with a D.O.T. stamp, just about any welding supply place will be able to help you.

4.9.2 Automated diffusion of carbon dioxide :

The only difference between a manual carbon dioxide diffusion system, and an automated one, is the fact that you need to add two components to the set-up : a pH controller, and an electrode (and a solenoid if you have not done so under the manual set-up).

The components that you require to set an automated system up comprise : a carbon dioxide canister, a set of gauges with pressure reducer, a solenoid/magnetic valve, carbon dioxide resistant hose, two CO_2 check valves, a CO_2 diffuser or, better, a CO_2 reactor, a pH controller with a two digit past the decimal point read-out, a good quality electrode (see earlier remarks about electrodes), pH calibrating solutions pH 7.00 and pH 9.00, pH electrode cleaning solution, pH electrode storing solution (optional but recommended), and a carbonate hardness test that measures dKH or meq/l (milliequivalents per liter).

The principle relied on is the fact that carbon dioxide lowers the pH. We can thus influence the pH by means of a controller, and stabilize the pH at the value that we determine to be right for our tank. Usually, a pH of 8.0 to 8.2 is suggested, depending on what hardness you maintain your water at. The higher the hardness, the higher the setting. For example if your hardness is more than dKH 15, set the controller for pH 8.2, if it lower, set the controller for pH 8.1.

What happens when you now add carbon dioxide is as follows:

• After you have installed the pH controller, by following the manufacturer's instructions, and taken a dKH test to ensure that it is at least 12, set the controller's set point for a pH of either 8.1 or 8.2. Again, follow the directions that came with the unit to do so.

• Set up the CO_2 system in the same manner as described earlier in the manual section. The only difference is that the solenoid valve is now plugged into the pH controller, and the controller is plugged into an outlet.

• Open the canister of and start adding the carbon dioxide. The pH will be lowered because the carbon dioxide forms carbonic acid when in contact with water. As the electrode senses that the pH is going down, it will close the solenoid when the pH falls below the set point. The reason for this is simple : it is the function of a controller to ensure that such is what happens.

• When the pH now goes up again, because of the hardness of the water, and the good water quality obtained by using a trickle filter, the controller will sense that the pH is above the set point, and re-open the solenoid, pushing more carbon dioxide into the water, and lowering the pH as a result. This, in turn, will prompt the controller to close the solenoid again, as soon as the pH goes below the set point. Because this process is continuous, you have, in fact, stabilized the pH around the set point value. Such is exactly what we wanted to do. CO_2 is now being added and the pH is stable.

We already indicated that one of the benefits of adding carbon dioxide is that it enhances the formation of calcium carbonate in the tank. This is a very positive side effect, as all corals need calcium carbonate for growth, and so do calcareous and crustose algae, the pink, reddish and purplish types that so often grow on rocks in reef tanks where the water quality is really good.

4.10 Dosing Pumps :

Hobbyists use a number of additives to improve the water quality of their reef tanks. These include : vitamins, trace elements, KH generators, iodine and strontium molybdenum supplements, and so on.

Because we have already indicated several times that stability of the water quality is a most important aim to strive for, it does not seem to make much sense to add all these supplements in large doses once a week or so. It would be much better for the water quality stability to add them evenly throughout the day and night. Such a system would only add a small amount of these supplements, but would do so all the time, keeping their concentration just about the same at all times.

Several types of special pumps are offered to do so : dosing pumps with diaphragm mechanisms, peristaltic pumps, gear pumps, etc. All achieve the same result. Cost and minimum quantity of fluid delivered per day should be your guiding criteria when selecting a dosing pump for your system.

Dosing pumps with peristaltic motors typically deliver the smallest amounts of fluid over any given period, especially if they allow the use of several types of internal diameter tubing. Indeed, the smaller the internal diameter of the tubing used, the smaller the amount of fluid dispensed per revolution will be. N° 13 tubing, also called spaghetti tubing by some, can be used on several such pumps. The better ones, but also the pricier ones, are made by Masterflex, a division of Cole Parmer, Chicago Ill. Many other excellent brands are available.

Thiel•Aqua•Tech sells a small, very quite and very reliable, peristaltic pump that delivers about 500 ml per day (slightly less than 16 fluid oz), and should be run on a timer, if the need to dispense even less fluid should arise in your tank. Use a timer that has multiple on/off settings, and set if for one cycle on, and then one cycle off. In that fashion you will be delivering ab0ut 8 oz per 24 hours. If you need less still, set if for one cycle on and two cycles off, and you will be delivering about 5.3 ounces per day. Timers with either 15 or 20 minute cycles are to be preferred.

An alternative way of using such a pump, recommended by some Authors, is to run the pump only during the day and not after the lights have gone off. In such a case you would be setting your timer on a twelve or so hour cycle (use the same number of hours as your lights are on). The reason usually given is that when the lights are out, and metabolism is low, not as many nutrients etc. are used and dispensing them is therefore not as necessary. The amount of water and nutrients that you will want to add should be selected in such a way that it makes up for evaporated water as well. In doing so, the peristaltic pump performs two functions : it is an automated water make-up system, and at the same time it dispenses all the additives that you normally add to the tank evenly throughout the day (and night).

The question is often asked how the mixture dispensed by a dosing pump should be prepared, and how one can easily determine the quantities of the various elements and additives used that need to be mixed in. Here is a suggested way :

• First determine how many ounces of liquid you wish to add to the tank per day. This will vary in every tank. It is dependent on the amount of evaporation, and on the size of the aquarium. If you do not know what that amount is, determine so over the course of a few days by keeping tabs of how much water you need to add, each day, to bring the level of water in the sump of the trickle filter, or in the tank, back to where it normally is.

• Let us assume for the purpose of this example that this amount is 16 fluid oz. per day.

• Next select a container that will be used to prepare the mixture in. When doing so, keep in mind that the container should hold several days of replacement water, but not too much either. For example, a one gallon container will hold 128 / 16 = 8 days of supply of replacement water. A

2 gallon container would hold 16 days. Anywhere from 8 to 12 days seems like an appropriate length of time. We select a container that can hold 1½ gallons (such plastic containers can easily be obtained from stores that sell kitchen supplies etc.).

• Fill the container with slightly less than 1½ gallons of distilled, reverse osmosis, or deionized water. Note that the water must be distilled, reverse osmosis, or deionized. Do not use regular tap water. It contains too many impurities that can react with the additives you will be using, and can affect them negatively.

• In our example, the container we used holds a 12 day supply of replacement water.

• The next step is to write down the additive you use, and calculate how much of them you use every day. This means that if you use them only once a week, you must divide the quantity added weekly by seven (etc.)

• Again, in our example we assume that we use the following supplements :

- trace elements	12 drops per day
- vitamins	20 drops per day
- KSM	120 drops per day
- Iodine	8 drops per day
- KH generator	100 drops per day
- Kalkwasser	100 drops per day

• If the above quantities are used in one 24 hour period, and if the container we have decided to use, hold a 12 day supply of water that will be dispensed evenly throughout those 12 days, adding 12 times the amount of supplements to that water, will at the same time result in all the elements and additives being dispensed in the tank evenly over the next 12 days.

• The next step is, therefore, to make up the mixture that the peristaltic pump will dispense so that it contains 12 times (in our example anyway) the amount of nutrients that we normally dispense every day. This means 144 drops of trace elements, 240 drops of vitamins, etc. (use your own figures to determine the required amounts to be added for your situation. The ones used here are just for illustrative purposes).

• Next, mix all this in with the water in the container (if you have too much water remove some first), and switch the peristaltic pump on, with or without a timer, to adjust the daily output to 16 ounces.

• Your automatic top-off and additive dispensing system is now set up.

• Replenish the water and additives in the container as required. If the amount you calculated the first time does not check out, make the necessary adjustments by recalculating all the numbers if need be.

Important remark : Peristaltic pumps use small diameter tubing to transport water from the storage container to, in our case, the aquarium or trickle filter. Because of the manner in which peristaltic pumps operate, that tubing is being compressed constantly, hour after hour, day after day.

        Such tubing has a rated life that is normally in the vicinity of 1000 to 1500 hours of usage. If you are running your pump 24 hours a day, you will have to replace it about every 45 to 50 days. If you do not, the efficiency of the pump will diminish, as the inside of the tubing will stick and transport less fluid. Possibly the tubing will burst, and some of the fluid that it is pumping may damage the motor or peristaltic mechanism. Make it a habit to change the tubing before you experience any problems. write the date you installed the tubing in your aquarium diary, or on a small piece of tape stuck to the pump itself. Use good quality tubing. Tygon, or better still Pharmed special number 13 tubing for peristaltic motors, should be used.

        Dosing pumps are very easy to set up and require little or no maintenance, except for changing the tubing from time to time. Make sure that whomever you buy your pump from, can also supply you with replacement tubing, or know an alternative source to obtain it. Check scientific supply house catalogues too. Peristaltic pump tubing can be expensive. Buy from the right source !

4.11 Water Changes :

One fact is certain : the need to perform water changes is not universally endorsed. Some Authors, and several manufacturers, would like you to believe that if you use their products no water changes whatsoever are necessary. This sounds very appealing, of course, and hobbyists are eager to listen to such claims, and any similar ones that mitigate the need to actually perform "work" on the aquarium they keep.

In all my years in the freshwater and marine hobby, both as a beginner and as a more dedicated researcher in the last ten, I have never been able to convince myself that all forms of pollution that are present in the aquarium can be removed efficiently and thoroughly enough, simply by using the four prevalent methods of filtration : mechanical, biological, chemical, and fractionation, advocated in books etc.

Such filtration can do wonders for the water quality, especially nowadays with the appearance of more sophisticated equipment and trickle filters, but a number of compounds still exist that will accumulate over time in the water, because they are not being removed rapidly enough to prevent such a build up.

Water changes, using the right kind of water, of course, can achieve that result simply and very efficiently. All the hobbyist needs to do, is include such water changes in the routine maintenance practices that should exist for every reef tank. A chapter, later in this book, is dedicated to what such practices should include besides changing water.

It is most important that the right kind of water be used. Replacing water of lesser quality, with water that is of not much better quality does not make sense at all. Nevertheless, hobbyists do it all the time. Tap water, the most common source of replacement water, can be heavily polluted with nitrate, phosphate, chlorine, chloramine, phenol, silicic acids, pesticides, fertilizers, ammonia, etc. Tap water should, therefore, never be used in its raw state. It should be checked for all such parameters first. Additionally, tap water should be treated, chemically filtered that is, before salt is added, especially since hobbyists cannot check for many of the compounds that chemical filters can remove efficiently.

The recommended treatment consists of running raw tap water first through a good quality activated carbon (one that does not add phosphates and heavy metals to the water, and many do), and then through another chemical filter to polish it even further and remove any traces of pesticides, phenols, amines, copper, zinc, and many other undesirable compounds. The medium suggested to achieve this is the Poly Filter ® from Poly Bio Marine Inc., or their molecular absorption discs which provide even stronger chemical filtration. Flow water through both very slowly. No more than 30 to 45 gallons per hour, to ensure a long contact time. Water that has been treated in such a way is of excellent quality and can safely be used.

Of course, you must also pay attention to the quality of the salt that you are using. It should not contain phosphates and nitrates, and should be free of impurities. The smaller the amount of residue remains after the salt has dissolved, the less impurities it contained more than likely to begin with. Such would, obviously, be a sign that the salt you are using is of excellent quality.

As already stated several times, if you are using activated carbon, you must ensure that it is of superior quality. We have already discussed this elsewhere in The Marine Fish and Invert Reef Aquarium, book however, it is important enough a matter for me to repeat it once more. Many carbons sold in the hobby will leach phosphates back into the water in your tank, and pollute the tank in the process. Excess phosphates, defined here as more than 0.1 ppm -yes, one tenth of one part per million- will soon give rise to micro-algae outbreaks, and will result in a very unsightly looking aquarium. Such algae will be difficult to deal with as they are hard to remove once they appear in the tank.

Having said all his, how much water should you change? There is no real scientific literature to back up the recommendation that I have made for a long time, which is to change about 4 to 5 percent per week, or better even, 2 percent every 2 days; but I have, over the years, had excellent results whenever I was doing so.

What could happen to your tank and corals if you do not perform such water changes?

Add Kalkwasser on a very regular basis

Probably nothing for a while, but as time goes on, you may find it difficult to keep certain types of animals alive, or they may just not look as good as they used to. This due to the already mentioned accumulation of noxious compounds. Often hobbyists run aquariums that look really good for months in a row, all type of corals and invertebrates do just fine, and thrive. Suddenly, for no apparent reason the hobbyist, however, senses that something is wrong. Things are not the way they usually are.

The difference may not be apparent to others, but it sure is to the hobbyist who knows his or her own tank. Something is wrong, you know it, you sense it, but you can't define it. The tank does not look as vibrant as it usually does. Your sixth sense tells you that something is not the way it normally is. It tells you that something that you cannot define is happening.

Has it occurred to you that this "malaise", so to speak, has to do with water quality, and that the progressive increase of certain compounds, noxious ones, perhaps from traces in the beginning, to parts per billion after a few months, is a possible cause for this undefined trouble, and is affecting the well being of the animals kept in the aquarium.

Because certain animals are more sensitive to certain types of compounds than others are, this malaise may manifest itself in several ways. Frequently the hobbyist will observe that he, or she, can keep anything in the aquarium, except for instance carpet anemones, or certain types of Tangs, or Flame angels, etc. The reason such animals do not make it in a tank has nothing to do with the hobbyist. It has to do with the water quality. Pure and simple. Water changes are therefore very necessary! Perform them regularly and improve the overall quality of your tank's water.

Another indication of trouble may be the fact that corals that used to open up and stretch to the point of what looked like "bursting", suddenly no longer do. Their general appearance can still be considered acceptable, but it certainly is not as magnificent as it used to be. Again, such is due to a deterioration of the water quality. Do something about it, change water regularly and eliminate the build up of noxious compounds as a possible cause of problems in your tank. If you change water regularly it does not become a chore, and when you only have to change a little at a time the task becomes easier, faster, and you are less likely to spill water. Because it is an easier task, you are also more likely to actually make the water changes. The easier the task, the more likely you are to perform it regularly.

Four to five percent a week, or 2 percent every 2 days is an average that I have been satisfied with. Every tank is a different ecosystem and may require some degree of adjustment. You may find that your tank does better with a slightly larger water change, for instance 5 or 6 percent a week, or as some hobbyists report 10 percent a week. The ultimate amount is up to you to determine, but changing some amount of water you must.

Keep in mind that it is most important to prepare the water that you will use to effect water changes in advance. Do not prepare it minutes before you plan to use it. Such water is too rough, too aggressive, too crude, and will stress the fish and other tank inhabitants. Prepare the water at least 24 to 36 hours beforehand, aerate it, and bring it to the right temperature and pH. This all ensures a greater stability of the water chemistry, and reduces strain on the filters and on the tank lifeforms. Less stress means healthier looking animals and a better looking tank.

It is a good idea, in fact, to have some spare prepared salt water ready at all times, as the need for such water will arise from time to time when it is least expected. If you have a few gallons of standby water, you will not have to use freshly prepared one that is not as safe to use. Aged water is definitely better. Thisis especially so if the need for spare water is created by some other emergency that may already have caused stress. Don't intensify the existing stress. Have some water ready.

4.11.1 Manual Water Changes :

Most of us who have kept aquariums for a while have been changing water for as long as we can probably remember. Whether we have, in fact, done so with the least amount of stress to the biomass in the tank remains to be seen. Changing water appears to be a simple process, and it is. But some precautions are necessary.

Large water changes stress the fish and invertebrates more than small water changes. Such should be pretty obvious because large water changes alter the water chemistry more than small ones. Large water changes = sizeable change in water chemistry = stress = may cause parasitic outbreaks.

If the amount of water to be changed is small, which is likely if you perform regular 4 to 5 percent a week, or 2 percent every couple of days, water changes, you will not need to set up an elaborate hose evacuation system that runs to your sink. A small bucket will usually do just fine. Use a hose with a ½ inch internal diameter and while removing the water, siphon out some of the detritus that is lying on the bottom of the tank as well. Such will benefit the overall water quality in the immediate, and if done regularly, as is suggested, will increase your redox potential slowly but surely in the longer term.

Regular water changes can be used to slowly lower the nitrate and phosphate levels in the aquarium, providing the make-up water does not contain nitrate and phosphate itself. We have already explained that you must check the water you use, pretreat it and chemically filter it, and make sure that the salt you are using does not contain nitrates and phosphates either. Although you may find these comments to be repetitive, I have done so on purpose hoping that the remarks will really sink in, and that you will from now on check all additives you use to prepare water for your tank, including the water itself on a regular basis.

If you are using a trickle filter, as we hope you are, add the new water to the sump of the trickle filter, not to the aquarium. In this manner it will mix more evenly with the main water body and create less of a change in the tank's water layers. Stability of all conditions is important, as pointed out several times already as well.

Often it is the attention paid to such small details that will make the difference between an aquarium that runs well, and an aquarium that looks in superb shape. Please remember it and tell your hobbyist friends about it. It will help them too. If you share with them, they will share knowledge with you, which in the long run helps everyone in the hobby.

4.11.2 Automatic water changers :

Automating the water changing process introduces an even greater degree of water chemistry stability, as it can now be done on an even more regular basis, for instance once, twice, or several times a day, depending on how much water needs to be changed. The equipment needed to do so is not expensive and is easy to acquire, as we shall see in the next paragraphs.

The only issue that you need to deal with is the evacuation of the excess water as, when you add new water to the tank, you will have to remove a similar amount for the tank not to be overfilled, and possibly overflow, especially after a few days. The following situations can exist: (a) you can evacuate the excess water by means of an overflow in the filter, to a drain, or (b) you cannot do so, and must use a slightly more sophisticated system to rid the tank of the excess water.

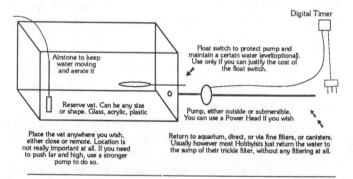

AUTOMATIC WATER CHANGER SUGGESTIONS AND OPTIONS

Digital Timer

Airstone to keep water moving and aerate it

Float switch to protect pump and maintain a certain water level(optional). Use only if you can justify the cost of the float switch.

Reserve vat. Can be any size or shape. Glass, acrylic, plastic

Pump, either outside or submersible. You can use a Power Head if you wish

Place the vat anywhere you wish, either close or remote. Location is not really important at all. If you need to push far and high, use a stronger pump to do so.

Return to aquarium, direct, or via fine filters, or canisters. Usually however most Hobbyists just return the water to the sump of their trickle filter, without any filtering at all.

Add Kalkwasser on a very regular basis

➡ **(a) Evacuating the excess water to a drain :**

The trickle filter must be outfitted with an overflow hole that is connected directly to a floor drain through which all the excess water can be made to flow away. If you have this type of a set-up, installing an automatic water changer will be simple. Refer to the instructions below. If no hole has been predrilled in your filter, do so using an electric drill and a hole saw (can be obtained from any hardware store). Drill slowly and carefully. Try it out on a piece of scrap plexiglass if you do not have previous experience with drilling through plastic. If your filter is made of glass you need to use method two, as you will not be able to drill a hole sideways. If the glass filter is new, and not installed yet, and you can have a hole drilled, so the better. In that case you can follow the instructions for this type of set-up outlined below.

➡ **(b) No floor drain is available :**

You must install additional equipment to evacuate the water to a sink, or a vat that can hold several days of water changes if no sink is close-by. What you need is a powerhead type pump, placed in the sump of the trickle filter, and a float switch that will switch the pump on when the water level rises above a certain level.

➤ **Installation when a drain is available :**

Run a piece of large diameter flexible hose from the fitting placed in the hole in the filter to the drain you will be using. If no fitting is installed in that hole, glue in a hose barb of at least 1" internal diameter. Hose barbs can be obtained from hardware stores and plumbing supply places. Tighten the hose down with a clamp. Glue the barb in with silicone glue, or a similar compound. Resin based bonding agents will make for a stronger bond. They are available from just about any hardware store. Most of them are 2 compound based, and are sold in separate tubes or plastic dispensers in a blister pack.

➤ **Installation when no drain is available :**

Place a powerhead in the sump of the trickle filter, or in the tank, and attach a piece of flexible hose to the output side of the power head pump. Plug up the air intake hole of the power head. If you don't, water will be pushed out through that hole back into the sump, or tank. Such is counter productive, so close off the hole. In line with the electric wire that is normally plugged into a wall outlet, install a float switch that activates the pump when the water level rises above a certain predetermined position or height. As you now add water (we shall see a little later how this is done), and the sump or tank level rises, the float switch will activate the power head, this will evacuate water, and the water level will go down again. See the section on float switches for exact wiring instructions of such devices, earlier in this book.

➤ Installation of the water changing equipment :

Prepare a vat with reserve water. The larger the vat, the longer the supply will last and the less frequently you will have to refill the vat. If it is rather large, for instance 10 gallons or more, you should sink an air stone in the vat and run the output of a good air pump through it. This will make the water in the reserve container circulate and re-oxygenate itself.

Determine how much water you will need to change a day. For example, if your tank is 100 gallons and you wish to change 5 percent a week, you will need to change 5 gallons divided by 7 (days of the week) every day. This the same in ounces, as 128 times 5 and then divide the result by 7. This works out to 91.5 ounces per day, or around ¾ of a gallon per day.

This is just an example, and you must do a similar calculation for your own tank. Set the timer you are using to make the water changer operate to its minimum setting. Because of the short span of time that you will want the pump to run, you should use a timer that allows for very short interval settings. Radio Shack makes such a timer. Its minimum setting is one minute. It is part of their Micronta range of products.

You must now regulate the output of the pump so that it delivers about ¾ of a gallon per day each time the pump goes on (at least that's the number needed in our example. Use the number that you calculated for your own tank), and decide at what time of the day you want to perform the water change. Set the timer for one minute "on" time and adjust the output further if necessary. If the amount of water that you need to dispense cannot be delivered in one minute by the pump that you are using, increase the "on" time progressively until you reach that level. In most cases the amount of water that you need is small, and any power head pump should be able to do so in one minute or less (therefore the adjustment of the powerhead's output. Most are. If not, tighten a small clamp placed around the hose attached to the output of the power head to reduce the output even further).

Lastly, you must dispose of the water that is evacuated by the powerhead/float switch combination, so the filter or tank do not overflow. The hose attached to the powerhead's output side can be guided to a sink, or if no sink is available, to a vat that can hold a sufficient amount of water for you not to have to empty it every day.

Ideally it should the same amount as the reserve vat itself can hold. If such is the case, you can then empty one vat (the one that holds the evacuated water) and refill the other one (the one that holds the new salt water) in one and the same session, which makes for a more organized maintenance schedule.

Automatic water changers can always be installed on a system, whether you have holes in the filter or not, whether you have a drain available to you or not. Some installations are a bit more involved than others and require more equipment, but installing such a system can always be done and will not cost an arm and a leg. At the time of this writing a float switch cost around $65.00, the Micronta timer around $25.00 and the powerhead around $20.00, or a total of just over $100.00. look through catalogues from scientific supply houses for other float switch and timer offers as well.

W.W. Graingers, McMaster Carr, Whitney, and others, all offer a wide variety of equipment that you may want to consider, if not for this application, at least for some other one that you are considering. When it comes to reef aquarium technology you are no longer limited to supplies available at your local pet or hardware stores in your area. Because the variety of equipment taht you may need, or can use, shopping around is strongly recommended.

Vats can be obtained from large hardware stores, from swimming pool places, from D.I.Y stores, from businesses that sell fiberglass molded vats, from catalog mail order companies, and so on. The whole set-up should cost less than $175.00, which is really a good deal, considering how much easier an automatic water changer can make your life, and how beneficial it is to the stability of the water quality and chemistry.

Should you set the water changer for more than one cycle per day? All depends on how much water you need to change. If only a small amount is involved such will not be the case, but if you have a real large tank, and you are changing several gallons a day, you may wish to split the changing over two or more cycles. The decision is entirely up to you and a factor of the quantity you are changing.

Remember, whether water changing is done manually or in an automated fashion is not the important matter. Doing it, and doing it regularly, is what really counts.

Because automating the system reduces the amount of manual work that needs to be performed to do so greatly, I recommend that you seriously consider setting such an automated system up.

5. Water Quality Parameters

5.1 Introduction :

Water is often referred to as the universal solvent, meaning anything that enters the water will, in some form or another, in some amount or another, dissolve in that water and affect its chemical make-up. Any gas that is in contact with the water will also dissolve to some extent in that same water. Some of these compounds, elements and gasses -many different names are used, depending on how semantically precise one wants to be- that dissolve are beneficial, and others are toxic and noxious.

The key, therefore, is to ensure that only beneficial ones remain in solution and that all noxious elements are removed in some way or another. That is, of course, exactly the purpose of all filtration, and it is also the reason why the success of a tank really boils down to the relative quality of the water chemistry. The more efficiently these noxious compounds are removed, the higher the water quality will be and the better a living environment for your fish, corals and invertebrates you will be providing.

This chapter deals with some of these compounds, the ones most frequently encountered in an aquarium environment, especially by hobbyists who use tap, well, river, lake and other such types of water. Distilled, de-ionized and water that is chemically treated with, for instance, resins, is much purer, and will not contain these elements as a matter of course.

The listing in this chapter, and the analysis of each compound, is by no means to be considered exhaustive. Many other chemicals and elements can be, and are, present in aquarium water. A complete analysis would require more than one book just on that subject. Many beneficial ones are not discussed in this chapter either, but can be found elsewhere in this book, e.g. oxygen, dissolved oxygen levels, carbon dioxide, trace elements, and so on.

Natural seawater contains all known elements in solution, in varying quantities, many in such small amounts that they are measured in the parts per billion, and even lower. Many of these elements are present in the artificial salts that we use, and provide the basis for the environment in which the fish and invertebrates are placed. A fair number are not available, and are often added by means of supplements such as trace element mixes, specialized mixtures, individual additives, and so on.

Whereas you may think that such solves the problem of ensuring the presence of all the required elements and nutrients in the water, this is unfortunately not so for two main reasons :

◉ trace element mixtures as well as other additives and supplements are not as complete as manufacturers would like them to be, and do not substitute efficiently for true seawater, as many elements are still missing. Upwards of 30 may not be present. Whether many of the missing elements are, in fact, really needed by the tank's inhabitants, has not been documented in hobby literature, at least not to my knowledge, and is often a matter of great debate.

To the manufacturer's credit it must be said that such additives cannot be made more complete because information as to what elements to add to make the mixes more efficient is scarce or non-existent. Unfortunately, in-depth research on the exact and complete requirements of invertebrates and fish is not as complete as we hobbyists would like it to be. Much progress can still be made in that area.

Fortunately however, as time goes on, many new discoveries are made. The recent introduction of a strontium and molybdenum supplement, and also an iodine supplement, by Thiel•Aqua•Tech is proof of that. Kalkwasser from the same company, an absolute must in reef tanks, is another example. Research is obviously not at a standstill, and new findings are acted upon as soon as they are known.

Add Kalkwasser on a very regular basis

◉ all these compounds are present in an environment that is chemically very active : your tank. The chemistry underlying what happens in an aquarium and the biochemical and other processes that occur in that water, are far beyond the scope of this book, but result in many of these elements, amongst others, being :

• removed from the water by the tank's inhabitants, during feeding, absorbing from the water and storing, metabolic processes, etc sometimes rather quickly.

• transformed into other chemical compounds that are not usable by the animals, but remain in the tank, either as dissolved or un-dissolved chemicals.

• precipitated out of solution, often due to the high pH of a reef aquarium, and thus not available to the animals,

• removed by chemical filters such as highly activated carbon and other types of chemical filters,

• removed by protein skimming, foam fractionation, air scrubbing, denitrification, assimilation, the use of special compounds, etc.

• stored by algae, especially certain type of macro-algae, (for more details see the chapter on macro-algae).

Artificial seawater not only contains all the additives that we purposely introduce, but it contains an even greater number of elements that we do not even know are there, because we do not test for them, or because no tests that can be used by hobbyists are available. Such elements enter the water in multitudes of ways, many of which you do not suspect, or are aware of. Here are a few:

• as by-products of chemical processes taking place in the tank, both chemical, biochemical, and redox processes.

• as leachings from rocks, etc. present in the aquarium. This is often the case when you place rock of unknown origin in the tank, e.g. red lava rock, rocks that came from aquariums previously treated with copper, medicine, and so on.

• as impurities of additives that you may be using, for example impurities in the salt, the foods, many grades of activated carbon, fertilizers, carbonate hardness generators, etc. Yes, even some of the latter contain more impurities than is good for your reef tank.

• as elements, chemicals, and compounds dissolved in the water used to perform water changes and top-off the tank. This is often particularly the case if you use tap or well water to top-off your tank and perform water changes, when such water is not treated beforehand.

• as pollution entering the water because it is present in the air.

• as pollutants that transfer to the water because of chemicals used in the daily maintenance routines of your apartment or house, of cooking, etc., referred to more generally as airborne pollutants.

For the majority, these elements, the ones that are unwanted, can be removed by using the appropriate form of filtration : chemical filters and foam fractionation and, in some cases, air scrubbing. Some can only be gotten rid of by performing water changes with water that does not contain such pollutants : either triple distilled water (H_2O), deionized or reverse osmosis water (but you must use a reverse osmosis unit that has the right kind of membrane, and such units can cost several hundred dollars).

The fact that such can happen is also the reason why I totally disagree with anyone suggesting that water changes are not necessary. Some pollutants just cannot be removed by filtration. They must be diluted, and kept at non-toxic levels, by changing water on a regular basis (see chapter on maintenance as well).

This chapter, then, deals with some of these elements; desirable ones and non-desirable ones that are frequently found in aquariums that you should be aware of. It is certainly not an exhaustive list. The chapter also includes a short explanation for some terminology that you will frequently found in hobby texts in magazines and books.

A last note : macro-algae can store certain elements in their internal structures in concentrations far higher than the ones normally found in seawater. These can be several powers of 10 greater than the concentrations normally found in water. Keep this in mind when you have an algal die-off, or when you rip algae out of the tank when trimming excessive growth. As the stems are broken, fluids leach in to the tank's water. These fluids contain many chemical compounds, some of which may be toxic. Performing a 10-20 % water change after doing so is, therefore, often recommended. The size of the water change depends on the amount of algae removed, and whether or not an algal die-off had, in fact, occurred.

Important Note : Some of the remarks made in this introduction may seem trivial to you because in many cases we are talking about such small quantities of these chemicals. Such may very well be the case, but keep two important factors in mind :

■ Small quantities soon build up to larger ones. Such somewhat larger quantities may become moderately toxic and may account for your corals dying, or at best not looking good.

■ the difference in maintenance practices between a tank that looks vibrant, really "alive", and one that looks all right, is the degree of attention to detail that the hobbyist pays. I have said so before, but have found this to be reconfirmed to me based on facts many many times a year, whenever I try to help hobbyists, or aquarium installers, solve problems they are having with their aquarium(s).

5.1 Alkalinity

Alkalinity, carbonate hardness, hardness, buffer, and other such terminology is often found in hobby literature. Frequently you will find them associated with references to the pH level. Explaining the exact chemical meaning of each, and the differences between them, is too elaborate a task for this short chapter.

What you need to be aware of is that the level of the buffer, or the carbonate hardness, as the latter is what is often measured to gauge the buffering capacity of the water -its ability to neutralize acids and withstand the tendency of the pH to want to drop- needs to be at a certain level for your tank and its corals and invertebrates to do well.

This is necessary for pH stability, as just indicated, but also because it definitely makes for a better environment for the corals (Peter Wilkens, 1979).

Many acids are continuously formed in the tank's water. Some are organic in nature, others are inorganic. Which ones, and why, is not really of concern to us here. What is important is that water conditions should be of a quality that prevents these acids from reducing the pH, or make the environment less acceptable for the corals. This means that you must keep the carbonate hardness, in this particular case, at a high level : between 12 and 18 dKH, preferably around 15. To convert dKH to meq/L (milliequivalents per liter), divide by 2.8. For example : 15 dKH is the same as 5.35 meq/L. I keep my own tank at even higher levels, but do not suggest you do too.

Hobbyists need not really worry about the details of the process that raise or lower the buffer. Commercial products are available that enable every hobbyist to maintain the KH or dKH level, as it is often called, at the correct magnitude.

KH generators come in tablets, powders and liquids. Here are, in my opinion, the advantages and disadvantages of each of them :

■ Tablet form KH generators may contain only one of the many compounds that are necessary to adjust the carbonate hardness. One brand on the market contains nothing but sodium bicarbonate (baking soda) and a dye. Tablets may also contain binders to hold the powder together. This may result in your skimmer overflowing when you add them to the water. Check the one you use to ensure that it contains at least four, or even five compounds, and no binders. If it is not complete, resort to another form of KH generator.

Tablets are of course easy to use, as all you need to do is drop them in the water and let them dissolve slowly. Such is a plus, but add them only after you have determined that they contain more than just baking soda (sodium bicarbonate), and make sure too that they do not contain "binders". If they do, and if you use them, watch that skimmer.

■ Powdered form KH generators : most of the ones available are more complete, and thus contain all of the compounds necessary to raise the KH, and in those we tested, no binders were used. Make sure that they do not leach phosphates into your water. Checking for phosphate is easy. Add some of the powder to water that does not contain phosphates, let the mixture stand for a few hours, and then use a phosphate test. If the product adds phosphates, do not use it. Phosphates will, invariably, lead to the appearance of micro-algae which you will have a very hard time eradicating, even if you use products such as Ridalgex and Micro-algae Controller, because every time you use the product, you are, in essence, re-adding phosphates as well, and the algae will reappear.

■ Liquid KH generators are the ones that I personally prefer. They are easy to add, and do not raise the dKH too quickly in too short a period of time. They also contain all the required compounds to raise the KH hardness, uniformly and evenly. Sediment will be present in most liquid KH generators. Such is normal. All you need to do is shake the container to mix all the ingredients up again.

Some, such as calcium carbonate, will remain in suspension and will not dissolve. They are added to the tank in that manner each time you dispense a small amount of KH generator. Such is also the correct way to add these compounds. If your KH liquid contains chunks of matter at the bottom, some of the compounds may have come out of solution because of a temperature drop. To redissolve them quickly, warm up the compound a little, and shake the container.

Any time you affect the KH level of your tank by adding tablets, powder or liquids, you will need to check the carbonate hardness itself by using a test. Such tests are now widely available in the hobby. You must verify that you are not raising it too much on one hand, and enough on the other. Suggestions as to how high the KH should be vary greatly depending on which author you read, and also depending on how much that author has experience with reef tanks.

Since prior to 1986 reef aquariums were very rare, most texts you will find suggest levels that are intended for fish-only aquariums. Good sources of reference information include : Peter Wilkens, Guido Hueck-stedt, Albert Thiel, and Klaes Aquaristik's literature and articles in hobby magazines.

My own recommendation is, and has been since 1985, that you raise the KH slowly to a dKH of 12 minimum, and 18 maximum, with 15 being the level I would recommend you keep your tank at. dKH stands for German degrees of hardness.

Why this "German" in the name? Because there are several methods used to express the hardness, and dKH is a very common one, especially all over Europe. In North America hardness is expressed in either meq/l, milliequivalents per liter, or in ppm, parts per million.

Converting from one to the other is easy. dKH divided by 2.8 equals meq/l. dKH times 18.9 equals ppm. meq/l times 2.8 equals dKH, etc. For example a dKH of 15 is the same as 5.35 or 283.5 ppm, a dKH of 12 is the same as 4.28 meq/l etc.

Pet Stores also sell "alkalinity" tests; such tests can be used as well. Although they are technically speaking different from carbonate hardness tests, for our purposes the difference is so minimal that it can be neglected. Aquarium Systems make such an excellent test.

You must adjust the KH slowly if it is too low. Do not make rapid changes in the aquarium. In fact, as already pointed out, this remark applies to any condition in the tank. No parameter should be changed too quickly. Such would stress the fish and the invertebrates, and can be one of the many causes leading to the appearance of parasitic outbreaks, or the the corals not looking good or as healthy as they normally should.

Is there too high a KH level? Research through aquarium literature indicates that very little has been written on the subject, and I can therefore only go by my own experiments which indicate that 24 dKH is about the highest you will want to go, and that at 29 dKH most tank inhabitants react very negatively. Anemones close up and may die off, corals close, etc. Although I have always recommended very high KH levels, and still do, keep the level in your tank around 15 and not over 18 dKH. You will notice a marked difference in the way your tank looks when you do.

Because all hard corals require more than just bicarbonates, also called hydrogen carbonates - they need carbonates as well - you must also use another additive when adjusting the KH : Kalkwasser, or limewater, which greatly enhances the availability in the water of calcium carbonate. Corals precipitate calcium carbonate to build their hard outer skeletons.

According to certain sources and texts, ortho-phosphate interferes with this process. This makes it even more important to ensure that you do not add any phosphates, in any form, to your tank. If corals cannot perform that function efficiently, they will die on you in a matter of weeks or months at the utmost. At best they will look in sad shape, dwindling away, and becoming smaller and smaller, or not opening up as much as they used to.

Kalkwasser is not widely available but can be ordered from TAT in one gallon sizes. You must do so if you wish to keep corals for any length of time, and want to see them thrive. At the time of this writing one gallon sold for $16.00, plus shipping, or order Kalkwasser from your local dealer. Get them to order it for you if they do not keep it in stock. TAT is mainly in the distribution to stores business, not in mail order. Such is also the reason that they do not accept credit cards.

5.2 Arsenic

Arsenic, a very toxic compound, enters the tank's water mainly through the addition of tap, or well water that has not been chemically treated by the hobbyist before it is used, and salt is added. Of course, that same salt contains some arsenic as well, granted in microgram quantities only, levels so low that they are not toxic. Remember, however, that if you do not change water, this quantity will increase over time and may reach levels that become slightly to moderately, to really toxic. Several forms of arsenic can exist in the tank. The really toxic one is the trivalent form.

All lifeforms that you place in the tank take up many elements from the water. This includes this one. Not reducing its levels can, therefore, prove dangerous over long periods of time. It can account for the sometimes hard to explain death of corals and invertebrates. This may not occur immediately. It usually doesn't. Problems only start after several months. Arsenic may be one of the causes, but there are many others.

The reasoning is as follows : maybe just one compound, for instance arsenic, would not be all that dangerous. It is when the synergistic effect of all of them starts to work against you that unexplainable problems occur. Keep it in mind.

Change water, and treat the water you are using chemically. We describe how to do so elsewhere in this book, and also in my other book: Small Reef Aquarium Basics, a companion book to this one, and one of the four that make up this series, together with Marine Reef, the newsletter dedicated solely to reef aquariums, of which I am the Editor.

I have already mentioned it, but attention to details, and maintaining a regular and complete maintenance schedule is what makes the difference between an aquarium that looks good even after many many months, and one that looks good for a while, and then starts deteriorating. If this is the type of problem that you are experiencing, or have experienced, you may benefit a great deal from the suggestions made in this book.

5.3 Boron

The chemical "boron" is, in nature, always found in bound form. Usually it is bound with calcium or sodium. Plants definitely require it, but it has not been demonstrated to be essential to invertebrates. Kopp (1967) has demonstrated that seawater contains higher levels of boron than, for instance, lake water.

Spotte (1979) reports that boron makes up a sizable portion of the seawater buffer, but does not find evidence that it is required by invertebrates. Artificial sea salts contain boron, and so do certain fertilizers used to stimulate macro-algae growth. Adding trace elements to the reef on a regular basis ensures that you supply adequate quantities of boron. We suggest you do so. Some KH builders contain sodium bi-borate, e.g. Aquarium Systems and TAT.

Note : additives are a controversial subject in certain circles. Whenever you decide to add supplements, follow the directions of the manufacturer. Use all additives that such a manufacturer markets. They

---
Add Kalkwasser on a very regular basis

often work together to give you the overall result that you are looking for (the so-called synergistic effect). A complete program of additives is offered by several companies : Energy Savers Unlimited with their Coralife range of products, Thiel•Aqua•Tech with their Tech•products, Hawaiian Marine, Sera and a few others. If certain newer additives are not offered by all of them, get them separately. They are needed, at least based on my experience and research. Read hobby magazines and books to keep yourself informed on the newest developments in this respect. With all the progress being made, this is a must.

5.4 Chlorine

As most aquarists already know, chlorine is extremely toxic to fish, algae, beneficial bacteria, and invertebrates. Its presence in the tank's water and in the water used to perform water changes and top-offs, must be avoided at all cost. Just about the only reason for chlorine entering the tank is as a dissolved compound in tap water used by the hobbyist. Since this is a process over which the latter has total control, removing chlorine should not be a problem.

The manner in which this is done is where the problem may be. Two types of approaches are commonly used : aerating the water for a number of hours, or adding chemicals or additives that contain chemicals that neutralize the chlorine. Chlorine removing liquids all contain sodium thiosulfate, a compound that eventually breaks down to sulfate in the water.

Using such compounds continuously, for weeks or even months on end, eventually changes the sulfate hardness of the water to a level that is no longer recommended. It also affects the ionic balance of the water by increasing the proportion one compound : sulfate.

Remove chlorine by aerating only. It is safer in the long run. All you need to do so is an air pump and an air stone. A few hours, to a maximum of overnight aeration will remove all chlorine. Alternatively, flow the water through a good quality activated carbon that does not leach phosphates into your water.

5.5 Copper

Your tank's water should not contain any copper whatsoever, except for some traces that enter the water as part of the salt mixes that you use. Such trace amounts are a necessary part of the nutrient mix that all living things require. More than traces is extremely toxic, especially to invertebrates. You must ensure that all excess copper is removed from the water you add to the tank before you actually add it. Not doing so will make it impossible, to very difficult at best, for you to keep invertebrates. It poisons and kills them. Test the water you use before deciding that you will add it to your tank.

If copper is present, the water must be filtered chemically to remove it before you add salt. Such is easy to do. All you will need is a set of Poly Filter® pads from Poly Bio Marine Inc., they are available from dealers and pet stores nationwide. Use either 1 or 2 pads, depending on how much water you are in reality treating.

Since you will also require Poly Filters® for the chemical filtering of the aquarium water, you will need more than those filter pads. Do not use the Poly Filters® that are dedicated to removing copper from the tap, or well, water for any other purpose. Use them only for that purpose. After each treatment, rinse the pads, and store them until the next time you need them. Typically if copper was present, the Poly Filters® will change to a blue or greenish color, depending on what form of copper is being removed from the water.

Some types of rocks that are placed in the tank, for instance some types of lava rock, some decorations and equipment used, and so on may leach copper into the system as well. This may sound farfetched, but it is not. Make sure that all the equipment you use is absolutely salt water safe and does not contain any metals other than 316 SS (stainless steel), titanium, and/or gold. Often hobbyists overlook this, and copper and sometimes zinc (another toxic heavy metal) end up in the aquarium water for reasons that they cannot determine. Alternatively, because they are not adding any copper based medications, they are convinced that no copper can be present in their tank, such is or can be a mistake. Indeed, copper can enter the aquarium in many ways.

For example : new copper pipes that are part of the water supply system in your house or building, will also cause copper to appear in your tank. My recommendation is, therefore, that whenever you use tap water, you first let the water run for about 2 to 3 minutes before actually collecting any. Then, filter the water chemically to remove ionic copper and other compounds that must be removed.

Alternatively use a reverse osmosis unit to purify the water. The better reverse osmosis units, with the very efficient thin film membranes, cost around $325.00 and can be used safely (I use such a unit, TAT sells them; they are very efficient) . Be aware though that reverse osmosis is a slow and somewhat wasteful process as, typically, you will only collect 20 % of the water being treated. This means that for every five gallons treated, one is collected.

You must also know that R.O. systems work at top efficiency when the temperature of the water being treated is around room temperature, and the PSI going into the unit is around 60. Any deviation from those numbers reduces the efficiency of the unit; either less pollutants are removed, or less treated effluent is collected (the amount of water wasted is greater).

Be aware too that at higher pH levels some copper will precipitate. It will not all be in solution. When you then test for copper, you will not really get an accurate result, or may think no copper is present. As the pH drops for any number of reasons (e.g. a water change, or the build up of organic acids, etc.), some of that precipitated copper may go back into solution and damage your invertebrates. This is extremely dangerous as you may loose some animal life. Animals that die pollute the water; this leads to, and increases the stress on the remaining ones, which can lead to even more problems.

Recommendation : Keep all measurable levels of copper to zero ppm. Treat all water before you add it to the tank. Do not use lava rock in the salt water aquarium. Use a chemical filter both in the tank, and in the treatment set-up used to clean up the water you will use (Poly Filters® are a must).

Check all additives used to ensure that they do not contain any copper. Do not use micro-algae destroying products unless you know they do not contain copper. Freshwater algaecides should not be used in saltwater tanks.

Be aware also that certain filters sold in hardware stores, and used to pre-treat water for taste and odor (as they are usually labeled) may contain filter material that is made of heavy metals that may leach into your water.

5.6 Cyanide

Cyanide is known to hobbyists as the controversial chemical used in catching fish, to stun them and make them easy to trap in nets by divers around reefs in the Indo-Pacific region. Although technically illegal, it is still being used widely according to several sources, not the least of which is the International Marine Association. It is a practice that should be stopped, regardless of whether it does damage to the fish or not. It is a practice that if continued, will destroy the reefs in the long run. Steve Robinson of Cortez Handcaught has been fighting for this cause for years, and should get all involved's support. Buy from dealers who will guarantee hand-caught stock.

The two main dangers associated with cyanide, irrespective of how it entered the water, is that it affects the animal's oxygen metabolism, and that at high pH levels cyanide will combine with hydrogen to form hydrocyanic acid, which is very toxic to invertebrates and fish.

Cyanide is destroyed by ozone, permanganates and chlorine. The latter cannot be used in aquariums, but the former are. Many hobbyists now use ozone in combination with protein skimmers, and sometimes with ozone reactors, greatly reducing the danger. Frequent water changing and using chemical filters are other suggested ways of ensuring that this highly toxic compound does not slowly poison your corals, fish and other lifeforms.

As a side note : vitamins are sometimes added in great quantities to supplement possible deficiencies in the food, or to make up for the deficiencies that occur as a result of various forms of filtration. Some hobbyists even add supplemental B_{12} vitamins. This is fine, as long as the hydroxocobalamin form is used, and not the cyanocobalamin variety. Adding vitamins is strongly recommended for those hobbyists who also use large amounts of ozone to clean up the water and increase the redox potential of the water. Mix it with the food, or add them separately, but make sure you use a high quality brand. Vita Chem, Coralife, Marineland and TAT are all recommended.

5.7 Mercury

Mercury is an extremely poisonous compound. It is not a problem as such, as under normal circumstances you will not find it in your water supply, but mercury can become a problem if you are using an older style thermometer and break it by accident in the aquarium. Indeed, such thermometers contain mercury, a silvery, shiny looking metal.

Should this happen, you must try to remove the mercury immediately, or make large water changes. Because mercury "beads", it breaks up in even smaller beads, you must use a siphon hose and hold it over the beads to remove them. Use $\frac{1}{4}$ inch I.D. hose to do so, and do it immediately. Mercury poisoning is fatal to all invertebrates, fish, and whatever else you may be keeping in the tank. Be very careful with old thermometers around the aquarium.

5.8 Phenol(s)

Phenolic compounds are of organic nature, and will appear as intermediate breakdown compounds of many of the chemical reactions that take place in your aquarium. Phenols are toxic, and that toxicity increases with higher salinities and lower redox potentials. The use of ozone will, however, rid the tank of the danger.

Additionally, chemical filtration, using highly activated carbon of good quality (e.g. pelleted coconut shell), or especially Poly Filters®, will remove phenol, and more complex types of phenols from the water as well.

5.9 Phtalate Esters

Another series of compounds that are not only very toxic and that, in addition, are taken up by your corals and invertebrates quickly. Sanders (1973) recommends the use of a properly sized protein skimmer, ozone, and good maintenance practices to avoid that these esters rise to dangerous levels (of only a few micrograms).

Of course this must be combined with regular partial water changes, and good general maintenance practices (see elsewhere in this book for more recommendation on changing water and a later chapter for maintenance and husbandry).

5.10 Lead

Lead does not serve any known function in animal and plant life, and is extremely toxic to all forms of life kept in reef and other aquariums. Nowadays lead poisoning is a highly unlikely event, but water supplies, in old houses with lead pipes, may need to be checked carefully for lead before that water is used.

Another often overlooked source of lead in the water, are leachings from painted decorations that are sometimes placed in tanks. Mistrust anything that is painted, varnished, or otherwise coated, unless you know for sure which compound was used.

The only occurrence of lead in an aquarium that I have been exposed to myself, was in an aquarium where a lead pencil had been dropped and left for a long time. It only became apparent when the tank was eventually taken down, and the long pencil lead was found in the gravel, the wood around it having totally decomposed.

5.11 Pesticides

All pesticides are toxic to invertebrates, and in certain concentrations they become very toxic to fish as well. You do not, of course, add such compounds intentionally. They enter the tank's water as compounds dissolved in either mains water, but more often so in well water.

Add Kalkwasser on a very regular basis

This is yet another reason why well water should always be treated chemically before it is used and added to an aquarium. Use Poly Filters® from Poly Bio Marine Inc. (best) or a very good quality activated carbon (as already indicated make sure that it is activated and that it does not add phosphates to the water).

5.12 Airborne Pollution

Many toxic compounds can enter the aquarium water from the surrounding air and, if they are not removed by some form of filtration (chemical) or regular partial water changes, they will build up to levels that may be just noxious enough to keep your tank in a drab looking state, or in a depressing looking shape.

The quantities present or the types of pollutants may not be of a toxicity level that kills fish and invertebrates quickly, and thus hobbyists do not pay any attention to them. In fact, in most cases hobbyists do not even suspect their presence.

It is, usually, only after hobbyists have exhausted all other methods and possible causes of pollution, and are at a total loss to understand what is going on in their tanks, that someone may suggest airborne pollutants. This is because when you have tried every method recommended by books and talked to pet stores in your area, you may start asking questions by calling around to manufacturers, reef specialists and so on. The latter may have a wider experience with this form of pollution.

These airborne compounds, which includes fumes from paint, compounds used around the house to kill flies and insects and such, kitchen fumes, nicotine from smoking, etc. can all be removed easily from the water as long as adequate chemical filtration is used. Again, Poly Filters® or very good quality activated carbon are the answer.

Besides entering at the air and water interface, these compounds will also enter the water because your air pump pushes ambient air into the tank, or into the filter, or both. If that air contains pollutants, the latter will end up in the water.

Because most of these pollutants do not cause instantaneous reactions, they are often overlooked. In fact, it does not even occur to most hobbyists that the air in the room where the filter and/or the aquarium are placed can be a source of problems.

In order to avoid them you may wish to filter the air that goes into your filter, or into your ozonizer, through activated carbon first. Alternatively, do as I do and fill an old air dryer with cut up pieces of Poly Filter®. It restricts the air less, and does not remove oxygen from the air (which makes your ozonizer work better).

5.13 Carbon dioxide - CO_2

Carbon dioxide transfers to the water at the air and water interface, and also inside the biological filter chamber. In addition, carbon dioxide is produced in the tank, by the tank inhabitants, as a by-product of respiration and metabolism.

Carbon dioxide in moderate amounts is certainly not noxious. It is, in fact, beneficial. Indeed, it is necessary for photosynthesis to take place. Zooxanthellae, the symbiotic algae that many corals depend on for their survival and well being, require carbon dioxide as well. So do all macro-algae. Zooxanthellae that do not obtain their required amount of carbon dioxide cannot photosynthesize efficiently, and as a result, your corals do not receive as much nutrients as they could. This will affect their appearance and survival rates.

Carbon dioxide itself is not noxious. The problem occurs when hobbyists decide to inject carbon dioxide into the water in some form or another, because not enough of it is present in the tank, but do so without really understanding, from a chemical point, what is really happening when such is done.

To safely inject carbon dioxide you must read the passage fertilization and carbonate hardness, earlier in this book very carefully, and make sure that you understand what is going on. If not, call us, or anyone else knowledgeable about CO_2.

Briefly, when carbon dioxide mixes with water, it produces a weak acid called carbonic acid. This acid, as any other acid, will have a depressing effect on the pH, unless the carbonate hardness (the buffer in this case) of the water is able to neutralize the effects of the acidity. The carbonate hardness of the water must always be above 12 dKH when you inject CO_2, and the amount of carbon dioxide added must be such that it does not affect the pH of the tank by more than a maximum of 0.2 pH. Adding carbon dioxide is, therefore, a process that you must monitor for a while when you first set it up, to ensure that nothing is happening to the system because too much CO_2 is being injected, too rapidly, and has lowered the pH dangerously.

As your system becomes more sophisticated in its holistic control of all parameters, equipment is often used that you are not as familiar with as you are with more traditional types of filters and controls. You must, for the sake of the aquarium and its inhabitants, take to time to understand these instruments and methods to prevent you from making costly mistakes. Many manufacturers will help you over the phone in setting up their products. Take advantage of these offers. Call them before setting up the equipment if you are not sure how to do so. Don't do it after you made the mistakes. This remark applies especially to setting up carbon dioxide injection systems, especially manual injection ones.

5.14 Nicotine

Often hobbyists are worried about the effects of nicotine and tar that enter the air as a by-product of cigarette, pipe and cigar smoking, and transfer to the water, as we have seen in the airborne pollution section.

The dangers associated with such compounds are real, but are completely neutralized by the use of Poly Filters® and/or activated carbon. They should not be a cause for concern if chemical filtration is used, especially if you also pre-filter the air that your pump blows into the filter and into the water.

Cigarettes butts thrown in your tank, for example while you have guests, will however do considerable damage.

5.15 Iron - Fe

Iron is a required fertilization compound by those hobbyists interested in growing macro-algae such as Caulerpa, and other species of larger green algae. Iron can however be toxic if too much of it is added to the tank.

Iron is also not the only element that such macro-algae require. A complete fertilizer needs to contain much more than iron. We are covering algae in more depth in a later chapter.

Maximum recommended levels are 0.05 ppm to 0.1 ppm of iron as measured with standard aquarium tests. Too high levels, e.g. 0.5 ppm can become dangerous if maintained for too long, not for fish, but for corals and invertebrates. Evidence exists (Thiel, 1988) that 1.5 ppm first affects Heteractis malu adversely, and results in its loss in a period of about 3 weeks, if those levels are maintained by the addition of chelated iron salts. Use iron responsibly and you will not have any problems with corals and other tank life forms.

5.16 Permanganates

Permanganates are used to improve the water quality in those cases where the organic load has increased so much, that the hobbyist is at loss about what to do to improve the quality of the water quickly and effectively, using more traditional methods.

Permanganates are very strong oxidizers and must be used with care. Adding too much of any one of them will raise the redox potential very quickly, and to levels that are either dangerous, or fatal to many forms of life that you have in your aquarium. Follow the manufacturer's instructions very carefully, and you will not have any difficulties in improving the quality of the water.

Permanganates are not meant to be used continuously. You should only use on an as required basis, and for short periods of time, perhaps a few days in a row. Perform a large water change after the treatment period is over. 20 to 25 percent is not unusual. Make sure that the water and the salt used conform to the parameters already outlined earlier:

• they should not contain nitrates and phosphates,
• they should not add other undesirable compounds,
• ideally you should chemically filter the water thoroughly before using it for water changes or top-offs.

5.17 Hydrogen Sulfide

This very toxic compound mixes with the water very easily. Conditions that are propitious to its formation must be avoided at all cost, if you are planning to run a successful reef aquarium. Hydrogen sulfide forms when decay occurs in areas where oxygen is very low, or non exis- tent. Because it contains sulfur, a foul smelling compound, one can detect the presence of H_2S at very low concentrations.

Hydrogen sulfide appears in tanks because the tank's water contains both inorganic sulfate (a great deal of it), and organic sulfur from the decomposition of protein. Small amounts of hydrogen sulfide will be re-oxidized to harmless substances in tanks that have high dissolved oxy- gen levels and good water circulation in all areas of the tank. As a result, they are no cause for concern.

In tanks with low levels of dissolved oxygen and in tanks with inefficient water circulation, for example behind rocks, hydrogen sulfide may not be re-oxidized or may be produced in larger amounts. This may result in a depressed water quality condition that cannot, seemingly, not be attributed to any particular cause. Higher temperatures increase the sensitivity of all life forms to hydrogen sulfide.

Rather than having to cope with its presence, the hobbyist should set up the aquarium in such a fashion that hydrogen sulfide is not a cause for concern. Maintaining high levels of D.O., combined with a good water flow throughout the aquarium, is the recommended method that will not fail you.

If you use one, pay particular attention to your denitrating unit.

Make sure that it is operating correctly and that no hydrogen sulfide is leaching slowly, and continuously, into your tank. Denitrators are very efficient at removing nitrate from the water, especially if you use them with the required nutrients (not everyone does, unfortunately), but you must monitor their operation regularly. Alternatively, acquire a unit that is of the second generation type, larger, and allowing for a more rapid flow of water, making it less likely to stop and become totally anaerobic or slow down considerably and go somewhat anaerobic (not totally, but in some areas of the denitrator).

Pay attention as well to all your mechanical filters. Clean them regularly. Once a week is a minimum. Mechanical filters that work efficiently obviously trap dirt and particulate matter. As the filter traps more and more such matter, some areas of the filter will plug, become trapped with so much dirt, that no water can circulate through it anymore. Water by-passes such areas, and anaerobic activity which produces hydrogen sulfide will soon start. Cleaning your filters regularly, and changing the material used for mechanical filtration from time to time, will avoid this pitfall.

Be aware that mechanical filtration occurs in other areas than you may think of. You may have set up a filter that you consider your mechanical filter, and you may be cleaning that filter regularly, thinking that your practices are in line with normal recommendations. But you may overlook the fact that other filters that are installed function as a mechanical filter as well.

The following should guide you in deciding what you need to clean regularly : any material in the tank or water circulation system that obstructs (offers resistance) to water circulation will trap dirt. Some faster than others. The former will need to be cleaned more regularly than the latter.

DLS in your biological filter, for example, is no exception but is often not considered a mechanical filter. Unfortunately DLS does trap dirt and can cause anaerobic areas within the biological chamber, the worst location to have such activity. If your roll of DLS has collapsed somewhat, getting lower and smaller, you may have a problem.

Add Kalkwasser on a very regular basis

This is also the main reason for my recommendation not to use DLS in biological filters. Granted, one can prefilter the water going to the biological filter thoroughly. The fact remains however the same. The filter will still trap dirt. It will just take longer for it to happen. Give yourself peace of mind, use a plastic filtering material. You may have to spend a little more, but it is worth the effort in the long run. Believe me, cleaning a biological filter that contains DLS or a similar material is no fun and is a messy affair.

5.18 Nitrates

The end product of biological activity, and the end product of organic breakdown is a compound known to hobbyists as nitrates. In aquariums it occurs bound with many other compounds or chemicals, and not on its own.

Untold articles and sections of books have been written on how nitrates appear in aquariums. Most of these articles make it clear that high levels of nitrate are detrimental and can cause many types of disease out-breaks. All these articles usually point out that nitrates are toxic if their levels become too high. Many of these articles are referenced by recent authors to illustrate what levels of nitrate they consider safe.

What is often overlooked, is that a lot of these articles were writ-ten several years ago, when reef tanks where not even on the horizon. This makes their use as a reference to justify certain nitate levels as being acceptable, doubtful to say the least., when applied to the reef tank.

Why such does not occur to authors writing about reef aquari-ums is not clear. Perhaps they assume that invertebrates and fish act alike in their responses to levels of nitrate (and also phosphate) pollution. Such is, in my experience, a great mistake. They do not !

Corals and invertebrates come from environments where the total nitrate levels are extremely low, close to zero ppm in many cases, and not much more than 4 ppm of nitrate at the highend. Suggesting that corals and invertebrate will do well in aquariums with nitrate levels of 15 ppm is, therefore, in my opinion, totally misleading. And that is indeed the number you will often find as a suggestion, even in very recently written articles.

Recommendation : keep your nitrate levels below 5 ppm of nitrate -NO_3, or below 1 ppm of nitrogen nitrate, N-NO_3. Check your test to determine which of these two measurements applies to your situation. Most of the ones on the market measure N-NO_3 and the 1 ppm limit is, therefore the one that applies.

Nitrate removal from the aquarium is a complex matter. It occurs in many forms, but perhaps the most frequently suggested, and rightfully so, is water changes. While such may not bring the nitrate levels down to zero ppm, or perhaps not even to lower than 5 ppm, it is certainly a step in the right direction. Water changes must, as we have already seen, be performed for other reasons anyway. You must make sure, however, that the water used to do so, and the salt used to prepare that water, do not contain nitrates themselves. Such would be totally counterproductive.

At times you may hear that nitrate (and phosphate) are a necessary nutrient of many life forms in the aquarium (even advertisers make such claims). Such is, of course, correct. What such statements usually fail to mention, however, is that nitrate (and phosphate) is already present in large enough quantities in aquarium water, making it totally unnecessary to add more as part of the water or the salt used.

If corals and invertebrates need to be kept at nitrate levels as low as 1 ppm of N-NO_3, adding nitrate as part of the water or salt used, is really bad advice. Don't do it. Removing nitrate (and phosphate) is difficult enough as it is, that you do not need to complicate it even more by increasing its levels knowingly. Check the water you use, and also the salt, for nitrates. If either contains any, change your supply source. Take my advice, do it.

Another method used to lower nitrates is the use of compounds that absorb it. X-nitrate, Thiel•Aqua•Tech's answer to the nitrate problem, is one such compound, and one that works extremely well. Because of its price, however, it is recommended that you first bring down the nitrate levels by water changes to the range of 15 ppm NO_3, and then start using X-nitrate. Such is also that company's recommendation. A 50 gallon treatment lot cost around $22.00 at the time of this writing, and lasts a couple of months.

All you need to do is place X-nitrate in line with the water circulation. The more water flows through it, the better it will work for you. Placing it in a bag is not the most efficient way to use the compound. Indeed, water has a tendency to flow by and over the bag, and not through it. If the water does not flow through the bag, it also does not flow through the compound. Place some of it in your corner overflow box, or place it the surface skimming siphon. Use a tray right underneath your biological chamber, or fill a canister filter with it, and run the canister filter by taking water from the sump of the filter and discharging the water either in the tank, or back into the sump. Layer the X-nitrate between floss to prevent it from getting into the tank, or into the pump and motor of the canister filter.

X-nitrate is a granular compound that will come to you some-what moist, rinse it well to remove dust and pulverised compound, and you are ready to place it in service. I use X-nitrate myself on a 135 gallon reef at my home which consistently shows very low levels of nitrate : below 1 ppm of N-NO_3.

Lastly, hobbyists also use devices called denitrators. These out-side filters, through water is flowed slowly and to which a special nutrient must be added to promote nitrate respiration by the bacteria present in the filter, is extremely efficient, but a little more touchy. It needs regular attention, especially in the beginning.

To make the water from the tank, the water that contains the nitrate that you want to eliminate, flow slowly through the denitrator, you must drip water slowly into the denitrator, rather than flowing water through the unit. That is where the problem is.

To establish a drip you must use airline style tubing and start a siphon effect, while at the same time compressing the airline tubing until the desired drip rate is attained. This leaves a very small opening inside the tubing for water to pass through, and that opening can easily clog. Such makes the drip slower at first, and then it may stop altogether. When this happens the filter goes anaerobic in matter of hours. Hydrogen sulfide is then produced. Since the filter is at a standstill, the noxious hydrogen sulfide is not being added to the tank, and the damage that occured is limited to the hobbyist having to restart the denitrator anew after cleaning it out completely. Not a pleasant task, but at least nothing detrimental to the tank's life forms has happened. It will take 4 to 5 weeks before the denitrator is functional again.

Even when the filter runs but runs too slowly, hydrogen sulfide may be produced, but this time it is evacuated slowly from the denitrator and pushed into the tank's water. Such is of course very dangerous as we have already seen. Again the unit must be taken out of line, cleaned and restarted. Unpleasant to do, but not as cumbersome as restarting completely from scratch. After water has been added, and the filter is restarted, it may take up to a week for the unit to operate properly again.

Several companies offer both the units and the nutrients, but some offer only the unit and claim that no nutrient is necessary. Such is completely erroneous.

The chemical process, when methanol is used as a carbon source (the nutrient), can be summarized as follows :

$$NO_3 + \tfrac{5}{6} CH_3OH \longrightarrow \tfrac{1}{2} N_2 + \tfrac{5}{6} CO_2 + \tfrac{7}{6} H_2O + OH$$

Because methanol is potentially dangerous when excess amounts are used, other carbon sources are often added in its place. These include ethanol, glucose, acetate and so on. Which nutrient you use is not as critical as using one. If you don't, the so-called denitrification process can not take place completely, and the filter will be very hard to regulate.

5.19 Phosphates

The reasoning and explanations outlined in 5.18 when talking about nitrates apply to phosphates as well. Phosphates, in large amounts, are detrimental to corals and invertebrates. In addition, large amounts of phosphate invariably give rise to the appearance of hard to eradicate micro-algae that make the tank look unsightly in a very short period of time, as many of you may have found out.

The recommended maximum level of PO4 is 0.1 ppm, while less would be much better. My own 135 gallon aquarium tests less than 0.05 ppm of ortho-phosphate.

Keep phosphates in your own aquarium as low as you can. Use caution with the water you add, and with the salt you use. Several brands tested contain phosphate in larger quantities than you should feel comfortable with. Be careful too with activated carbon. Many brands sold in the hobby leach phosphates into your tank.

To ensure that your water, salt and activated carbon do not, all you need to do is test them for phosphate levels. First thest the water you use. Make sure it does not contain phosphates. Then add salt, respectively activated carbon, to some of that water, wait a couple of hours and test again. If your test shows phosphate levels higher than what you originally had, you know that the phosphate is coming from the salt or the activated carbon.

In the latter case my recommendation is that you use a different type of salt, and a different activated carbon, if such is necessary. If you do not own a phosphate test yet, you should get one soon. Both qualitative and quantitative tests are now available. The former is less expensive and can be obtained from TAT and its dealers. PAT, who already sell an oxygen test, now also offer an ortho-phosphate one.

Although your tank will also contain organic phosphates, no tests presently exist that the hobbyist has access to. Organic phosphate is mineralized by bacterial activity, and will show up in your testing as ortho-phosphate once that process has been completed. Testing for ortho-phosphate is all you need to do.

Molded Venturi Valve as used in TAT Venturi Skimmers
Extemely efficient skimming valve.

6. Water Flow in the Reef Tank

Any hobbyist who has kept aquarium for a while, and any hobbyist who is just starting off, knows or has heard of the importance of water circulation. Turning over water, or turnover rates per hour, as it is called, is dealt with in many articles in hobby magazines and books. Suggested turnover rates vary from a low of three times to a high of eight times the content of the aquarium, per hour. All indicate, or so it seems, that such is necessary mainly for filtration and oxygenation purposes. Which is of course true, but only partly so.

What is overlooked in most cases, is the fact that water circulation for filtration purposes is only one form of necessary water circulation. The second, and perhaps as important one, the one usually not mentioned, is the "current" or water movement inside the tank, which is required by all invertebrates and corals, because such is exactly what they are accustomed to around the real reef.

There is a great difference between the two. Current can be obtained by placing, for example, power head type pumps in the aquarium and directing them at certain angles to ensure that all areas of the tank experience moderate to strong current. This set-up can then be improved upon by alternating the on and off cycles of those power head pumps with a device that periodically changes the electrical current going to each one at preset intervals, making it a cyclical and recurrent pattern, just like in the ocean around the reef.

Commercially sold devices to achieve this are now available in pet stores and from reef specialists such as Thiel•Aqua•Tech, about the only company making it a strong point of their technology to bring out equipment that allows hobbyists to keep their stock alive for much longer periods of time, thus contributing, albeit to a small degree only, to the preservation of the natural reef and a reduction in its depletion. Other companies include Route 4 Marine Technology, Lifereef Systems, and Marine Technical Concepts.

Water circulation for filtration purposes is achieved by means of "circulator" pumps and need not be as high as the levels sometimes indicated in literature, as long as the hobbyist provides strong current inside the tank as well. Two to three times the content of the tank per hour, is plenty, in my own experience.

Because the life forms you keep depend on the quality of the filtration (especially the biological one), care in selecting a good quality circulator pump is a must. Too many hobbyists buy the cheapest pump they can get away with. Such is a mistake. Your circulator pump must run hour after hour, day in and day out, for months if not years, without failing you. This requires a pretty decent piece of equipment, not just any pump.

Remember, when your pump fails no filtration takes place, and your filter bed -the bacteria- may die within a matter of hours, or sooner, depending on what type of medium you are using inside your trickle filter. Plastic media give the best survival rates. Bio•Techs, Super•Techs, Bio-Blocs, Bio-Cubes, Bio+, Mini Balls, Jaeger Tri-Packs, and so on, are all excellent media to use inside your trickle filter's biological chamber, and can weather longer power outages or pump breakdowns.

Buy a pump that can withstand this though service, one that has been made for continuous use in salt water aquariums. Most pumps sold in the hobby are chemical pumps used in other industries, and offered for sale in the hobby. Iwaki pumps, for example, come for the most part from the photographic processing industry. Although they are excellent pumps, they run a little too hot in my opinion. I no longer use them.

Sizing the pump is another area of confusion. Hobbyists use the following rationale : "my tank holds 100 gallons so, so based on what I have read, I need a pump that can move 300 to 400 gallons of water per hour". Such is wrong. The output of pumps is given at zero feet of head pressure (no back pressure on the pump, or said simply, not taking into account that the pump has to push several feet up, and through pipe or hose that may be going at many different angles). Height, fittings, the type of pipe used, all influence the pump's performance, and can reduce that output considerably.

To achieve the actual 300 to 400 gallons per hour that the hobbyist set out to achieve, he or she will more than likely need a pump that is rated at 800 to 900 gallons per hour. Make sure you keep this in mind when you select a pump for your own system. Spending money on a pump, only to have to change to a stronger motor a couple of weeks or months down the road, is really a waste of money, and time.

Make sure too that all parts can withstand being in saltwater for extended periods of time, and that the pump you buy is rated for continuous use. Saltwater safe pumps should not contain any parts that are not totally salt water resistant. This means that the pump housing and inside parts need to be of a durable inert plastic, or 316 stainless steel. Brass, zinc, monel, and so on are not acceptable. Keep in mind as well that you may be using ozone. Ozone will make any material deteriorate very quickly, unless you have a real high quality pump. I am not suggesting that you should buy a pump that is rated for ozone service. Such would cost you over $1,200, but you should get the next best thing, usually a pump with totally enclosed magnetic drive parts, casing made out of Kynar® or virgin (not mixed) polypropylene, impeller out of the same materials or 316 SS, Viton® seals, and so on.

Additionally, you must know that many pumps cool themselves by transferring heat to the water. This increases the temperature of the water in your tank by several degrees, which is not desirable at all. Keeping the water in your reef tank low is a big enough problem as it is. Get air-cooled pumps for your tank. They are sometimes referred to as blast-cooled.

Clean your pump(s) from time to time. Dirt, slime, algal debris, and so on, get inside the impeller chamber whether you like it or not and all impede the water flow. Besides, they may even build up to a level where the pump is being damaged and runs warmer because it has to labor harder to push the water through the pipes. I suggest you clean your pumps at least every 10 to 12 weeks. More often will, of course, not hurt.

To do so, you must take into account, when installing your system, that you will need to be able to take the pump out of service from time to time. The only way of safely doing so, is to install true union ball valves on each side of the pump. You can then shut off the valves when you need to service the pump, and remove it from the lines easily without much water spillage each time it needs servicing or cleaning. True union ball valves are somewhat more expensive than plain shut-off valves, but because of the union part they can be opened, the pump moved out of place and cleaned, and then re-installed. Once you have done it a few times the whole process should not take you much longer than 10 to 15 minutes.

Pumps come with in and outlet size fittings deemed best by the manufacturer to operate their pumps efficiently, and obtain the water movement ratings listed on the specification sheets. Although you can downsize the outlet side of the pump, or install a ball valve in-line to regulate the flow and service the pump, you should never ever downsize the intake side of the pump. Doing so may not bring enough water inside the impeller chamber and cause the pump to "cavitate" and break up the water so forcefully, that all dissolved gasses come out of solution. You then end up with a myriad of little air bubbles in your tank, you place a lot of strain on the pump and may ruin it, and you will heat up the water considerably. Besides, the tank will look very unsightly. If the intake side of the pump calls for one inch pipe or hose, keep it that way, if the intake is half inch, keep it that way as well. Do not, under any circumstances, change the intake size by changing the hose or pipe size.

Always buy a pump with a rating much higher than what you have determined your need to be. For example, in a 100 gallon tank, with the filter underneath the aquarium, and a moderate amount of 90 degree elbow fittings to bring the water to the tank, you should use a pump rated at zero feet for about 900 gallons per hour, or about 600 gallons per hour at 4 feet of head. You will probably end up with a true 400 gallons per hour going through the tank.

Such is about what you really want, because you can now adjust the exact output with the ball valve you installed, until you are comfortable that the water circulation is adequate for your 100 gallon aquarium.

Although I can recommend how much greater than your need the pump you buy should be, I can only do so after I know more about the exact manner in which the hook-ups are done, and how much "head" the pump will have to push. Generalizing is usually not a good idea, since such does not apply to everyone. Moreover, some pumps are good at overcoming head, and others are not. Circulator pumps can usually not handle a great deal of back pressure and loose their output very quickly as a result. All this complicates the picture somewhat.

My recommendation is therefore to first determine the approximate head that your pump will have to push, and then to specifically ask the output at that number of feet from whomever you are buying the pump from. Compare that number to the flow you want and decide whether or not to buy that pump.

How do you calculate the head ? You can, I have to admit, not calculate it accurately unless you have access to special manuals and understand fluid mechanics. You can, however, take a pretty good guess at it, and you will usually be very close.

First measure the number of feet upwards that the water has to travel. If you are returning the water through the bottom of the tank, you must measure the height of the water column in the tank as well. Count the number of fittings used, excluding elbows (If you are not familiar with fittings, see later in this book for more details on PVC fittings and valves). For each fitting that you have used, add $\frac{1}{5}$ foot of head. For each elbow used add $\frac{1}{4}$ foot of head. Add 1 foot for the pipe, and add 1 foot for the valves used. Head can, as you must have realized, build up quickly !

As an example : a 55 gallon tank, with water being returned from the top. Height to top of aquarium, including stand is 4 feet. 3 fittings and 2 elbows are used. The pipe size is half inch (same size as the output size of the pump). 2 ball valves and 1 check valve are used.

Rough head is : $4 + \frac{3}{5} + \frac{1}{2} + 1 + 3$, for a total of $9\frac{1}{5}$ feet.

Now that you now the approximate head that the pump will have to push, determine what the output of the pump (and brand model or number) you are thinking of buying is at 9 to 10 feet. Does that match the amount you had determined that you needed for your tank ? If yes, and the pump meets all other criteria set, buy it.

Another factor to be reckoned with is that heavily loaded small tanks need higher amounts of flow through the filters. For a 55 with a heavy load, 200 gallons per hour, plus good extra circulation inside the tank by means of power head pumps, is a must. If you do not install power head pumps that number needs to be increased to about 275 gallons per hour.

Noise is another factor to take into account, especially if your tank is in your living room, and most are. Manufacturers do not, as a matter of course, give noise ratings. Talk to a friend, a pet shop, the aquarium society in your area, or another equipment manufacturer to find out more about the noise generated by some of the pumps offered for sale in the hobby. Several real quiet ones, and a few very acceptable ones are available to the hobbyist. Because we assemble our own pumps, TAT models fit all criteria outlined in this chapter. So do the modified Grundfos 4500 3-speed, and 6400 1-speed stainless steel pumps we sell.

6.1 Designing the Water Flow

We stated earlier that, ideally, two types of water movement are necessary in an optimum reef tank : circulation through the aquarium and the filter, and current inside the tank itself.

Because of the nature of a reef tank and what is placed in it, areas with low water circulation are common. One such area is the entire back of the tank, behind the coral and base rock. Often the circulation in that area is low to non-acceptable because it is hard to create an even flow in such an area, unless the hobbyist designs it on purpose by using special water returns, or by placing power head pumps in the right locations. Indeed, rocks and coral base rock inhibits the even and continuous passage of water, and usually areas with very low water flow exist next to areas with good flow. Of course, as long as you are aware of it, and are willing to do something about it, this problem can easily be solved.

Several water return arrangements are possible, and we need to look at at least several of them :

6.3 Aquariums with holes in the bottom :

Whether to return the water to the tank through the bottom plate of the aquarium, by drilling holes through it, or whether to return the water from the top is a very personal decision. The advantages of returning the water from the bottom of the tank are that a better flow can be achieved easily, without sacrificing the outside view and esthetics of the aquarium. Indeed, returning it from the top makes hiding the pipe and hoses used to do so more difficult. But it can be done. The decision is entirely yours.

Drilling acrylic and plexiglass tanks is easy. All you need is a strong drill and some plastic hole saws. The size of the hole in the corner overflow box depends on the fitting you will use.

Get the fitting first, then decide on the size of the hole needed to pass that fitting through. A 1¼ fitting needs much more than a 1¼ hole. Drilling glass is not as easy, especially if you, or your local glass shop, do not have a glass drill. Best, usually, is to get the glass shop to acquire the tools, and volunteer to pay part of them if necessary. Mind you, they will have quite a bit of use out of them once they have them available, and you may be able to convince them to buy the required tools themselves. Check also with aquarium stores in your area. Some have glass drills, especially if they specialize in reef tanks, or have some experience with them. Determine whether your local aquarium society can be of any help.

6.3.1 One hole arrangement

Water is returned to the tank through one hole in the bottom of the tank only. This hole can be positioned anywhere on the bottom of the aquarium. The best size to use in tanks up to 100 gallons, is ½ inch. If the output size of your pump is greater, downsize the pipe or hose to

½ inch just at the bulkhead fitting used (the one that goes through the glass or acrylic). For larger aquariums use ¾ inch or 1 inch.

The first diagram shows the hole positioned on the left. You can place it more forward, more backwards, on the other side, etc. It really is a matter of personal preference and how you will be decorating your tank with the various types of rock offered for sale for reef tanks. Its exact positioning does not affect the flow, providing you angle the output end and flow, on the inside of the tank, in a way that it is not obstructed by rocks.

Hole on the Left.
Not to scale

Hole on the right.
Not to scale

6.3.2 Two hole arrangements

The two hole arrangement is nothing more than a variation on the one hole type return. Underneath the tank the water coming from the pump is broken up by using a Tee fitting, and guiding the output from one one end of the fitting to one of the holes in the bottom of the aquarium, and the output of the other end to the second hole. Shut-off valves (ball valves) should be used in each of the lines to adjust the output and water flow coming out of each return.

You may want to set the valves for a even flow from each return, or you may want to push more water through the one furthest away from the corner overflow box (if you are using one). Again the choice is up to you, and depends largely on the way you decorate the tank.

The two water return arrangement can be modified to include one water return in the open, one one side of the tank (left or right), and a second one, behind and underneath the coral, to move water away from the back of the tank, and prevent areas where water stagnates.

Not

to

Scale

This last method is to be
preferred because it moves
water away from behind the
coral and rocks

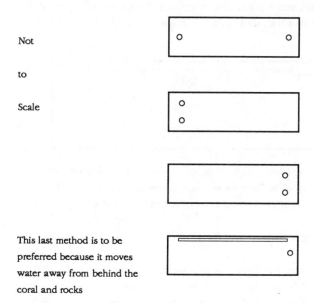

        The hole that brings water into the tank behind the rocks and
corals (last drawing) needs to be made in such a way that all water entering is distributed evenly throughout the back of the aquarium. To this
effect, a piece of PVC pipe is capped off and small holes are drilled at
equal distances. The size of he holes varies with the amount of water
being pushed through the pipe. Up to 600 gallons per hour I recommend
that these holes be a maximum of $5/32$ inch, from 600 upwards they can
be somewhat larger : $3/16$ to a maximum of $1/4$ inch.

6.3.3 Three hole arrangements

        The three hole arrangement is nothing more than the above two
combined, as the diagram clearly shows. Again a piece of pipe that has
previously been perforated is used to create good water distribution
behind all the corals and rocks.

        Point and adjust the two water returns that are on either side of
the tank in such a manner that the water is forcefully pushed towards the

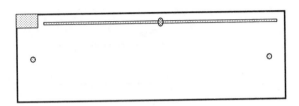

side panels of the tank, the short ends, and at a 45 degree angle upwards. This will push water out of the corners, move it upwards, and towards the outflow area that leads to the mechanical and biological filter.

Shown, but not to scale, are the three return holes, one on each side of the tank
and one behind the coral and rock. Corner overflow box is shown
in left back corner as well. See text for more details

6.3.4 Adding a corner overflow box

A corner overflow box arrangement, of the type discussed earlier, can be added to any of the above water return arrangements. It can be positioned on the back left, on the back right, in the back middle of the, along the short sides of the tank, and so on. Where it is placed is not crucial. Mostly hobbyists will position it in the area where it interferes less with the aesthetic appearance of the tank.

Corner overflow boxes should be large enough to accommodate a good flow, but not so large that they look disproportionate in the tank. In smaller aquariums up to 70 gallons a box that is $3\frac{1}{2}$ x $3\frac{1}{2}$ is sufficient. The outflow hole should be $1\frac{1}{4}$ inch. On somewhat larger tanks the box should be $4\frac{1}{2}$ x $4\frac{1}{2}$. On tanks over 150 gallons the box can be made 5 by 5 or 6 by 6, or two boxes can be used, one on either side of the tank. Make sure when you do so that the tank is absolutely level. This will ensure an even flow through both corner overflow boxes.

Multiple corner overflow boxes can be used on larger aquariums. Two is more than enough. Usually, one is placed at the extreme left, and the other one at the extreme right of the tank, but there is no reason not to put them in a different pattern if you prefer, since their efficiency will not be affected by their location.

Add Kalkwasser on a very regular basis

6.4 Aquariums without holes in the bottom

If no holes are drilled, the water needs to be brought down to the trickle filter by means of a siphon overflow, surface skimming arrangement. We discussed such devices earlier in this book. You may wish to re-read that section if you are not clear about which type is best for the reef tank.

The water from the filter is returned to the aquarium by guiding the hose or hard pipe attached to your pump first back to the top of the tank, then over the tank and finally into the aquarium. You can split that line up, of course, and make it into two water returns. One from each end of the tank. All you will need to do so is a Tee-fitting and some extra hose or pipe. Angle the returns in a manner that gives you an as wide coverage of the whole tanks as possible. Spray bars are not effective a doing this.

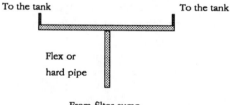

To the tank   To the tank

Flex or
hard pipe

From filter sump

If these returns are submersed they can act as back-siphons. To prevent this you must install check valves in line. Use salt water safe ball checks or Y-checks, not flap checks. If not, a lot of water could siphon out of your aquarium during a power failure or when your pump stops because of failure. The more the end of the return is submersed, the more water could possibly back siphon. Keeping the returns out of the water completely will prevent all back siphoning, but will make it hard to adjust the water distribution inside the tank, and may also result in a lot of splash and salt creep.

Factor all these remarks into your thinking before you decide on which exact way you will plumb your water returns to the tank. If you are unsure talk to someone who has already installed such a tank, or discuss it with your local pet store or a manufacturer. Fluid mechanics in an aquarium are not difficult to understand, but someone familiar with them must, preferably, explain them to you.

6.5 Conclusion

Good water flow and good water circulation are an absolute must in a reef tank. Do not overlook its importance. Acquire the best pump you can afford and protect it with a float switch, as explained in an earlier chapter.

All animals and most other lifeforms you keep in a reef tank are accustomed to strong water current. Provide it. You will be making the environment inside your tank closer that what they are used to in nature.

Such will benefit their well being and ensure that nutrients reach them as they should. Such will also make your tank look more realistic, especially if you use current alternating devices which will make the invertebrates sway from left to right, and vice-versa.

7. Fittings and Valves Used on Reef Tanks

It may seem odd to find a plumbing section in a book on aquariums. This is, in fact, not so. Around reef tanks a lot of pseudo and real plumbing often needs to be done, and experience tells me that many hobbyists are not very familiar with the many different types of fittings and valves that are used in this pursuit. Moreover, there are so many of them that a little more information on the types frequently used around reef tanks, will hopefully help quite a few readers.

As the aquarium gets more elaborate in the number of components that make up the filtration system, more and more types of fittings need to be used to make the system safe and prevent back siphoning, while at the same time allowing for an easy adjustment of the flow.

Hard piping a system, meaning using PVC or some a similar type of pipe, is the most durable way of installing a tank. It is usually also the one that will look the most professionally finished. There is, however, nothing wrong with using flexible hose. If you decide on the latter, do not use the cheaper variety of hose, rather invest a little more and use flexible PVC (sometimes referred to by one of its brand names : Tygon).

PVC is used by plumbers, pool installers, and so on, and local building and construction regulations set the safety and materials standards that such pipe must meet. Because different types of installations require different types of pipe, PVC pipe can be bought in various grades known as "schedules".

The most commonly used schedule is schedule 40, often referred to as "sched 40". It is also the least expensive. Usually sched 40 pipe is white. In some areas of the country, however, and in Canada, sched

40 is gray. The next schedule offered for sale is sched 80, a type of pipe that is usually gray, and has a thicker wall making it better for high pressure applications. It is not necessary to use sched 80 around reef tanks because we do not run reef tank systems at high pressures. Yet a sturdier variety, called sched 120, is available as well. It also has no applications in the hobby.

Although the outside dimensions of any size pipe in schedules 40, 80 and 120 is the same,the inside diameter diminishes as the schedule number increases. For example, 1 inch schedule 40 has a larger inside diameter than 1 inch schedule 80, which in turn is larger than 1 inch schedule 120.

Besides schedules 40, 80, and 120, you may come across thin wall pipe referred to as SDR pipe. Such pipe is excellent for use around reef tanks as well, but it is more expensive than regular schedule 40. If, however, you want to use gray pipe, and you do not want to pay the higher price of schedule 80, or CPVC pipe, use SDR.

CPVC, as opposed to PVC, is another form of pipe, made mostly for higher temperature and higher pressure installations. We do not need such pipe around reef tanks.

To be complete we should mention that you can also obtain clear PVC pipe, but at a considerably higher price. Besides the ones already mentioned, special application type pipe is available as well, mostly in highly sophisticated materials. As you probably already guessed, such pipe will be very expensive. Who uses this pipe ? More often than not it is used for food grade applications (for example polysulfone) or for the transport of strong chemicals (for example polypropylene).

7.1.1 Coupling :

A fitting used to connect two pieces of pipe of the same size. The pipes to be connected slide into the fitting, one on each side. Put some PVC primer and glue on all pieces first, push them together, give both a quarter inch turn, wipe off the excess glue with a rag, hold firmly together for a few seconds, and the two pieces of pipe are now permanently one.

Couplings are not usually necessary in short pipe runs, but come in handy if you have a number of leftover pieces that you would like to use rather than throw out.

Couplings also come in threaded variety, in which case you will need the matching fittings as well. Male adapter fittings have their threads on the outside, female adapter fittings have them on the inside.

Sometimes you will measure the length of a piece of pipe that you need to make a connection, cut it, or saw it, and make a mistake. If the piece is too long, you can always cut off a short bit. But if it is too short, you must either throw it out and cut another piece of the right length, or you can make it longer by using a coupling.

7.1.2 Ell or Elbow 90°, 45°, 22.5°:

These fittings are used to make 90°, respectively 45° or 22.5° angled turns with pipe. They are available in slip (no threads on the inside) or threaded. Slip is sometimes called socket/weld as well.

Elbows are perhaps the most frequently used fitting when plumbing an aquarium, indeed, because of the limited amount of space underneath the tank, many bends usually have to be made.

90° and 45° elbows are easy to find at plumbing suppliers' and are stocked by many hardware stores as well. 22.5° elbows are not as common. If you think you may need them, you would be wise to have them ordered in advance for you.

Of course, if you run out of 90° elbows, and you need to make such a turn in the pipe, you can always use two 45°, or four 22.5° ones. The end result may not look as good, but it will do the trick.

7.1.3 Tee-fitting :

Tee-fittings, also called tee-connectors, or just Tees, are used to split one line up into several. The most commonly used Tee is the 3 way Tee, allowing you to split one line up into two lines, something that is often necessary around the aquarium. Four-way Tees are also available and allow you to split 1 line up 3 ways. In all cases, one end is used for the input, and the others for the outputs.

Tee-fittings are, amongst others, often used for :
◉ splitting up a water line into several lines, e.g. as with two water returns to the tank.
◉ making a bypass around filters, for example around an in-line micron filter, or around a Fin-L-Filter®.
◉ making an extra water line available off the main one to run a protein skimmer.
◉ making extra lines available to pipe to reactors, e.g. for carbon dioxide, and oxygen.

7.1.4 Male Adapters - Female Adapters :

A fitting with an outside thread that can be screwed into a fitting with an inside thread is called a male adapter. The one with the inside thread is the female adapter.

Common male adapters have one side threaded and the other side will usually be slip, so pipe can be glued into that end. The female fitting has thread on the inside on one end, and a slip end on the other, again to glue in pipe.

These fittings are needed to hook up pumps, and can be screwed over the threads of the fittings that the pump housing itself is outfitted with. Always use Teflon® or PTFE tape when using fittings with threads. Alternatively, use a liquid, pasty, material that serves the same function: preventing leaks from threaded fittings. Tighten down by hand, or use a wrench if necessary. Never over tighten. You may crack the fitting.

7.1.5 Bushing-Reducers :

A fitting that is used to reduce the size of another fitting to the size that you need. For example, to connect a 1 inch piece of pipe to a ¾ inch piece, you will need a coupling that has been bushed down with such a fitting on one side to ¾ inch.

Add Kalkwasser on a very regular basis

Such fittings are also needed when you need to split up a water return line from, for example, one ¾ inch line to two ½ inch lines. In such a case you would use one ¾ inch Tee and two ½ inch bushings.

Instead of using separate fittings, in this case bushings, to do the job, you can also buy fittings that have the sizes you need. Such fittings are then referred to as reducing couplings, or are giving their fitting name with the dimensions of each opening. For instance, a Tee fitting to do the job above, can be referred to as a Tee ½ by ½ by ¾.

This may sound somewhat confusing, I know. There are so many different fittings available that even plumbers get confused sometimes.

7.1.6 Barb or Hose adapter :

A fitting that is made to take plastic pipe on one side and flexible hose on the other. Barbs come in male threaded, slip, and female threaded versions. Specify which one you need when ordering. The side that takes the flexible hose is ridged to give the hose a better grip once it is on. If you have problems fitting the hose over the barbed end, submerse the end of the hose in boiling, or very hot, water for a minute or so. This will soften the plastic and make it easy for you to make the connection.

Whenever you soft pipe (use flexible hose) your tank, you will need several barbs to do the job. For example, on the input and output side of your pump you will have the use the required barbs before you can hook flexible hose up to the pump.

Whenever you use barbs, you should also use worm clamps to tighten the hose in place so it can not slip off, or leak due to the pressure in the line. Use 316 SS worm clamps. They will resist salt water for much longer. Alternatively use then newer plastic clamps that you can tighten with a wrench.

7.1.7 Nipple :

A fitting that has outside thread on both sides. You may not have any need for this fitting around the tank, other than making a male adapter out of a female one, by screwing the nipple into the female fitting, after you have used a little Teflon® tape around it.

You could also use it to connect pipes that both end with female fittings.

7.1.8 Union :

A fitting used to make a connection between two pieces pipes, but in such a manner that the connection can be undone.

For example, if you had a union in the pipe on either side of a pump, you can take the pump out of the arrangement by unscrewing the unions. Of course, if you have water in the sump, which is highly likely, you would use a ball valve / union combination. Such a ball valve is called a true union ball valve.

Unions are frequently used in long runs of pipe to make removable connections. In aquarium set-ups you may wish to consider doing so too, for example if you think you may need to take the piping down at some point (e.g. if you were moving). All pieces can then be easily reassembled later when needed.

7.2.1 Ball valve or Shut-off valve

Ball valves and shut-off valves are used to control the flow of water through your system, or to isolate parts of the system so you can remove portions of it, e.g. the pump, or a canister filter that houses a micron cartridge.

In the former case you would use just a plain ball valve, in the latter case you would want to use a true union type ball valve, as the union part will allow you to disassemble the portion you want to take apart, without water spillage.

It pays to buy a good ball valve. Pressure from the tank on the valve will cause it to leak if it is not. Moreover, if you use ozone in the system, some valve will not last for very long. Recommended brands include Hayward, Asahi, Chemtrol and G+F. Keep in mind too that ball valves need to be cleaned from time to time. Not doing so may damage the valve, or cause the valve to leak when you try to shut it off because detritus is trapped inside thes shutting mechanism.

7.2.2 Check Valve :

Check valves are meant to do just that : check. This means that they will prevent water from flowing in the opposite direction of the one that you wish it to flow. They are one-way valves. Check valves are necessary in any water line around your tank that could back siphon is your pump failed or if you had a power failure.

Ball checks and Y-checks are the better ones to get. Check valves with a piece of rubber or similar compound, in the form of a flap will not hold up for very long around the reef aquarium. Salt in the water, and maybe even ozone, will ruin such valves in no time.

Keep in mind that the difference between a good and a bad check valve is very important to you. It could save you from a flood and an empty tank with, probably, many dead animals if you do not notice what happened for a number of hours.

They area safety feature. You must install check valves in all systems that work on water returns through the bottom of the tank. You must also clean check valves regularly. Hopefully you will never need them to protect the system, but if you do and if they do not work properly, you will have a big water problem on your hand, and more than likely you will have lost most of what is in your tank as well.

Check valves are best installed vertically so the back pressure of the water forces them closed if the need arises. Although dirty check valves may check partially, small amounts of water that can get through will empty your tank in a matter of hours, if you fail to notice what is going on. Why do they get dirty ? Slime, parts of algae, and so on, can get caught around the seat of the ball and prevent the ball from correctly seating itself in the space provided for it, thus preventing water from flowing in the other directions (towards your sump rather than towards the aquarium).

Of course, as long as your pump runs check valves serve no real purpose. But installing a check valve is the same as taking out insurance. You hope you never need it, and you may be upset about its cost, but when you do need it, you will be glad you have it.

7.2.3 Flow meters :

Devices that are piped in line to determine what the exact amount of water that flows through your pipes, and through your tank, is.

Not a necessary part of your system, but handy, especially if you want a high degree of control over what is going on in your tank. The price of the flow meter is determined by the degree of accuracy that you are looking to get. Calibrated flow meters are the best, but cost quite a bit. Check with·scientific supply houses if you are interested. Prices vary from around $50.00 for the least accurate ones, to about $250.00 for the real good ones.

7.2.4 Needle Valve - Angle valves :

Unlike ball valves, shut-off valves, and true union ball valves, these types of valves allow for very small adjustments in the flow rate.

Very good to have, for instance, to adjust the flow rate going into your columnar protein skimmer. Needle valves are usually only available in real small sizes. Angle valves which also allow precise control over the flow, can be bought in much larger sizes as well. Plan on spending between $20.00 and $30.00 depending on the size, and the quality that you are looking for.

7.2.5 Foot Valve :

Similar to a check valve. In fact foot valve contain a check system, but are, in addition, equipped with a screen to prevent large particulate matter from getting through. They are not a substitute for a fine filter, because they only prevent larger types of material from getting into your pipes and tank. The real fine particulate matter needs to be removed with a proper fine filter.

Can only be used in submersed form. Not in-line. Although some hobbyists use them, they do not have a wide application around reef tanks.

7.2.6 Gate Valves :

A form of shut-off valve. Same principle, but far less precise adjustment. For just opening and closing off a water line they are all right to use.

Often used in very large aquaria, but not so often in home reef systems.

7.2.7 Solenoid Valves :

Solenoid valves are lectrically controlled valves. They serve only an on or off function. Nothing in between, they do not allow for a flow adjustment. Such is not their purpose.

Two types are commonly available : normally closed (NC) and normally open (NO). When energized, meaning when an electric current is sent to them, the valves change internal position. The NO valves close, and the NC valves open.

Solenoids are used for many applications. For example, they are used in conjunction with pH controllers to dispense carbon dioxide. When a NC solenoid is energized, it opens and lets CO_2 through. When the pH has changed, and the controllers shuts off the power to the solenoid, it closes and stops carbon dioxide from getting through.

They can also be used with columnar protein simmers to prevent the skimmers from emptying itself when the power goes off, or when the pump fails (this is appealing to many hobbyists who have filters with small sumps that cannot hold the excess water coming out of the skimmer, during such a power failure).

Many other applications for solenoids exist, too many to mention here. Some of them are discussed in Advanced Reef Keeping Made Simple (I), for instance their use in conjunction with a gravity fed water refill system and a float switch.

7.2.8 Actuated Valves :

Electrically actuated valves do not have much of a use in home reef tanks, but are sometimes used, in line, to create an alternating water current between two different water inlets into the tank.

For more details you may wish to refer to Advanced Reef Keeping Made Simple (I) as well.

7.3 Conclusion :

Although you may not have used many fittings and valves in previous aquariums that you have kept, around reef tanks, especially the more sophisticated types, you will find that they are either a requirement, or that they will increase safety, or that they will make your life a lot easier.

If your are setting up such a tank, refer to my two other books for more details on many other applications not mentioned in this one.

Surface Skimming Syphon
by
Summit Aquatics
Mike Helton and David Nykodem
of Fulton Mo.

THIEL ▪ AQUA ▪ TECH   203 - 368 2111

Date	N°	Remarks	Time	KH	Fe	CO_2	O_2	O_3	NO_3	PO_4	NO_2	NH_3	pH	MV	Cu
	1.														
	2.														
	3.														
	4.														
	5.														
	6.														
	7.														
	8.														
	9.														
	10.														
	11.														
	12.														
	13.														
	14.														
	15.														
	16.														
	17.														
	18.														
	19.														
	20.														
	21.														
	22.														
	23.														
	24.														

Test Tank Conditions Regularly. Make Elaborate Notes. They will help you evaluate tank conditions better. © A. Thiel 1989.

Add Kalkwasser on a very regular basis

8. Testing the Water

8.1 Introduction

It is well known that one should regularly test the aquarium's water, to determine the relative levels of certain compounds and certain water characteristics that will give the hobbyist an indication of the level of purity, and the adequacy that the water in the tank possesses and offers for coral, invertebrate and fish life.

Although such is well known and often suggested in hobby literature, few hobbyists actually perform a number of basic tests regularly, and fewer yet keep note and records on sheets such as the one reproduced on page 194.

Testing the water is more than just adding chemicals to a sample of tank water and looking whether or not the result is "normal". Indeed, what is normal, and who determined it to be so? Unless the hobbyist really understands the results of the tests, knows how to influence the water quality safely to alter these results, and is a able to interpret what is going on in his, or her, tank while such is taking place, **the tank controls the hobbyist**. The hobbyist should never let this happen as it will, invariably, lead to problems with the tank in the short run, usually not more than a couple of months, at best seven to eight.

Many tests are offered for sale through the mail or at pet shops, but most were developed when fish-only aquariums were the norm. Such tests may not be accurate enough, or they may not offer enough precision for our purpose : running a vibrant looking reef aquarium. The hobbyist must re-evaluate the types of tests that he, or she, now needs to use. Unlike in fish-only tanks, most should now meet laboratory grade quality

and accuracy. LaMotte Chemicals, Chemetrics, Hach, and similar companies offer such tests.

This does certainly not mean that regular aquarium tests can no
longer be used, or that they are of inferior quality, many are not, but reef
hobbyists should only use them if they were developed specifically for
the reef tank.

Are there in fact "correct and precise" levels for many of the compounds and characteristics that we are testing for ? Usually not, because
even around real reefs these conditions vary, but only within narrow ranges. What we must try to achieve as best as we can in our own reef tank,
is to keep all water chemistry parameters within those ranges, because
if they are common around natural reefs, they can obviously be considered safe, and if they are acceptable there, why change them.

8.2 Suggested Values for water quality parameters :

Below is an overview of the test values that I personally recommend for reef aquariums, and that I maintain in my own 135 gallon reef
show tank that those who have seen, can testify to be vibrant looking:

dKH	Fe	pH	Mv	Cu	Sal.	T°	O₂	NO₂
15	.05	8.25	390	0.00	35p	76°	8.00	0.00

PO₄	NO₃	CO₂	NH₃
0.05	5.0	4.0	0.00

Small variations from these numbers are in order, providing they
stay within close limits of the ones suggested. For each of the parameters
measured the variations are unique, meaning no variation magnitude that
applies to all of them can be given. Some parameters can vary a little more
without any damage occuring, others cannot vary for any length of time
or stress will build up and lifeforms may, as a result, suffer from the not
so adequate water chemistry.

Here are some suggested levels that seem to be tolerated by most
fish and invertebrates that you may keep in your tank :

dKH	12 to 21 German degrees of hardness
Fe, Iron level	0.05 ppm to 0.15 ppm
pH	7.95 to 8,35
Millivolt (redox)	250-475
Copper	must be zero at all times
Salinity	32.5 to 35 parts per thousand
Temperature	73 to 79 degrees Fahrenheit
Oxygen level	6.00 to 10.00
Nitrite	0.00 to 0.01 ppm
Phosphate	0.00 to 0.10 ppm
Nitrate	0.00 to 15 ppm
Carbon dioxide	2 to 4 mg/l
Ammonia	must be zero

Although some of these numbers are quite a bit higher than the ones suggested in the first list, such does not mean that it is all right to keep your tank's water chemistry towards the high end of these parameters' values. All it means is that for short periods of time the higher values do not seem to result in damage.

For the benefit of your tank's lifeforms you should try to stay with the values suggested in the first list. Your tank will look much better and all lifeforms will fare much better as well.

Once you attain those closer to ideal numbers, your task is to maintain them at that level. Such is, of course, easier said than done. Good husbandry, not overfeeding, not overstocking the tank, cleaning filters regularly, and more, are all part of the success equation. Keeping a reef tank is fascinating but it does require a fair amount of work and maintenance. Don't fool yourself into believing it doesn't.

Advertising slogans that purport, for example, that if you use brand X products no water changes are necessary, sound great and draw a lot of sales. Why ? Because such is exactly what the hobbyist wants to hear. Similar slogans that "guarantee" results appeal to certain of the hobbyists' weak spots and make him or her buy, but often fool you into thinking that you can then slack off in other areas, frequently in the "maintenance" area. Doing so can be very dangerous, as many may already have found out after having used such products for a while. Unfortunately, there are no short cuts when it comes to ending up with a really nice looking reef aquarium and keeping it that way, at least not yet.

In my experience, to be successful, what the hobbyist needs to do is to strive to be as close the the natural reef conditions as one can come given the available technology. This requires using certain products and certain types of additives, quite a few in fact, no question about it. But advertising for such products should not lead you to believe that you can safely take shortcuts in husbandry techniques and in other similar areas. Don't believe it. Don't do it. If you do, you are asking for problems down the line.

Last but not least, whenever one or more parameters are out of line with the suggested values, you must initiate corrective measure immediately. Do not put them off till the week-end, or to some other time that happens to be more convenient. Your corals and invertebrates may not be able to take the stress for that long. Don't take any chances.

8.3 Carbon dioxide

CO_2 is a gas that mixes with the water very easily to form carbonic acid, and is available in the tank, either in free or in bound form. The more free CO_2 is present or injected, the more the pH will be affected downwards. Too much CO_2 can, therefore, be harmful. Because the effects of carbon dioxide, and the resulting carbonic acid, can be neutralized by the aquarium water's buffer (we have called it the carbonate hardness), maintaining a high dKH level is important as we have already discussed in another section.

Carbon dioxide is necessary for photosynthesis by all green algae, especially symbiotic Zooxanthellae living inside the tissues of your corals and invertebrates. Photosynthesis takes place in the presence of light, more so when strong light is available. Just think for a minute about the amount of light that is available to such algae on the reef, day in day out, except for a small number of days of stormy or overcast weather. The levels and amount of lighting over a natural reef always far exceed what the average hobbyist normally provides.

If only a small amount of light is provided to the reef tank, photosynthesis will be low and the amount of carbon dioxide dissolved in the water may be sufficient for it to take place at a low level. Such carbon dioxide enters the water as a by-product of metabolism, fish and invertebrate respiration, and from the air around the tank.

As you increase the amount of light -and over a reef tank you should, especially if you are trying to recreate the natural environment-the natural amount of CO_2 available in the water may be too low for proper photosynthesis to take place. Adding supplemental carbon dioxide may then become necessary. This can be done either manually, or by using an automated injection system, as we have seen in another chapter already. In most tanks the manual injection will work fine.

Because the appearance of your corals greatly depends on the amount of nutrients they receive and can absorb from the water, light intensity becomes an important limiting factor. If you provide low levels of lighting, photosynthesis will be low and your corals will suffer. If you provide high lighting, but you do not provide enough carbon dioxide, your corals will suffer as well. Their appearance is directly related to the nutrient amounts available to them. Limiting one nutrient, in this case carbon dioxide, is not recommended when what you want is for your corals to look healthy and vibrant. Although lighting is a prominent part of this natural cycle, light is not the nutrient, light is the catalyst for the process to take place efficiently.

Because photosynthesis is a process whereby macro-algae take up carbon dioxide from the water and produce oxygen as a by-product, ensuring that photosynthesis takes place in the tank has the added benefit that oxygen levels will be increased in aquariums with good algal growth.

This process can, in fact, be observed. When small streams of very tiny bubbles rise from algae towards the surface, oxygen is, in fact, being released. Some of this oxygen dissolves in the water, and increases the quality of the environment that your aquarium is. It has also been suggested that this type of oxygen dissolves three times faster than regular atmospheric oxygen, making it perhaps the best manner in which to maximize the aquarium's dissolved oxygen level.

Testing for carbon dioxide is not as easy as most hobbyists would like, because the chemicals used do not give easy to interpret results, or are affected by the high pH of the tank's water. I personally never test for carbon dioxide, but I always make sure that my tank's carbonate hardness is high. When such is the case, and you inject carbon dioxide into the water as well, its level at a pH of around 8.00 will be between 3 and 4 mg/l. Since that is the value that we should strive for, no direct testing for carbon dioxide is necessary.

Read the section on carbonate hardness in 8.7 carefully, as the use of carbon dioxide and the level of the carbonate hardness are very closely interrelated. You must understand that relationship, and feel safe using CO_2, as knowing what you are doing when using CO_2 puts you in the driver's seat, not the opposite. "You" should always be in control, not the tank, or the instruments and other equipment used to run it.

8.4 Phosphates

Not identified as a source of problems until perhaps 1985, phosphates are finally being recognized as one of the reasons for the frequent micro-algae outbreaks and blooms in reef, and also in other types of fish tanks. Thiel (1985 and 1988) suggests that their level should be below 1 ppm. Since then he has changed his recommendation to a level 20 times lower : 0.05 ppm. This rather substantial change is based on further experience with adding phosphate based compounds to reef tanks and observing the effect of ever increasing levels on corals and invertebrates (Thiel, Lab notes 1986-1990).

Thiel's research was a continuation of experiments conducted on freshwater tanks by several German plant experts, but had not been tried on marine reef tanks until then. All his experiments at levels higher than 0.1 ppm led to severe micro-algae problems in the tanks the tests were performed on, and result in the new recomendation of 0.05 ppm to a maximum of 0.1 ppm of phosphate for the reef aquarium.

Phosphates enter the aquarium in many insidious ways. Many are deceptive and subtle, often ways that you do not even think about or suspect. Case in point : the water you use to top-off the tank, the water you use to change water in the tank, the activated carbon you use, KH buffers you my be adding, food that you administer, additives that are dispensed, the salt itself that you use, leachings from rocks you place in the tank, pH altering compounds, mineralization of organic phosphate produced in the tank, and so on. The manner in which this occurs is actually baffling, often because you do not, and have no reason, to suspect products that are sold for use in reef aquariums by reputable companies.

The only way to protect yourself, and your tank, is to test all your additives and supplements, the salt and the activated carbon you use, and anything else used before adding it to the tank. Test especially the salt, the activated carbon, and the water. My recommendation is that you change brands if they add any phosphates to your tank. Indeed, why add compounds to the water that you will spend time and energy removing, at sometimes great expense, when you can prevent adding them to begin with and avoid the problems associated with phosphate altogether?

Of course, phosphate is a required nutrient of all macro-algae that grow in your tank. Advertising therefore suggests that if it is contained in your salt or water, all you are doing is providing a required nutrient for those algae and for other lifeforms in the tank. Deceptive, because phosphate is always present in your tank in small and sufficient quantities anyway, mostly as a result of the mineralization of organic phosphates that occur as a by-product of protein and other organic compounds also present in the water. Why would you want to add more of something that is already available to the lifeforms that need it in sufficient quantity, and risk micro-algal blooms or outbreaks in the process ?

Always keep phosphate levels as low as you can. Use Poly Filters® from Poly Bio Marine Inc, water changes, and other chemical filtering compounds to remove excess PO_4 from your tank. Keeping phosphates low should be high on your list of priorities.

Water changes are the recommended way to go if your levels are now high. After you have brought them down to the <1ppm range, rely on Poly Filters® to bring them down even further and keep them low.

I have yet to come across another compound that will lower them safely, but am convinced that some will appear. The hobby evolves all the time, and phosphate removing and lowering products will be offered for certain at some point.

Some hobbyists resort to the use of Ferric chloride, a very dark powder or crystals, to lower phosphates. Tests on water that contained phosphate levels of 2.5 ppm show that after a few hours the phosphate level is actually down to close to zero, and that a floc, a sludge like material, has built up on the bottom of the container used.

Using the additive in aquarium conditions presents a problem : the floc is dispersed and ends up clouding the water for several hours, especially if a fair amount of Ferric chloride is used. Trapping the floc in micron filters is not an ideal solution either, because the cartridge used to do so plugs up rather rapidly requiring its frequent replacement. Such cartridges can cost in excess of $5.00 a piece, even when bought in quantities !

Both the pH and the redox potential are affected downwards, but only for short amounts of time when the Ferric chloride is added to a large amount of circulating water. This would be the case in aquarium conditions. No data on the long term use of this practice has been studied to my knowledge. If you decide to experiment with Ferric chloride, be careful with the quantities used, and do so on a tank that is not your pride and joy. Use it on another tank. More information will hopefully become available as time goes on. We are continuing our testing and will make whatever results we find of interest to the hobbyist available in Marine Reef, the newsletter we publish.

8.5 Ozone and Ozonizers

Until Sander of Germany introduced ozonizers for use on home aquariums, only large systems were being treated with ozone to improve the water quality. Hobbyists might have read about the possible use of ozone and its beneficial effects, but that is about where it stopped. Things have changed quite a bit, indeed, nowadays American made units are available from at least two manufacturers.

Ozone is a special form of oxygen, an allotropic form. It has an extremely high oxidative power (over 2700 mv redox) and can, therefore, be used to our advantage to clean up the water in our tanks. Ozone oxidizes many unwanted compounds, especially organic ones, breaking them down into different compounds that do not affect the water quality as much as the original ones, or can be removed, for example, by protein skimmers.

By oxidizing compounds completely, some only partially, ozone greatly assists in the mineralization of many organic compounds present in the water. Mineralized compounds are complex compounds broken up in simpler forms, most of which are not as noxious as the original compounds themselves. Some of those mineralized compounds are then re-used by the tank's lifeforms, or removed by other forms of filtration.

Because of its very high oxidative power, ozone can do as much damage as it can do good if it is not used properly. Many hobbyists refrain from using it because they are afraid it will kill off everything in their tank, or will damage system components. In fact, when ozone is not used with care and knowledge of what it can do, it may do both.

I am certainly not trying to scare you and suggest that you should not use ozone. I am not trying to depict a bleak picture of all the harmful results that ozone can bring about if used without care.

On the contrary. I am a very firm believer that ozone is a must on a reef tank and that it has to be part of the overall filtration of such a tank. It is highly unlikely that you will be able to attain, and maintain, the high water quality parameters necessary for a reef tank without using ozone. But you must know how to do so safely before resorting to its use.

My premise is as follows : *use as much ozone as you wish, as long as no ozone is present in the water in the tank itself, and as long as it cannot find its way into the biological chamber of your trickle filter. Best is when using ozone to control the unit producing it by means of a redox potential controller. I said best, not required. Use ozone resistant materials wherever they are required, especially the hose between the ozonizer and the skimmer must be of ozone resitant material.*

Always take the following into account when injecting ozone into your system, and check some regularly if necessary :

➡ All tubing that transports air and ozone mixtures must be totally ozone resistant. Norprene™ (not the same as Neoprene™) and Polysulfone are the two recommended types of tubing to buy. Such tubing is more expensive, but you will gain by using them in the long run, as you will not only not have to replace tubing constantly, but you will be injecting all of the ozone produced by your ozonizer into your skimmer, without loss of ozone because of the chemical reaction taking place between the tubing and the ozone. Other types of hose will either harden, crack and leak ozone in the air, or will disintegrate in a matter of weeks, or a few months at best. Regular airline tubing does not do the job at all. Flexible PVC tubing, e.g. Tygon™, will give several months of service.

➡ All parts of your system that come in contact with ozone must be either ozone resistant or made of material that can resist ozone for a long period of time. This applies mainly to the protein skimmer you use. Not all skimmers will resist ozone's action for extended periods of time. Be especially concerned about small fittings used to make connections, and tubing that conducts the ozone to the air stones that are used in columnar skimmers. Viton™ and polypropylene offer a good life expectancy. ABS and similar resins (often black) do not.

➡ No ozone should ever be present in the water in the tank. All ozone that is present in the water coming out of your skimmer must first be removed by means of a good quality activated carbon. You must flow the water coming out of the protein skimmer, or ozone reactor, over such carbon before it is re-mixed with the main water mass in the sump and tank. Change the carbon on a regular basis. I do so once a month. One pint of carbon is enough, but you must remeber to change it.

➡ Test for residual ozone on a regular basis, using one of several tests available in the hobby. Most pool O.T.O kits do not work on salt water. They are meant to test for chlorine, not for ozone. They contain hydrochloric acid in addition to the O-Tolidine which is used to test for the presence of ozone. Although residual ozone tests and chlorine tests use the same make-up chemicals, they are used in different proportions, resulting in the tests not being interchangeable. Pool tests will not indicate the low levels of ozone that you are concerned about. As little as 0.02 ppm on a continuous basis is harmful.

➡ Always use an ozone safe check valve in line with the hose going from the ozonizer to the skimmer, or reactor, in which ozone is injected. Such check valves cost a fair amount of money. The main reason they are so expensive is because of the materials that they have to be made up of, to make them ozone safe and resistant. Ozone is a very strong oxidizer, remember. A $8.00, or so, check valve will not do the job, believe me.

➡ place the ozonizer higher than the water level of the device in which you are injecting the ozone. This will protect the unit and especially its electrical parts. Always clean up water that may have gotten onto your ozonizer during maintenance, or water changes, immediately. Remember : your ozonizer is an electrical device. Water and electricity do not mix. Salt creep on the ozonizer will lead to electrical shorts, because salt conducts electricity when moist.

➡ Should the fuse in your ozonizer fail, replace it only with a fuse of "the same strength" as the one in the ozonizer. If it fails again within a short time (seconds to hours), it is likely that your ozonizer needs servicing. Do not attempt to fix it. Call the manufacturer and make arrangements to send it back. Most ozonizers work on very high voltage, several thousands of volts in most cases. Unless you are an electrician you are not qualified to deal with such current. Again, do not put larger fuses in the unit. Such can be very dangerous. Ozonizers are touchy devices and prone to more than an average number of failures. Get one with a long warrantee. TAT, for instance, offers a 24 month warrantee on theirs. See their warranty card for more details.

➡ You do not need an ozonizer with an output adjustment. In my experience they fail in a short matter of time anyway. Rheostats used to do so, do not seem to hold up for very long when used on ozonizers.

➡ If your unit is sized properly ozone output wise, you will need to operate it with an air dryer. Indeed, moist air -and around an aquarium the air is always very moist- will only allow you to produce about 40 to 50% of the rated output of your unit. My suggestion is, and has been for a long time, that hobbyists should get a unit that is rated for about double the amount of ozone they really need. Even when such a unit is then operated without an air dryer, it will still produce enough ozone.

➡ Ozone is a very pungent gas. You can smell as little as $\frac{2}{100}$ ppm in the air. To prevent ozone from escaping into the air one can use a so-called "ozone cap" which is placed on top of a columnar skimmer, or a bag of activated carbon placed over the collection cup of a venturi skimmer, or both. Activated carbon traps ozone very effectively. Remember to change it from time to time.

➡ If you still smell ozone, even though you are using activated carbon in the way just described, suspect a leak somewhere, and check for such leaks and cracked tubing in the lines bringing ozone to your skimmer or reactor. If the ozonizer itself is at fault, send it back to the manufacturer for repair or exchange for a new one.

➡ Because ozone increases the water quality easily and can do so substantially in a short period of time, many hobbyists nowadays use redox potential controllers to switch the ozonizer on and off at preset levels of redox potential. Such is safer in the long run, especially if you are using a very strong ozonizer. It is however not an absolute requirement. Why redox potential controllers ? Because the level of that redox potential, as we shall see in a later chapter, is a very good gauge of the quality of the water. The higher the number, the higher the water quality is.

Ozone has had a poor reputation in hobby circles for some time. The main reason is that those using it, either did not fully understand what ozone does, or did not know how to prevent it from ending up in the tank's water. As a result, many problems occurring in a tank on which ozone was used were blamed on ozone. Often, ozone was not even closely to blame. It just made for an easy explanation for problems that otherwise were hard to figure out. Knowledge and understanding are important, not only when it comes to using ozone, but in all areas relating to your tank. Read up on ozone in other books as well, and ask manufacturers of ozonizers as many questions as it takes for you to feel comfortable with its use. The more you know about ozone, the safer you will feel using it, and the less likely you are to have problems.

As the redox potential rises, meaning as the water quality improves, you will need less ozone to keep the water quality at that level. If you need less ozone, you must have a way of controlling its input. If you do not own a redox potential controller that may sound impossible. It is not. Use a timer that allows for on/off settings of 15 or 20 minutes each, and adjust the on/off timing until you can keep your redox potential within narrow bounds. This may take a little while for you to figure out, but it can be done. Allow for 6 to 8 hours to do so. Do it on a vacation day, or on a week-end when you have all the time needed to safely adjust the ozonizer/timer combination. It will be a lot less expensive than buying a $500.00 or so redox potential controller, unless you are ready to do so. It is a trial and error method, but if you take the time you will soon have it right.

8.6 Copper

No copper whatsoever, except for traces that are part of the salt used, should ever be present in a reef aquarium. Copper is very toxic to corals and invertebrates and will cause them to die, or never open to their fullest. You can, therefore, not treat reef tanks with any medication containing copper, even when parasitic disease is present in your tank. You must treat disease differently.

Where does the copper that some hobbyists find in their tanks come from ? We have already pointed to copper pipe as part of a house, or building's water supply system, as one source. Other sources include rock that has been used in another tank in which copper based medication had been used. If the rock you want to place in the tank appears to have been used before, do not add it to a reef tank. You must first examine it to make sure it does not contain any precipitated copper.

To do so, place the rock in copper free fresh water. Lower the pH of that water by adding some acid to it, e.g. a little muriatic acid found at many hardware stores. Let the rock sit in that solution for 12-24 hours. Move it around forcefully in the water from time to time. After 12-24 hours perform a copper test on the water. If copper is present it obviously came out of the rock(s). Don't use it in your reef aquarium.

Lava rock, especially the reddish variety, is inexpensive. As a result many hobbyist want to use it as the base on which they will place other rocks, rocks that have lifeforms on them. Because you do not know where such rock actually came from, and because you do not know either what it will leach into your water, I strongly recommend against the use of such rock in reef aquariums. Stick with lime based rock.

Alternatively, soak some pieces of rock in 5 gallons of acidified water for several days and test for leachings of heavy metals such as copper and zinc, sulfur and so on. If none are present, go to the next step.

Now prepare the water in which you had the rock, the 5 gallons, and add salt to it, as if you were going to add it to your tank. Do not add it to your tank however. Transfer it into a 5 gallon aquarium. Adjust the pH and temperature if necessary. Now add a small anemone to that tank and see what happens to it over the course of a few days. If it dies, seems to close up completely, and generally does not look good, chances are the rock has leached compounds in the water that you do not want in your reef tank. If it does all right, the rock is probably all right to use as well and may be placed in your reef aquarium.

As a last remark : Once you have determined that no copper is present in your reef aquarium, test for copper on an infrequent basis any-way, maybe once a month, just to be sure that it has not suddenly appea-red, even in low levels, and is building up to amounts to could become toxic if not removed.

Copper can be removed from your system by performing water changes with copper free water, or by using Poly Filters from Poly Bio Marine Inc. Do not resort to using chemicals. All such chemicals do is precipitate the copper out of solution. This does not remove it from your tank, and the copper may go back into solution later on. If you use Poly Filters® in your system, you should not have to worry about copper buil-ding up, as they are very efficient at removing it.

8.7 Carbonate Hardness, KH level

You must test the KH level of your tank frequently. I recommend you do so at least once a week. Twice is better. Keep records too. Use the sheet shown on page 194, or something similar. Keep the KH level between 12 and 18 dKH, 15 is the recommended level (Thiel, 1985). Some authors recommend even higher levels, for instance Peter Wilkens' often suggests as much as 18-22 dKH.

Adjust the KH level whenever it has fallen from the previous rea-ding that you obtained while testing. Use a KH generating compound that conforms to the characteristics I described earlier in the book. Keep the

KH level up especially if you are using carbon dioxide to prevent acid fall. When the KH is low, and when you add CO_2 the pH can drop quite rapidly. Do not let it happen. Check the KH level regularly and adjust it whenever necessary.

Besides adding KH generating fluids or powders, also add Kalk-wasser on a regular basis. Daily is best. Kalkwasser affects the KH level too, as it adds calcium carbonate to the water. Calcium carbonate is requi-red by all your hard corals. When raising the KH you can, and should, in my opinion, use a combination of KH generator and Kalkwasser. If you don't, you will find it difficult to add limewater once the KH is at the desired level, since Kalkwasser also raises the KH somewhat. I use equal amounts of each.

Never increase the KH level rapidly. As with any changes made to a reef aquarium, go slowly. If you test regularly, and if you adjust each time you test and an adjustment is necessary, the change and the amount required to adjust the KH level should not be large anyway. The carbo-nate hardness does go down, but it does not fall rapidly.

Sodium bicarbonate, better known as baking soda, will raise the KH level quickly. Do not use it. It will affect the pH a little downwards at first, and then it will gradually build it up to around 8.5 or 8.6. Because of the chemical nature of sodium bicarbonate you will have a hard time bringing the pH back down.

Besides, baking soda contains only one of the four or five (better) compounds that a good carbonate hardness generator should contain. It may sound like a good product to use because it is inexpensive and fast, but it is not. You are looking for problems especially if you use too much of it. At worst use it in an emergency situation, but not continuously. Too many hobbyists have had problems with too high pH levels as a result of overdosing. Some have reported a calcium fall-out, a situation where calcium comes out of solution, and coats everything in the tank, including the glass and pipes.

Unfortunately too many hobbyists still use it, and in too large a quantity. Hopefully you will not be one of them.

8.8 Dissolved Oxygen Level

Oxygen is a necessary and life sustaining element that all life-forms in the aquarium including the bacteria in your filter need, and they need it in large amounts and all the time. Maintaining high levels of dissolved oxygen, therefore, reduces the stress on all such lifeforms because they have to labor less to get it. Because the bacteria in your biological filter require lots of oxygen as well, maintaining high level of D.O. ensures optimum biological filtration.

In light of this it would be totally counter-productive not to make sure that D.O. levels are high. How high ? Around all natural reefs the dissolved oxygen level during the day, when photosynthesis is really at its peak, is at saturation or higher. Such is, of course, what you must try to achieve in your own tank. Why do anything different than what is tested around natural reefs ?

Saturation is a somewhat misunderstood concept. Water can absorb oxygen from the air above the tank, or from air injected in the biological chamber, but there is a natural, chemical that is, limit to the amount of oxygen it can hold in solution. That level is called the saturation level. The saturation level is also dependent on the temperature of the water. At lower temperatures the amount is higher, and at higher temperatures the amount is lower (an inverse relationship). Running your tank at 75-76° Fahrenheit, rather than at 79-80°, therefore, naturally increases the mg/l of dissolved oxygen that can be present in the water.

Using oxygen reactors, devices inside of which air and water are maintained under over pressure, usually between 3 and 6 psi, will also result in higher levels of dissolved oxygen, because air contains around 21% oxygen. Such reactors are described in a later chapter and are usually installed in tanks where the filtration is somewhat too small, or where the load is hight, or more often than not, both.

Any device installed on the tank, any method used, any practice adhered to, that increases the dissolved oxygen level of the tank is a beneficial one and is to be recommended, as it reduces the stress on all lifeforms. Less stressed lifeforms means better looking tanks.

On the not so positive side, many processes that take place in the aquarium constantly and continuously reduce the amount of oxygen available. Metabolism, fish respiration, biological activity, decay, unclean filters, small amounts of hydrogen sulfide, over feeding, over crowding, and so on, are all ways to describe processes that lower the dissolved oxygen in the water in your reef tank. All must be avoided if you going to have an aquarium that looks vibrant.

Is oxygen over-saturation dangerous ? Some have alluded to the fact that while injecting pure oxygen in an oxygen reactor, their animals reacted negatively. Such is correct insomuch as pure oxygen has a very high redox potential, or said differently, a very high oxidative power.

Too high an oxidative water quality will result in the same harmful effects one would have if ozone were present in the tank itself. Scuba divers will understand this much better, since breathing pure oxygen, especially at shallow depths, will cause the same deleterious effects. It surprises me that the test was even conducted. We do not recommend the use of pure oxygen and never have. At best, enriched air can be injected into a reactor, without any damage occurring. Do not return the water from the reactor directly to the tank, and do not return it to the biological chamber either, it is too aggressive and needs to be mixed with the rest of the tank water first. Return it to the sump of the trickle filter.

Several dissolved oxygen tests are available. LaMotte Chemicals, Chemetrics, and a few others are offered for sale in pet shops and by companies specializing in reef tank equipment. Get one. Testing for dissolved oxygen levels is an important aspect of being able to interpret the quality of the water in your tank. Most tests are based on the old Winkler method which was first developed in the 1880's, and that method is still advocated by many national organizations concerned with the environment. Electronic meters are available from scientific supply houses as well, but are rather expensive. A quality meter and its electrode can easily cost around $800.00.

Because the level of oxygen dissolved in the water is so important you must ensure that you do everything possible to keep it at as high a level as you can. This includes :

❑ Cleaning your mechanical filters at least once a week or more to prevent decay, which uses oxygen, from taking place.

❑ Keeping the temperature of your tank's water at the recommended 75° to a maximum of 77° degrees Fahrenheit level.

❑ Not overfeeding. Uneaten food will decay. Decay uses up oxygen. Besides using up oxygen it increases nitrates and phosphates as well.

❑ Not overcrowding the aquarium. Too many fish and too many invertebrates quickly tax the filters and lower the D.O. levels.

❑ Ensuring that no anaerobic activity takes place anywhere in the tank or in the filters. Pay particular attention to your denitrator if you use one.

❑ Blowing lots of air into the biological chamber of your trickle filter.

❑ Using a drip plate at the top of the trickle filter to disperse the water coming from the tank over the medium in little streams and droplets. This promotes a better diffusion of oxygen into the water.

❑ Using ozone in conjunction with your protein skimmer to clean the water of organic material before it breaks down and consumes oxygen.

❑ Changing your protein skimmer to a more efficient columnar or venturi protein skimmer.

❑ Creating good water movement in the tank.

❑ Removing dying and dead algae from the aquarium as soon as you notice them. Do not let them decay.

❑ and so on.

Quite a number of points to watch out for, and quite a number of husbandry steps to consider. But they are all to the benefit of what you already have in the tank and what you plan to add at a later date. Do yourself and the tank a favor, adhere to a regular and complete maintenance schedule. You will have far less problems with your tank than someone who doesn't.

Some authors recommend the use of hydrogen peroxide (H_2O_2) to deal with oxygen deficiencies quickly. Don't do it. I have tried it many times and have always experienced very negative results, especially with corals. Fish can take the treatment if you do not overdose, but invertebrates and corals react extremely adversely. It may seem like a quick-fix, but it is bound to give you more problems that you bargain for.

Last but not least, what is an acceptable D.O. level ? As indicated, temperature is a factor that influences the level, and so is the organic load of the tank. If your test results in a level of less than 6 mg/l you must look for the cause(s) and correct them immediately. If you follow the list of steps on the previous page, you should be able to maintain a level higher than 7 mg/l, preferably higher than 8.00 mg/l. Higher levels are better.

8.9 Ammonia

No ammonia should ever be present in a reef tank other than during the period of it's filter's maturation. During the cycle, as it is called, ammonia and ammonium ion will appear as long as your filter is not populated with enough bacteria to deal with the life forms load in the tank, and the by-products chemically and biologically developing as a result of their metabolism and your feeding.

Ammonia/ammonium is much more toxic at higher pH levels, which is the reason that it is a bigger problem in salt water tanks than it is in freshwater aquariums. Why is this so ? In water of higher pH levels, ammonium ion, usually present as ammonium hydroxide and relatively less toxic, changes to ammonia gas which dissolves very easily and is much more toxic.

The presence of ammonia at anytime other than during the cycle should be a real reason for concern. It means that your biological filter is not performing as it should, or that it is too small. That, in turn, may be an indication that your tank is overcrowded and that you must either remove animals (unlikely in my experience) or that you must increase it biological filtration capacity to enable it to deal with the amount of pollution created by all the animals you stock in the tank.

Increasing the biological filtration ability of your filter can often be achieved by resorting to a better filtering medium, for instance one of the many plastic filtering media now available. You may wish to change from an older type of filtering material to a much newer one, one that promotes more gas exchanges. It does not always mean that you must buy a new filter. You may also need to blow air in the biological chamber, if you are not already doing so.

Other methods include adding a canister filter, and fill it with a high quality medium to increase the amount of biological filtration that can take place. You may also consider adding an oxygen reactor, as such devices also provide biological filtration. The point is, no amount of ammonia is acceptable. If any is present, you must do something about it immediately. Talk to your pet store, to a friend who is also in the hobby, or call one of the reef specialist companies, and see if they can help you. Read other books, and think the problem through. You will probably come up with a solution that is not too difficult and not too expensive to put into place. You may also want to read my 2 other books for more ideas on what can be done.

Before deciding that major changes are necessary, review what you have done or changed to the tank in the last week or two. Have you added a number of animals, did you use any type of medication that may have interfered with the filter's performance, and so on. If you can attribute the presence of ammonia to any such change you may not be as bad off as you first thought. Water changes, and patience, may just solve your problem, and hopefully no damage will have been done to your animals.

8.10 Nitrite

As already recommended, nitrite levels should be zero ppm at all times. If your testing determines any level of nitrite whatsoever, your biological filter is not operating optimally. Very low amounts of 0.01 to 0.1 ppm may be an indication that some amount of denitrification is taking place somewhere in the system. This may not be a cause for concern but you should try to eliminate the reason for it. Nitrite interferes with the oxygen metabolism and is therefore extremely noxious.

If you determine that nitrite is higher than those values, you may have a similar situation as the one described under 8.9, Ammonia. Review what you have done in the last week or two, and determine whether such may have brought about the nitrite problem. If not, your biological filtration may be too small for the amount of livestock that you keep in the tank. Again, increase the amount of such biological filtration.

One often overlooked cause is of lower water quality is dirty mechanical filters. Clean them and determine whether that improves the situation. It often will.

Because ozone neutralizes nitrite by chemically breaking it down further, you may wish to experiment with increasing the amount of ozone that you are injecting into your protein skimmer or ozone reactor. This may or may not help. It will not if your biological filtration level is clearly too low. In such a case you need to resort to providing more biological filtration to the tank. But if the presence of nitrite was due to a temporary increase in organic material that your filters can normally cope with, but are still adjusting to, ozone will solve your problem.

Nitrite that appears a few days after adding new animals to the tank should not be present longer than 7-10 days, and then only in very small amounts. If it is, you must do something about it. Perhaps those last few animals that you added just taxed the system too much.

Because many hobbyist assume that once the cycle is passed they no longer need to test for nitrite since they have a biological filter to care of that problem, nitrite is frequently overlooked as a cause for low water quality levels. For example, we may get a call at Aardvark Press from a hobbyist stating that all is OK with the tank, he or she tested both nitrates and phosphates and both are really low, but the redox potential just does not want to go up. Such is often a sign of under-filtration on the biological side, and the presence in the water of nitrites. But since the hobbyist did not test...

8.11 Nitrate and Nitrogen Nitrate

Unlike phosphates, hobbyists have been testing for the presence of nitrates in their tanks for years. As far as I can remember in fact. Nitrates have been recognized as a problem compound in fish-only tanks by many authors and hobbyists are, as a result, aware that such levels must be kept within certain ranges.

What is not as clear, is that fish-only tanks and reef aquariums do not place the same requirements on the water quality. Far from it, reef tanks need much higher levels of water purity, and nitrate levels in reef tanks (and many other compounds as well, not just nitrate) need to be much lower than in fish-only ones. This poses a problem insomuch as a lot of the literature that hobbyists read was intended to be supportive of the hobbyist who was only keeping fish. Not realizing this, many hobbyists still assume that nitrate levels advocated for such tanks apply to their own, when such is not so at all.

As a result, nitrate levels found in reef tanks are usually much higher than what they should be, mainly because the hobbyist feels that such levels are acceptable, having read so in books, magazines, and so on. Until more literature that deals with reef tanks becomes available, this mistake will be made over and over again.

Water quality parameter demands in reef tanks are much more stringent, and nitrate, and many other levels, must be considerably lower than what one finds recommended as acceptable for fish-only tanks.

My recommendation is to keep nitrate levels below 5 ppm of NO_3, or 1 ppm of $N-NO_3$, much lower, in my experience, than the levels most hobbyists keep their reef tanks at.

If the nitrate level in your tank is too high, you can resort to any of the following three methods, either on their own, or in combination, the latter being done by many hobbyists:

● using a compound that reduces nitrates as part of your filtration system,
● using a denitrator,
● or performing larger regular water changes to keep the levels down.

Of course, cutting down on feeding, lowering the amount of life forms in the tank and using a more efficient protein skimmer will greatly help as well.

It can be demonstrated that corals open much wider in tanks with low levels of nitrate (and phosphate), and you can see so for yourself by lowering them in your own tank. It is a time consuming effort and one that requires perseverance. Do not expect immediate results with any of the three methods recommended. All will take weeks for any significant differences to become apparent. But they will, if you keep at it. Denitrators for example require 4 to 5 weeks before you will see any significant changes in nitrates in the tank. Patience is, unfortunately, not always a trait the hobbyist excels at. This is not meant in a derogatory way, but it is a fact with the majority of hobbyists that I have been in touch with, and that is quite a few.

We refer to two types of nitrate levels in this section : NO_3 and $N-NO_3$. NO_3 is the highest of the two measurements and, obviously the one that you must watch, because it is the most complete type of measurement. $N-NO_3$ is always the lowest as it measures only partly what the total NO_3 content of the water is. The conversion is as follows : 4.4 times $N-NO_3$ = your real NO_3 level. For example : 10 parts of $N-NO_3$ is the same as 44 parts of NO_3.

10 parts per million may seem in the correct range to many hobbyists, but since you now know that such is only part of the total NO_3, and that the real total is 44 parts per million, you can well imagine how easy it is to believe that the water quality is fine when in fact it is not. Many hobbyists make that mistake because they are not aware of the difference between the two, and because most tests available to the hobbyist measure, in fact, $N-NO_3$ and not NO_3.

Keeping your tank's nitrate levels low is one of the major objectives you should focus in on, and should also be high on your list of priorities. The approach should be two-fold :

1. do not add anything to the tank that artificially increases them,
2. take all steps necessary to ensure that naturally occurring nitrates are efficiently reduced.

Nitrate can enter the tank artificially through the salt and water source you use, in the same manner as phosphates can. Both must be tested to ensure that such is not the case. Review your feeding techniques and reduce the quantities fed if your nitrate level is now high. Do not feed several times a day. Remove all dead or dying algae as soon as you notice them. Letting them decay, even if that is what is happening, will increase your nitrate levels for sure. Do not use old coral rock, from other tanks, unless you first scrape off all dead material that may still be on it, and after rinsing it thoroughly and several times. Clean all your mechanical filters regularly. Be especially careful with fertilizers for macro-algae. Test them before you add them to the tank to make sure that they do not contain nitrates and phosphates. Use an efficient protein skimmer, one that really removes organic material from the water, because once the skimmer has removed it, it can no longer break down and increase nitrates.

8.12 Salinity, Specific Gravity

Keep the salinity at 35 parts per thousand. Such is the level around most natural reefs and it is, therefore, what most of the animals that you keep in your tank are accustomed to. If they do fine at that salinity around the reef, why change it ?

Many hobbyists measure the specific gravity rather than the salinity. The specific gravity (s.g.) that I suggest, which corresponds to 35 ppt salinity, is 1.0234 at 77 Degrees Fahrenheit. Because the s.g. is temperature dependent, you must always match the s.g. up with the temperature at which you are measuring. Conversion charts for specific gravity can be found in, for example, Martin A. Moe's : The Marine Aquarium Handbook, Beginner to Breeder (Green Turtle Press).

If you do not have a really accurate hydrometer, use a salinity test such as the one sold by LaMotte Chemicals, instead. Alternatively, use a refractometer that gives a salinity reading as well. Such units cost around $300.00 and are worth the investment. They make the test so easy that you are more likely to perform it.

All one does is place a few drops of aquarium water on the front of the unit, look through the visor, and read the salinity on the scale. They can be ordered from companies such Cole Parmer, Markson's, Extech, and several others. All these companies have (800) numbers which you should be able to get from directory assistance in your area, or from the (800) directory assistance operator. TAT also sells such units.

Because of evaporation, the salinity in your tank will change continuously. Salt does not evaporate, only water. As a result, the salinity has a tendency to go up. To counteract this fresh water is added to the tank on a regular basis. This brings the salinity back in line. The more frequently the topping-off occurs the less pronounced the variations in salinity will be.

As I have already pointed out several times, one of the keys to success with a reef tank is keeping the water chemistry as stable as possible. Top your tank off every day, or set up an automatic system to do so, either as a drip method or using a small dosing pump, combined with a timer, if necessary, to reduce its output further.

Some articles suggest that you should keep the salinity at a lower level, as such would protect your tank from parasitic disease outbreaks. Levels as low as 1.019 are recommended. I do not recommend this approach in reef tanks at all. I have not found it to work for any length of time anyway, because parasites can adapt to a changing environment just as well as the fish you keep in it. Moreover, invertebrates and corals do better at the salinity that they are accustomed to around natural reefs.

Should you keep the salinity higher ? Depending on which type of tank you run, you may wish to increase it somewhat. This is especially so if you keep a lot of Red Sea lifeforms. Do not increase it over 37 ppt though if your tank is filled with animals of mixed origin.

8.13 Water Pretreatment
8.13.1 Introduction

The water chemistry in the tank is dependent not only on the amount of pollution that is generated continuously in the aquarium but also, and to a great extent, on the amount of pollution that is introduced into the tank because it is part of the water used to perform water changes and top-offs. We have already touched on this earlier in the book, and it is important for you to remember.

Although, technically speaking, not a test in itself, the values of all tests performed later on the tank's water can be greatly influenced by the quality of the water that you use to fill the tank, and so on, because such water may contain a number of compounds that are not acceptable for reef tank water, and that will result in much higher readings when you test the tank.

With that in mind, pretreating the water that you use, not only makes a lot of sense, but becomes a requirement in many areas of the country where tap and well water are of such inferior quality that they must be purified before they can safely be used on the reef aquarium.

Well water may contain leachings from nearby fields, traces or more of phosphate and nitrate based fertilizers, PCB's, VOC's, pesticides, insecticides, and so on. Often these are present only in very small quantities, in the ppb range (parts per billion), but over time such ppb levels will build up to levels that become toxic, if not removed in some form or another.

Pretreating the water also gives you the peace of mind that you need not suspect the water source when anything happens in the tank. For example : you determine during a routine test that your phosphate levels are 0.15 ppm. Obviously because this is about 3 times higher than it should really be, you must determine the reason. Since you always pre-treat the water that you use, and have tested the salt, you know that the cause lies elsewhere. Perhaps overfeeding, overcrowding, another type of activated carbon you obtained, etc. are the cause.

In the long run, treating water yourself it is much less expensive than buying distilled or deionized water from an outside source, at any-where from $0.60 to $0.99 a gallon. This may not seem a lot on a per gallon basis, but for hobbyists maintaining a 55 gallon tank, who perform 5 percent water change a week, and need another two gallons a week for top-offs, this can work out to $15.50 a month, or $186.00 a year. A similar calculation for a 70 gallon tanks yields respectively $22.00 and $264.00. Taking a closer look a such numbers quickly convinces hobbyists that it is far cheaper to buy a small water treatment system and prepare their own water.

Consider too that when you have your own installation you do not have to lug bottles of water around, and that it is "always" available, even on week-ends, or on holidays, when the shops you get water from may be closed, or may have run out.

Last but not least, whatever installation you buy will serve more than just one purpose. Such systems make excellent drinking and ice water for yourself. Everything prepared with it tastes better too.

8.13.2 Reverse Osmosis Filters

Reverse osmosis filtration is one way to remove nitrates, phosphates, sulfates, silicates and many organic impurities from the water, including pesticides and so on. R.O. systems can be extremely efficient at removing impurities if you buy the correct type of unit. Many types are offered for sale but not all are suitable for use around the reef tank. Depending on the type of membrane used the efficiency of the unit will vary, and so will the price.

The better reverse osmosis filters use thin film membranes and give efficiency rates of over 99 percent, not 90-95 percent as several units we tested do. Efficient reverse osmosis units cost more money because the components that must be used to increase the efficiency to the 99% level greatly increase their production cost; indeed, the increase in efficiency from an average of 95% removal to 99% removal requires the use of much more expensive materials.

If what you are interested in is truly removing all impurities from the water -and that is the type of unit you should be looking at buying- you must buy a unit that includes the following three forms of filtration:

• a micron filter to remove particulate matter that comes in with well and tap water and that, if not removed, will shorten the lifespan of your R.O. membrane. Membranes are expensive to replace.
• a carbon filter to remove, amongst others, chlorine because chlorine damages the membrane quickly.
• a thin film membrane reverse osmosis filter, the heart of the filter itself.

When buying such a unit ensure that you can service each of the above parts separately and easily. The micron cartridge will have to be replaced every couple of weeks, the frequency will depend on how much particulate comes in with your tap or well water; the carbon filter may need changing every two to three months, especially in areas where strong chlorination is the norm; the reverse osmosis membrane is probably not in need of service for up to 12-15 months or even more, depending on the quality of the water in your area.

Keep the following in mind when using a reverse osmosis system:

• You will only collect about 25% of the total amount of water that goes through the filter system. Said differently, for every 5 gallons treated, only 1 gallon will be collected, the rest will either go down the drain, or can be stored for a different use (not reef tank use).
• Cold water reduces the efficiency of reverse osmosis units. The ideal temperature is around 75 to 77°Fahrenheit. At that temperature efficiency is maximized and waste minimized.
• Water pressure through the unit must be around 60 PSI. This may require the installation of a "booster" pump to increase the pressure of the incoming water by those hobbyists drawing the water that they are treating, from a well.

The effluent from reverse osmosis filters, especially from the three part filters just mentioned, is of very high quality. It can be used immediately, or can be stored and aerated. If you aerate it, filter the air going in to the water through activated carbon first.

The advantages of reverse osmosis are many :

• the system is very simple to install,
• the system is easy to operate,
• individual parts in 3 component filters can be serviced in minutes,
• the effluent is of very high purity,
• the cost per gallon of water produced is low, usually in the few cents per gallon range.

The only disadvantage that I need to point out is that reverse osmosis wastes a lot of water. This may be a problem in areas where drought or water restrictions are common.

8.13.3 Deionizers

Deionization by means of 2 separate treatment columns, one with cation resins and the other one with anion resins is another very efficient ways of pretreating your tap or well water. Alternatively hobbyists can use a single column unit in which the bed of resins is already mixed. The latter are normally less pricey than double type units. They are, however, more difficult to recharge or regenerate.

Good deionizers remove all the pollutants that the hobbyist needs to remove before using such water and operate at degrees of efficiency as good as reverse osmosis units.

You must flow water slowly through the resins to increase the contact time, and to attain the highest cleansing possible. 20 to 30 gallons per hour is better than higher velocities, although many units will still operate relatively efficiently up to velocities of 1 gallon per minute, or 60 gallons per hour.

Although some resins leached phenols in the water a number of years ago, this problem has now been resolved, and all units that I have tested, using resins from Dow Chemical and Rohm and Haas, are now safe. Because of the very large number of resins, and the great disparity in the price of such resins, it is important to buy your deionizer from a company that has experience with them, has tested many resins, and can service your unit if need be. The latter is most important.

Some resins may cost only around $100.00 per cubic foot at the distributor level, whereas others may cost around $600.00. You can well imagine that a company using the latter will have to get more money for their units than one using the former. It should also be clear that the more expensive resins do a much better job at cleaning up the water than the industrial type, inexpensive ones.

As the resins inside the deionizer unit polish the water that flows through the columns, they load themselves progressively more and more with impurities. A point will soon come where the resins are saturated and need to be cleaned, so they can be reused effectively.

The more resin you are using the longer if will take for this to happen; the purer the water to be treated the longer this will take to happen; the more loaded with impurities the water to be treated is, the sooner it will be necessary to recharge your deionizer. Cleaning resins of impurities is called regeneration or recharging. This is not an easy process and it requires the use of several chemicals. One for each type of resin. The most frequently used chemicals are hydrochloric acid and sodium hydroxide, both usually in 4% or 5% solutions.

In mixed bed resin deionizers the resins need to be separated before the treatment can begin, making the regeneration process yet a little more difficult. Separating the resins is usually done by blowing air mixed with water from the bottom to the top of the column. Because the two types of resins have different weights, one is much lighter, the action of the water and air mix will tend to make the lighter resin migrate to the top. This top layer can then be separated from the bottom one, and both resins can now be treated independently of each other. In the middle, between the two layers, a small band of mixed resin will remain, and should be treated separately or discarded.

Regenerating is not hard to do, but it does require time and the use of chemicals that must be handled with care. Recharging resins, and using deionizers, is discussed much more extensively in my other book called "Small Reef Aquarium Basics" and has also been reviewed in many articles in Marine Reef, the newsletter published by Aardvark Press. You may wish to refer to either, or both, for more details.

The advantages of deionizers are :

• low cost per gallon of effluent produced, usually in the 10 to 15 cent per gallon range,
• rapid production of usable effluent,
• excellent water purity if the correct resins are used

The two disadvantages that need to be pointed out are that to recharge the unit you must use strong chemicals, and that such chemicals may not always be that easy to obtain, especially not in small quantities.

On the other hand, some companies, for example TAT, offer a re-charging service for a nominal fee per year, something that will make the regeneartion process a lot easier.

8.13.4 Using Activated Carbon

Although activated carbon, for instance acid washed pelleted co-conut shell carbon, removes many undesirable compounds from tap and well water, and although it is easy to use, I have not been able to attain the water purity that I find is needed to run a reef tank by using activated carbon on its own to pretreat the water used on my home tank.

Combining carbon filtration with a micron filter, placed before the carbon filter, is one step in the right direction, because such a micron filter will remove particulate matter as well. The lower the micron rating of the cartridge in the filter housing, the better the filtration will be, but the more often you will have to replace that cartridge.

Ideally, one should use a Poly Bio Marine Fin-L-Filter® because such filters work at the sub-micronic level and remove bacteria, parasites and other such small life forms as well. Well water often contains many of them. Used on water lines with high input pressure, such filters can treat great amounts of water before the sub-micronic filtering assembly is in need of replacement. Using Fin-L-Filters® is as good as cold sterili-zing, meaning that the water is completely free of any bacteria etc.

Such a dual set-up, using either micronic or sub-micronic filtra-tion, combined with a third form of filtration : molecular absorption, gives the best results and delivers effluent that can be used directly in the tank. I use such a system myself. A drawing showing how to hook one up can be found elsewhere in the book. Molecular absorption filters use a special form of Poly Filter®, in disc form and with a greater absorption capability than the rectangular pads. They are made by the same company : Poly Bio Marine Inc. Although I have absolutely no interest in that company or in their products, I find Poly Filters to be the best of all chemical filtra-tion media presently on the market, and one that every reef keeping hobbyist must use. No ifs or buts.

The advantages of a triple system such as the one just described are multiple :

• the water quality of the effluent is extremely good,
• particulate matter has been removed, and so have bacteria if you used a sub-micronic filter, rather than a micronic one,
• the effluent can be produced at a rather high flow rate,
• the cost per gallon is low, in the 15-20 cents per gallon range,
• all parts can be individually serviced and replaced and all are readily available.

There are no disadvantages that I can pinpoint. The only remark, in all fairness, is that this system requires the largest initial investment : possibly as high as $ 450.00, but in the long run it is the one that gives the least amount of problems.

8.13.5 Tangential flow filtration

Yet another form of filtration, closely related to reverse osmosis, but not presently used in the hobby, is tangential flow. Water is flowed through a cartridge under over-pressure. The housing in which the cartridge is placed allows the water to escape either by going through the

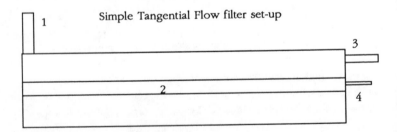

Simple Tangential Flow filter set-up

1. Water to be treated going into the filter unit.
2. The cartridge itself.
3. Untreated water coming out.
4. Treated water coming out.

cartridge, or by escaping through a smaller diameter hole than the input one, untreated, to rejoin the mainstream of the water.

The treated water will be much purer as a result of having passed through a cartridge that is designed to remove certain compounds. Typically, these cartridges can remove nitrate and phosphates and a number of other compounds as well. The more they remove the more expensive they become. Unfortunately, at this point in time, all cartridges are much too expensive for use in the hobby, fetching well over $125.00 as a minimum, and all require frequent replacement. Perhaps, as time goes on, cartridges that are priced more at the hobby level will become available.

8.14 Using Activated Carbon in the System

Activated Carbon can be used to pretreat the water, as already discussed in 8.13.4. If is often used as well in the main system, to treat the tank water continuously.

Because of the many problems associated with the types of activated carbon available in the hobby, even under very fancy names, the hobbyist must pay careful attention to the brand he buys, and test it to ensure that no phosphate or heavy metals are leaching from the carbon into the tank's water.

Good quality carbon must be used in all systems that rely on ozonization, and reef systems should. All water exiting a skimmer, or reactor, in which ozone is injected should first be flowed over activated carbon and then be remixed with the main water. Such will remove residual ozone and prevent any from ending up in the tank and possibly damaging the corals and invertebrates.

A.C. is a form of chemical filtration, and we have already seen that some form of chemical filtration is a must on a reef tank. Use activated carbon and/or Poly Filters® but make sure that the water to be treated flows freely through the carbon and the pads or discs.

Do not use large amounts. Such is not necessary if you follow my recommendation to use Poly Filters® and/or molecular absorption discs. This is unlike what I have recommended in previous printings of this book. If you decide not to use Poly Filters®, you must use more activated carbon, and you must test your tank water from time to time to determine whether or not your carbon is still detoxifying the water. This is done by using a small piece of plastic on which a few faint yellow marks have been made. Submerse the plastic in the tank, and look at it from a distance. If you can no longer see the faint yellow lines, you must change your activated carbon immediately as it is no longer effective since yellowing matter (Gilvin, Gelbstoff, Yellowing matter) is present in the tank.

How much carbon should you use ? If Poly Filters® or discs are also placed in the system, a maximum of 1 pint to 1.5 pints per 50 gallons of water is enough. If you do not use the Poly Filters®, place 3 to 3.5 pints per 50 gallon in the filtration, making sure that water flows through the carbon easily and continuously. So-called carbon bags are not always the best solution, as often water has a tendency to flow over them, rather than through them. If the water does not flow through the bag it is not in contact with the activated carbon, and you are not using the activated carbon efficiently.

8.15 Laboratory Water Tests

A time may come when, after you have tested your water extensively and find nothing wrong using all tests that are available in the hobby, the animals in your tank are not opening, are dying, or just do not look good. All water quality parameters test out well within acceptable ranges, your redox is high and your dissolved oxygen levels are good. There does not seem to be a logical explanation for what your tank is going through, but you know there is a problem, even though you have followed all my recommendations and adhere to a strict husbandry program.

Such may be the time to consider using a water testing service, and have a real thorough analysis done to determine whether some compounds are present in the water that are harming the corals, invertebrates and so on. Usually a "drinking water analysis" will tell you enough about your water, to allow you to make a determination as to what the problem may be. Such a complete water quality test is not inexpensive, so make sure you really need to have one done before going ahead with it. Since the results of such an analysis are given to you with both the acceptable levels, and the ones in your water, their interpretation is rather easy, and abnormalities will be obvious.

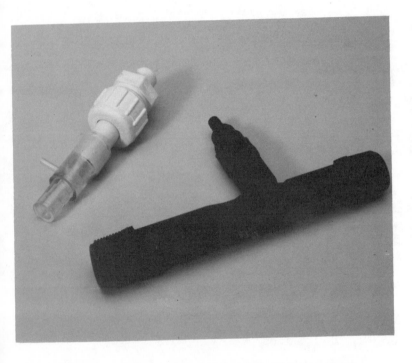

Molded Venturi Valve (black) and Manually made Venturi valve

9. The Maintenance and Husbandry Schedule

Throughout this book references are made to many husbandry and maintenance practices, and how important both are to the well being of the tank and what you keep in it, as well as to the life expectancy of the equipment and instrumentation that is used to run it.

Maintenance is defined here as taking care of your equipment to keep it working and in optimum condition, so its useful life will not be shortened, and in the case of instruments, so they will give you accurate readings. A lot of the equipment and the instrumentation differ so greatly from what hobbyists have been accustomed to use that they fail to see the need to care for either. True, most of the filters you bought earlier were in need of very little maintenance, which was a plus and made the hobbyists' life easier. Unfortunately this is no longer so. The equipment used on reef tanks needs to be maintained to keep it in good shape. The instruments need to be adjusted from time to time, and the electrodes need to be cleaned and calibrated.

Because most of the items used on reef tanks are more sophisticated and in many respects more temperamental, the hobbyist needs to spend time caring for them. This is not unlike what you would do with a sports or high performance car, for example a Corvette or a Porsche, or with camera and video equipment. Advanced technology used on reef aquariums falls in the same category. It must be taken care of and cared for if you plan to get it to work for you for a long time.

Husbandry is the agglomeration of all other tasks that need to be performed to keep the tank in vibrant looking condition. It includes all what is done to maintain the water quality at optimum levels, and the testing necessary to achieve it. Cleaning the tank and the filters, and testing water quality parameters are a major part of it. Husbandry is always necessary. This is especially so when the tank looks in good shape. The reason : you want to keep it looking that way. Slacking off on your husbandry will, without fail, result in lowered water quality and all the problems associated with it. Don't lull yourself into believing that because your tank seems to be doing fine that you do not need to service it. Quite the opposite.

Husbandry includes three other major tasks that you must perform continuously : changing water on a very regular basis to prevent the build up of compounds that are not removed by any of the traditionally used filtration methods; topping off the tank when the water level drops due to evaporation; and most importantly taking remedial action whenever the water quality parameters are out of line. All three work together to give you the objectives you are after : a tank that looks "alive", and animals that live for a long time.

The listing given here is as complete as possible, but is not exhaustive as you may, possibly, be using equipment that we have not included, or are not aware of. You may, therefore want to add to it if necessary.

A complete husbandry and maintenance schedule looks overwhelming to many hobbyists. It really is not, because you are not performing all the work in one session. Adhering to it as closely as you can is important, as the text of the book should have made clear by now.

The listing includes certain tasks that may not have to be performed on a regular basis but are included to remind you that they should be considered as well, one example is obtaining a complete water analysis from your town or city's water supply company.

Obtain water analysis	:	At least once a year. Twice a year is better. Free in most cases.
Mechanical Filters	:	Clean a minimum of once a week. More often is better. Change medium frequently.

Chemical Filters	:	Clean once a week, if needed. Change activated carbon as required by test (yellowing test). Change Poly Filters® when color tells such is needed. Usually when dark brown.
Pumps	:	Open and clean once every 3 months or sooner if noisy or if algae have gotten into volute.
All ball valves	:	Clean at least once every 3 months.
Check valves	:	you should clean frequently. ±6 weeks. Test your check valve by turning off pump and check whether any water comes through.
Skimmer	:	Empty scum cup as often as needed. If too much moist foam collects, re-adjust the skimmer.
Skimmer Collection container	:	check level every day and empty when necessary.
Ozonizer (depending on type)	:	Clean when needed (see instruction manual). Some do not need cleaning.
Air stones in skimmers	:	as soon as bubbles become larger. Usually every 3-4 weeks.

Tubing on ozonizers	:	Check for leaks every few weeks. Ozone smell around unit should be an indication if needed sooner.
Overflow box	:	Once every week is a real minimum. Visually inspect more often.
Siphon overflow box	:	Once a week if needed. Clean pre-filter as often as needed Prevent if from clogging and restricting the water going down to the trickle filter.
Uneaten food	:	Do not overfeed. Remove as soon as you notice any. Prevent decay, take it out immediately.
Foot valve (if used)	:	once a week. Clean the screen.
Power head pump intake	:	once a week if needed, inspect visually first.
CO_2 reactor	:	clean every 4-5 weeks. More if needed.
Oxygen reactor	:	check often to adjust pressure is needed. Run between 3 and 6 psi.
Spray bar (if used)	:	clean holes frequently every few day if yours seems to slow down
Drip plate	:	check at least once a week
Teeth around siphon box (comb-like)	:	inspect often to prevent water from rising in the tank
Sump	:	remove visible detritus whenever you see any.

Balls or Plastic media	:	Do not touch at all. Always leave biological media alone. Touching it and cleaning it destroys bacteria.
Air pump	:	replace diaphragm on regular basis to ensure good air supply at all times.
X-nitrate	:	replace when nitrate level starts to go back up.
Denitrator	:	inspect visually often. Odor will tell you a lot. Test effluent once a week. Look for possible blockage of water flow. If needed clean that area.
Molecular absorption discs	:	rinse once a week, replace when color is dark brown or black.
Bottom of tank	:	remove visible dirt and detritus as soon as you notice it. Prevent decay. Don't let it sit there. Remove it.
Algae	:	remove dead or dying algae at once. Prevent decay.
Lights	:	replace fluorescent tubes based on manufacturers recommendation. Metal halides should not need replacement for a long time, 1000's of hours.
pH electrode	:	visual inspection once a week. Determine whether cleaning needed. If so, clean. Calibrate after each cleaning. Clean at least every 4 to 6 weeks.

Redox electrode	:	same as pH electrode. Clean more frequently ± every 4 weeks. Check accuracy with 465 mv solution every 4 weeks or more
Heaters	:	inspect every few weeks and clean if needed. Remove accumulated dirt, it reduces heating efficiency, and can cause problems.
Aquarium glass/acrylic	:	clean as often as needed based on amount of algae growing on it Use Ridalgex to reduce such growth
Resins	:	Recharge when no longer removing nitrate, phosphate and/or silicate. Test effluent of each batch you prepare.
Substrate	:	Clean frequently remove all visible dirt, detritus etc. Siphon off whatever accumulates on the bottom that should not be there.
Air dryer	:	re-charge every 3 days, or sooner during humid weather. Or get a stronger ozonizer that does not need an air dryer

Micron cartridges	:	change when water flow has been reduced by 50%
Sub-micron filters	:	inspect every few days and wash and or change as needed when water flow has diminished by 50% or more.
Micro-algae	:	remove all micro-algae when they are still small in number. Scrape off, or use Ridalgex and then siphon dead material out.
Macro-Algae	:	Trim if growth is excessive. Change 10-20% water if large amount has been taken out.
Venturi Skimmers	:	Clean venturi when amount of air drawn in seems lower than usual. Use pipe cleaner or very small brush
Water changes	:	4 to 5% a week, or set up an automated water changing system.
Top-offs	:	as required by your rate of evaporation.
Salt	:	when changing brands test for phosphates and nitrate. Also test the salt you use now at least once.
Activated Carbon	:	test for phosphate leaching before you use it.
KH Generator-buffer	:	test the one you use to make sure that it does not leach phosphate or nitrate into the water.

Tap water (if used)	:	Check regularly for nitrate and Phosphate.
Well water (if used)	:	Check from time to time for nitrates and phosphates.
Deionizer effluent	:	check each batch for nitrate and phosphates.
Reverse osmosis unit	:	after a couple of months of use start testing for nitrates and also for phosphates.
CO2 lines (if used)	:	check for leaks to prevent loss of carbon dioxide.
Accuracy of Redox	:	check electrode reading with 465 mv standard solution frequently to ensure that your redox electrode is reading accurately. It many need cleaning.
Canister filters (if used)	:	check for good flow. Clean inside on a weekly basis. Detritus builds up inside. Prevent decay. Remove it.

Tests

KH test	:	once or twice a week adjust immediately if necessary. Use equal amounts of KH generator and Kalkwasser.
Residual Ozone test	:	Whenever you make a change to the ozonizer setting, or at least once a week.
Salinity	:	Check about once a week. More often if a lot of evaporation.
Specific Gravity	:	same as salinity. Only one test is needed.
pH test	:	monitor continuously with meter or controller, or test the pH at least once a week. Adjust if needed by using KH generator and Kalkwasser.

Nitrate test	:	once a week is the minimum suggested.
Phosphate test	:	once a week is also the minimum.
Nitrite test	:	once every 2 weeks, unless you notice that your tank does not look good. Then test more often.
Ammonia test	:	every 2-3 weeks, except when tank does not appear in good shape.
Iron test	:	once a week but only if you add fertilizers. If not, test once every 3-4 weeks.
Copper test	:	once a month to ensure no Cu has gotten into your system.
Redox Potential	:	Monitor as often as you can and keep records.
CO2 supply	:	check bottle pressure whenever you are nearby. Ideally, have small spare bottle available, so you won't run out.
Dissolved Oxygen test	:	test once a week or more often, especially if something seems wrong with the aquarium
Temperature	:	look a it often and correct if necessary. Lower the heater setting or consider getting a chiller.

Although this list is rather complete, and may include items that you do not use on your own tank, there many be some that are not included that you "are" using. If so, add them to the list and use the manufacturers' recommendations to determine when and how often they should be checked, cleaned, etc.

Don't be overwhelmed by the list. Many of the husbandry/ maintenance steps take only seconds to perform. Many involve only a quick look at the device or item, and action is only needed from time to time. Testing is important as it will often tell you, in advance, that you may be looking at more serious problems if you do not act on a lesser water quality condition now.

Do not use old tests. Many of the chemicals used loose their potency, or their accuracy, as time goes on. No one can do anything about it. That is the nature of the chemicals. By old we mean tests that you have had for 7 to 8 months, and that may not even look that good anymore. Performing the test with such chemicals, and getting an erroneous result, does not tell you anything about the conditions of your tank's water.

Because tests can be expensive, shop around and buy from companies that offer kits, or test sets, that allow you to perform 50 or more tests with one set. Usually this will bring the cost of the test down to a reasonable level of less than a dollar a test for nitrate, phosphate and dissolved oxygen, and far less for KH and iron.

Whenever you are unsure about a result, do not use the ostrich approach. Don't put the result aside and forget about it. Do something. Call a shop, or call a company that specializes in reef products and get them to help you. If a water quality parameter is out of line you must correct the situation for the benefit of the tank's animals.

Always keep in mind that because a tank is a very small closed system, one small problem can very quickly lead to several larger ones. This is somewhat like a downward spiral. If one animal dies because the water quality if off, the water gets polluted even more because that animal died. This may lead to more die-offs and an even worse water quality, which can lead to even more dead fish etc. This can go on and on until you lose everything in your tank.

Do not let things get out of hand. React as soon as something wrong is established and identified. Reacting quickly will also give you the best shot at correcting the problem quickly without any damage to corals and invertebrates.

10. Redox Potential and the Reef Tank

10.1 A Definition

Redox potential is definitely a new concept to the hobby. Many articles have been written about it, and more confusion has resulted because of the many ways in which redox potential is explained. Chemically speaking, redox potential, also referred to as oxidation reduction potential, abbreviated to ORP, is a most difficult concept to explain. Because the hobbyist does not really need to understand the chemical meaning of redox potential, but only how it can be used and interpreted with respect to his, or her, tank, its explanation can, in my opinion, be kept fairly simple and easy to understand by every hobbyist interested in it.

Very simply, the redox potential of the water in the tank is a measure, usually expressed in a 3 number millivolt value, of the oxidation potential of that water. Organic material in aquariums soon starts to decay and requires oxygen in the process. The greater the amount of decay taking place, the more oxygen is used. The more oxidative power the water has, or has left, the better it will be able to deal with organic material in the tank, the material that pollutes the water that we want to reduce to a minimum for the benefit of all animals in the aquarium. The more efficiently this takes place the better off the tank will be.

Highly oxidative media demonstrate high millivolt readings. Case in point oxygen: ozone, chlorine, fluorine, and so on. All these compounds, two of which are of interest to us, oxygen and ozone, have a very large ability to oxidize organic material in the tank.

If media that have high oxidative powers also have high redox potential values, it follows for the purpose of our explanation, that if the tank's water has a high redox potential, it also has a high oxidative power.

Because the oxidative power of a medium gets "used" as it chemically goes to work on organic material in the tank, such power will be reduced, and the redox potential of the medium will be lower, some of its power having been employed in the process of oxidizing the pollutants present in the water.

Putting all of the above together we can say the following : Water of high purity must exhibit a rather high redox potential value, because if it was not pure, its oxidative power would have been used up, lowered that is, in the process of cleaning up the water and dealing with the organic material that was present in it. Decay lowers the number, so in water with low numbers, decay is taking place. We do not want such water in our tanks. We want water where no decay is taking place, or very little. Consequently we are looking for our tank to demonstrate a rather elevated redox potential value. More on numbers later.

Given that high numbers = high oxidative power, pure water must have a high number as well because if it was not pure the high number would have been reduced as a result of the lower quality (the decay that is taking place). So we know that the redox potential of the water in our tank should be high. How high ? We will get into that a little later, as just indicated.

Since we keep animals that come from natural reefs, many a diver/hobbyist/author has taken measurements of the redox potential around natural reefs. Because the redox potential of any medium, in our case salt water, is influenced by many factors, there never is a unique number that can be found around the reef, applied and suggested. The redox potential around reefs varies considerably during any 24 hour period.

Why ? Because of light, temperature, metabolism, the number of animals, the pH of the water, the level of dissolved oxygen, and so on. Many factors influence ORP, and its value can change for any number of reasons.

10.2 Types of Redox Potential Equipment

How is redox potential measured ? Several instruments are offered for sale in the hobby that will indicate the ORP level in either 2 or 3 digits. Some of these can act as controllers at the same time, because they have a relay built-in that can switch another device on and off. This concept is of great interest because we can use the relay trigger to add compounds to the water that will clean it up if its redox potential falls below a certain number. Again, more on this later.

Besides the instrument, whether a plain meter or a controller, one needs a sensing device, called an electrode or probe, that can send a signal to the meter or controller, which can then in turn display a value: the redox potential.

Two decisions the hobbyist interested in measuring redox potential has to make, after deciding whether he, or she, wants a meter or a controller, are :

• which type of meter or controller to buy,
• what type of redox electrode to acquire.

These are important decisions because the equipment we are talking about is not cheap, and once you decide to spend several hundreds of dollars, you want to be sure that you have spent them on the right piece of equipment. Good meters and good controllers cost quite a bit of money, and so do good electrodes.

As a general rule, several types of meters and controllers exist, and so do several types of electrodes. All are excellent for the purpose they are intended for. They are not bad units. There are just buyers who buy the wrong unit for the application that is theirs.

Because redox potential is such a new concept, and because some resellers in the hobby do not fully understand the differences between various units either, several meters and some controllers are offered for sale that are not accurate enough for use in the hobby around reef aquariums.

Two general type of units exist : industrial quality and laboratory quality. Industrial units allow for general range measurements and offer a fair amount of accuracy, whereas laboratory quality units are obviously very accurate. And since the degree of accuracy determines the price...

Meters and controllers also come in two general finishes : bench types with a full enclosure, and panel mount units, with partial enclosure. Bench types are plug-in ready, and you can use them immediately, whereas panel mount units usually aren't. You may have to do quite a bit of wiring yourself. They often also have fully exposed and unprotected wiring in the back of the unit, which is not recommended underneath an aquarium because of the high humidity (over 90%) and the salt which will corrode the unit.

Industrial units are on average not accurate enough for our purpose, but have the benefit of being inexpensive. Companies such as Extech, Markson's, Cole Parmer, and others, sell such units starting at prices in the $200 to $300 range without electrode. Many of these units are, in fact, now sold in the hobby, albeit at much higher prices. Often they are panel mount types. All resellers do is get a unit that you can buy yourself, place their name on it and mark it up substantially. If industrial is the way you decide to go, buy the units direct from the companies mentioned, and save.

Laboratory units are much more expensive, and are far more accurate than what the hobbyist really needs. Meters and controllers from companies such as Hach, Beckmann, WTW, and Fisher, can cost well over $1000 without electrode. But if money is no object, and/or you want a top of the line unit, this is the way to go.

These differences in type and finish pose a problem insomuch as to offer a unit that is affordable, most resellers offer industrial units, either as they come, or with some wiring added to it in the case of panel mount meters/controllers. Hobbyist buying such units end up with industrial type meters or controllers that are, in my opinion, not quite good enough to use on your reef tank.

How much less accurate are these units ? Large differences exist, but often the error is expressed as a % of scale. Ask the question before buying. A 2% of scale error in meters/controllers that read from -1000mv to +1000mv is equal to a possible 40 millivolt difference. Similarly a 1.5% of scale works out to 30 mv, and 1% of scale is still 20 mv in such meters.

The difference between a reading of 400 mv and 440 mv is significant in a reef, especially when the number read by the controller is used to trigger the on and off cycle of an ozonizer. Buy a unit with low error rating if you can. They are offered for sale too.

Because only two companies offer controllers specifically made for the hobby, they should be your first preference, because they are made taking the requirements of the reef tank into account. Next, consider getting a bottom of the scale laboratory unit, they are still more accurate than industrial types, and only then an industrial type, using it while you keep its inherent drawbacks in mind.

The problem of selecting the right set up does not end here. Great variations exist also in the types of electrodes that can be used to measure redox potential. This is similar to what was described about pH electrodes. The far greatest problem, I have found, is that most electrodes are not suited for continuous immersion in salt water. It takes a special electrode to resist the harsh environment that a reef tank is, with all the salt, the organic material in the water, and ozone being used etc.

Of course, when buying an electrode, not necessarily from the same people you buy the meter or controller from, make sure it can take that rough treatment. Again, only 2 companies offer such electrodes besides the catalog places already referred to. When dealing with the latter, talk to their technical department first to determine which one you should order. Expect to spend in excess of $150.00 for the type of electrode you need. Get an ORP electrode cleaning solution and a standard reference solution as well (for example a 465 mv).

Depending on where exactly you place the meter or controller, you may need an electrode extension cable as well. Cost : approximately $25-30.00 for a good one with "silver" connections and cable that does not distort your reading even if 15 feet long.

Available only from Thiel•Aqua•Tech : the Kalkwasser Reactor
Promotes the addition of dissolved calcium carbonate to the
water for the benefit of all stony corals, the ones most hobbyists
want to keep in their tanks

The resolution of the unit you buy should be at least 3 digits, meaning it should read in hundreds of millivolt. The read-out should indicate at least 3 numbers, not two.

Some meters/controllers are sold with LCD's (liquid crystal read-out). Think twice before getting them. LCD's do not hold up well at all in a moist environment. Buy units with LED's (light emitting).

10.3 Measuring Redox Potential

Electrodes can be placed in the water just about anywhere it is convenient for your particular set up. They do not need to be in a specific location. Once you decide on one, however, leave it there. Such will allow you to keep accurate records being you are always measuring the redox potential in the same location. As already indicated the ORP is influenced by many factors. To get a stable reading you should not keep moving the electrode around.

Here are a few factors that you must be aware of in order to be able to interpret your own tank's redox accurately, and decide where to place your probe (read them carefully and decide which ones will apply to your tank) :

• pH and redox potential are inversely related. When the pH level goes down, the redox potential goes up, and vice-versa. 1 pH degree = 59 millivolt.

• the level of metabolism taking place in the tank changes the redox and reduces it as the rate goes up. Thisis also an inverse relationship. This is the reason that your redox potential will have a tendency to go down as soon as the lights come on.When the lights come on, metabolism increases. This can also be expressed as time sensitivity. Do not compare a redox reading taken at 9.00 am one day, with one taken at 2.00 pm on another day, or even on the same day. Because the metabolic processes are different your readings will be different as well.

• carbon dioxide will influence the reading you obtain, especially if your redox electrode is placed too close to the area where the water/carbon dioxide mix re-enters the tank, or the sump of your filter.

• raising the buffer will affect the redox potential reading downwards. Because a high buffer is necessary for corals and for pH stability, such is a fact you will have to live with.

• different types of electrodes will give different readings for the same water, in the same spot, as the same time of day. The two main types of electrodes are Platinum/silver/silver chloride and Calomel. Use only the former in a reef tank. Calomel electrodes contain mercury.

• because ozone has a very high redox potential, never place an electrode too close to the area where the water from your skimmer, or ozone reactor, is re-entering the sump of your filter. Your reading will be much higher than it really is, if you do.

• changing the stocking level of the tank will affect the redox potential. Indeed as you increase the load the filter has to deal with, the water quality will suffer somewhat, and your redox will be a little lower as well. If the system does not go back to the level it had before you added those animals, you are getting close to having an overloaded tank. If you add several animals at a time this drop can be significant.

• changing water and adding top-off water will affect the redox potential for a while, because by adding new water (and salt in the case of a water change) you are changing the chemical composition of the aquarium's water. Your electrode will reflect that, especially since newly prepared salt water has a lower redox potential,

• feeding, which is really adding a lot of organic material to the tank, will lower the redox. The system should, however, come back to its original number in a matter of 1 to 2 hours. If it does not, you have a highly loaded tank.

• trend analysis of your redox potential is very important. When comparing values taken over a period of several days, or weeks, a trend emerges. Comparing numbers taken over a period of weeks, but only the ones taken at the same time of day, gives an even better idea of the water chemistry of your tank. Example : if your redox is showing a small but constant increases in values for all redox potential levels measured at 9.00 a.m., your tank is obviously doing well, and the water quality is in fact improving slowly.

• as the temperature of your tank rises, its will redox potential will go down, and vice-versa. This is similar to its dissolved oxygen content. Yet another good reason to keep the temperature of the tank within the recommended ranges.

• redox potential electrodes accumulate dirt and small algae. This causes the read-out to be distorted, either upwards or downwards. Clean your electrode regularly as suggested in the maintenance and husbandry chapter. Upward distortions occur when micro-algae grow on the tip. When they release small amounts of oxygen, as a result of photosynthesis, a higher than actual redox will be displayed. When plain dirt settles on the tip, and prevents water from touching it, a lower than actual redox is the result. Either way, the reading will be erroneous.

• many redox potential electrodes react much slower to changing conditions than, for example, pH electrodes. This is especially so the first time you use a new one. Since the cap that is placed over the tip may have been on the electrode for quite some time, the tip itself is saturated with whatever solution was in the cap. This is the same solution as the one inside the electrode, more often than not it will be silver chloride. When you now place the electrode in the tank's water, quite some time can go by before the super saturated tip rids itself of the silver chloride and starts reading the actual redox of the water in your tank. Ergo the long time before you get a reading that is accurate the first time around.

• always place the electrode in an area where good water circulation exists. This is important as in doing so the water passing by and over the electrode sensing end will always be representative of the water in your tank.

• since CO_2 lowers the pH, and since lower pH levels are associated with higher redox levels, it is not a good idea to place the electrode too close to the effluent of a carbon dioxide reactor.

• since ozone has a redox potential of over 2700 mv, you should not place the electrode too close to the effluent of a skimmer or an ozone reactor. Your reading would be much higher than actual.

10.4 What lowers the Redox Potential ?

Redox potential can also be defined as the ability of the water in your tank to deal with the pollution of all kinds present in that same tank. The higher the redox the better it can deal with such pollution rapidly and efficiently. Chemically speaking such is not a good explanation of redox potential, but for our purpose it is accurate and suffices.

The higher the redox value, the better the water can deal with pollution and in the process the redox will be lowered. If the redox value is high there can not be a lot of pollution, because if there was, the redox would no longer be high, as it would have been "used" up in the process of dealing with that same pollution.

High purity water = water with a high redox = less stress on the life forms = a better looking tank and more vibrant looking animals. If the redox potential is low, decay must be taking place because decay and its by-products lower the redox potential and the quality of the water. To keep the redox potential high we must, therefore, eliminate all sources of pollution. Any process that involves reduction of organic material lowers the redox potential even more rapidly.

Below are some reasons for low redox levels (and the list is not exhaustive either) :

→ Over feeding or feeding too frequently, especially feeding repeatedly during the same day.
→ Dead material in the tank, whether it be algae or fish or small animalcules etc.
→ Dirty filters, especially dirty mechanical filters
→ Clogged undergravel filter areas. If you still use such a filter make sure you clean it regularly.
→ Clogged or low oxygen areas in layers of substrate that are too thick.
→ Dirty pre-filters in trickle filters and siphon boxes.

→ Spent activated carbon that has not been changed and has picked up a lot of detritus.

→ Dirty sponge material in filters, canisters, and so on.

→ Unclean corner overflows.

→ Over crowding of the tank. Too many animals tax your filters.

→ Too small a trickle filter.

→ Unsuitable medium in the biological filter.

→ Low dissolved oxygen levels.

→ Nitrite in the water.

→ Denitrators that are not operating as they should.

→ Excessive amounts of liquid foods

→ Using too much nutrient additives that are high in organic components.

→ Salt of low quality that does not contain all required chemicals.

→ Salt that contains too many impurities.

→ Certain fertilizers, trace elements, and so on.

→...

Many reasons indeed, and all can be controlled by the hobbyist who is willing to take the time and make the effort to take care of his, or her, tank according to a regular schedule of maintenance and husbandry, such as the one described, for example, in Chapter 9 .

There are still other reasons, more acceptable, or normal ones, that you need to accept as a fact of life, because they are, in most cases, unavoidable :

→ Whenever you perform a water change you are adding water of a redox potential that is the range of 220 to 240 mv. Indeed, freshly prepared salt water, and salt water that has been standing around for 24-36 hours has a redox that is relatively low. This water of a lower redox will lower the redox of the tank water for a short period of time.

→ When you feed, and you should, but not excessively, the redox will go down. Perhaps by as much as 60 to 75 mv. The original level should come back within 1 to 2 hours at the maximum.

→ Fresh unused activated carbon can lower the redox for a short period of time. So will other products that you need to use. Some additives, especially when you add a large amount of them, rather than dosing them with a pump, will reduce the redox for a few hours.

10.5 Increasing the Redox Potential

Every hobbyists' challenge is to keep a good looking aquarium, and all such tanks are typified by high redox potential levels. Increasing the redox should, therefore, also be on your list of priorities.

Many factors must be combined to achieve and maintain high redox potential levels, and all are within the reach of the average hobbyist. There is no magic to it. It is not complicated and does not require years of experience or special schooling. Often common sense combined with the right equipment will do it for everyone who tries. Let's review a few that I recommend :

10.5.1 Protein skimmers

Reef aquariums that are operated without a protein skimmer will greatly benefit from the addition of such a unit. Size it correctly, so you do not find yourself operating a unit that does not do the job for you. Columnar skimmers can be very efficient at removing organic material that would otherwise pollute the water and tax the filters.

Checklists on how to size the right filter for your tank are available, and will tell you exactly what the correct one for your tank is. Sometimes you will hesitate between two units, I suggest that when in doubt you buy the larger unit. The best skimmers, at least the most efficient ones, are venturi operated skimmers. They have the additional advantage of not requiring an air pump and also not requiring air stones. Not all venturi skimmers can be operated with ozone; if you plan to use it make sure you buy a unit that can.

The principle behind skimming, or foam fractionation as it is better called, is that if you remove organic and other material from the water by using a device to do so, that material can no longer break down in the tank and pollute the water, because it is no longer part of your system.

Typically, adding a protein skimmer to an aquarium that was not equipped with one will raise the redox potential by 75 to 100 mv (Pieters, 1985). If ozone is used in addition to the regular skimming, the redox can be raised even further, and the level is really only limited by the amount of ozone used.

To run a protein skimmer efficiently you must follow certain guidelines, here are a few :

• Flow at least 1 to 1.5 times the content of your tank through the skimmer, per hour. More will usually not hurt, but may not be necessary.

• In columnar skimmers a large amount of air must be blown into the column by means of a strong air pump. I particularly recommend the Wisa 200 and Wisa 300 air pumps. I use them myself and have done so for many years.

• Columnar skimmers operate with air stones. They must deliver real small bubbles for the skimming to occur efficiently. Air stones wear out rapidly. Change them about every 3 to 4 weeks. Use limewood or oak. The latter make even smaller bubbles than limewood ones, but offer a far greater resistance and can only be operated with real strong air pumps.

• In venturi skimmers no air pump and no air stones are required, but you must clean the venturi valve itself from time to time. Every week is probably a minimum. Salt creeps up inside the valve and reduces its ability to suck in air forcefully. Use a pipe cleaner or a small brush.

• Tanks operated without a skimmer will not show immediate results when one is installed. G. Bepko (1987) reports that it can take up to 2 weeks or more for a significant change to become apparent.

• If ozone is used, make ozone safe connections between the ozonizer and the skimmer input, to prevent the ozone generated by your ozonizer from being used up in the chemical reaction between the ozone and the materials used. Such is totally counter-productive and is the reason Norprene™ hose is recommended.

• Prevent the ozone from entering the main body of water in your tank by flowing the water coming out of the skimmer over activated carbon. Use a residual ozone test to make sure no ozone can find its way into the tank itself.

• Ozone should not be allowed to enter your biological chamber because it will destroy your bacterial filter.

S. Spotte and M. Moe in their books "Seawater Aquariums, A Captive Environment", respectively "The Marine Aquarium Reference" go into great detail about how to set skimmers up and how to run them. You may wish to refer to those books as well.

10.5.2 Permanganates

Permanganates are very strong oxidizers which can be used to rapidly increase the amount of oxidation that takes place in the tank. In the process your water will be cleaned up. Because of their high potency you must be extremely careful when using them. You can do more damage than good if you are not.

Always follow the instructions that come with the product carefully and do not overdose under any circumstances. Permanganates raise the redox potential very very rapidly and can, in the process, make the environment so harsh that your fish, corals and invertebrates will suffer greatly.

Pure potassium permanganate comes in purple crystals that are hard to handle in small quantities. It is very easy to use too many of them. If you resort to permanganates use a product that is not 100% straight, or use the liquid form that has been redox stabilized.

As you add permanganates a purple color will first develop. As the oxidation proceeds, this will turn to a brown slime or tinge depending on how long you use them for. The residue from the oxidation, and the color, can both be removed by water changes, by your mechanical filters, and with activated carbon. Skimmers will also remove the by-products of the oxidation efficiently.

Use permanganates only when all other methods have failed. Do not overdose and do not use them continuously. Permanganates are not a product meant to be used as a regular basis, but a palliative for situations that have gotten out of control. Talk to the manufacturer if you are not sure about the dosage and the way to introduce it into the tank. Don't take any chances. Get informed.

10.5.3 Ozone

One of the better ways to increase the redox potential, but a method that requires the hobbyist to be careful, as we have seen earlier in this book. The problem most frequently encountered is that the hobbyist is at loss when it comes to how much ozone needs to be used.

As I have stated earlier, the amount of ozone used is not the issue. The issue is that whatever that amount is, it must be used in such a way that no ozone is found in the water in the tank. Removing it efficiently from the water coming out of the skimmer, or from the ozone reactor is what the hobbyist must focus in on. Activated carbon and a residual ozone test will allow this to be done.

Additionally, a point will come where the water quality is at the level that the tank requires, as we shall see later in this chapter. When that point is reached, the amount of ozone needed to keep it there will stabilize itself. Indeed water of high quality does not require a lot of additional ozone to remain at that level. At such time the hobbyist must limit the ozone input by either using a redox potential controller, or by operating the ozonizer on a timer. In such cases a pen-type redox meter of good quality is really an instrument that the hobbyist should acquire. Coralife should have such a unit available for a very affordable price, by the time you read this book.

10.5.4 Iodine

Another of the additives that increases both the oxidation and the redox potential of your tank's water is Iodine, usually available in the potassium iodine form. It is used for a totally different purpose however. Iodine is needed by all living things and especially by macro-algae. It is removed rapidly from the reef tank by protein skimming and ozone, as pointed out again, recently, by Moe (1989).

Because it is a required nutrient some hobbyists add it as as supplement, which is fine and should be done on a regular basis. The danger resides in the fact that one can overdose rather easily on iodine and make the redox potential rise to fast. Follow the instructions on the bottle that it comes in carefully.

Do not use Iodine as a redox potential altering additive. Use it only as a supplement required because it is a nutrient. Use any or all of the other methods to alter the redox potential.

10.5 Suggested Redox Potential Levels

Rarely will you see a complete listing of suggested redox potential levels, and rarely will they be qualified. Below is such a table, painstakingly arrived at after many years of testing and observation of many a tank (mostly tanks in my own basement and home). It involved keeping notes and charts in a total of 7 different notebooks.

These numbers can be used as really safe guidelines. I fully stand behind them, having arrived at them through a lot of empiric evidence and observations by myself and others who were asked questions about tank appearance in general, specific animal appearance, macroalgae growth or lack thereof, micro-algae growth or lack thereof, fish appearance, and so on.

These millivolt ranges apply in aquariums with a medium to high load (not a heavy lead), with a pH of between 8.15 and 8.25, a temperature of around 76°-77° Fahrenheit, and a salinity of 35ppt (‰). Because of the type of filtration used on the tanks tested, the dissolved oxygen levels were always at saturation or higher. Columnar and venturi protein skimmers and ozone were used as well.

Look at the numbers carefully and determine where your tank fits in. If you are not in the right range, use one or several of the many methods suggested in this book to increase the redox of your tank.

Very little will be alive	:	below 100 millivolt
Very Bad	:	below 140 millivolt.
Bad	:	140 to 180 millivolt
Poor	:	180 to 200 millivolt
Too Low	:	200 to 220 millivolt
New salt water	:	220 to 240 millivolt
Low	:	220 to 270 millivolt
Medium	:	270 to 310 millivolt
Good	:	310 to 340 millivolt
Better	:	340 to 360 millivolt
Best	:	360 to 390 millivolt
High	:	390 to 450 millivolt
Too high	:	over 450 millivolt
Dangerous	:	over 525 millivolt
Very dangerous	:	over 575 millivolt

All readings were taken using a platinum, silver, silver chloride electrode, cleaned on a regular basis. Several controller were used: Sander, WTW, and TAT. Readings were taken after the lights had been on for two hours. Metal halide lighting of three different kinds was used during the course of the experiment over the aquariums : Osram Power Stars, Venture Lighting 4300 K, and recently the new Coralife 5500 Kelvin degree bulbs.

Because redox potential is such a sensitive and changing measurement, you must be careful when comparing these values to the ones in your own tank. Pay attention to the type of electrode used and the conditions existing in your own tank, especially the pH.

No one level is ideal, but from the chart above it is easy to see that the range of 360 mv to 390 mv is obviously a very desirable one to be in. Aquariums can be maintained for short periods of time at higher levels, but you must pay careful attention to all life forms if the tank if you do. If they react negatively you must lower the redox immediately by, for example, switching off your ozonizer, or adjusting the set point on your redox controller to a lower number.

Many German hobbyists tend to run their tanks at slightly higher levels than the ones suggested here : often around 430-450 mv. This is still in the safe range, but on the high side of it. They report that it greatly reduces the annoyance of micro-algae.

My personal experience with running aquariums at the recommended redox potential levels is of a different nature. Yes, micro-algae problems were far less a factor, in fact, it was a non-issue, but that was, in my opinion, mainly due to extremely low levels of nitrates and phosphates in my tanks. I keep nitrates below 5 ppm of NO_3, and phosphates below 0.05 ppm of PO_4.

What I was able to notice over and over and document as well, is that corals open wider, so-called picky fish eat without any problems, and the overall tank appearance, all greatly improve at the suggested levels of 360 to 390 millivolt. You may want to experiment and see it for yourself.

10.6 Working with Redox Potential Levels

Knowing your redox potential value is one thing, being able to interpret and use it is yet another matter altogether. Once you have the value in the right range, its absolute number becomes less important, it is mostly the trend that you are and should be interested in.

To illustrate this premise we will use an example and some redox potential values, and then take a closer look at that aquarium's conditions and water chemistry :
(Conditions : Tank 100 gals, pH 8.2, salinity 35 ppt, T° 76°, load medium, D.O. saturation, Lights on at 9.00 am and off at 9.00 pm.)

10.6.1 Aquarium with stable readings over 5 days

Redox	7.00	10.00	15.00	19.00	22.00
Day 1	401	387	379	375	391
Day 2	400	389	375	375	394
Day 3	398	384	374	370	396
Day 4	397	386	377	371	392
Day 5	397	388	372	373	390

As you notice, the readings are taken 5 times a day, and all exhibit a fairly stable value over a period of 5 days. The values are all in the correct range (360-390 for the majority) and the tank shows no signs of stress.

Take, for instance, all 3.00 pm readings (15.00 hours) : 379, 375, 374, 377, 373. All are within a narrow range and no great fluctuations exist. The same applies to values taken at other times of the day, either before the lights are on, or even when the lights have been off for a while.

Because the trend is good and does not fluctuate up or down much, these can be considered readings taken on a tank that must be doing very well. And so it was. It looked in real good shape, animals were wide open after the lights were on for about 1 to 2 hours, and no micro-algae could be seen except for some very minimal amounts if one looked carefully. So little that it was actually beneficial to the overall look of the aquarium. What I mean by the latter is that the tank did not look like a sterile environment.

10.6.2 Aquarium showing signs of stress

Redox	7.00	10.00	15.00	19.00	22.00
Day 1	390	355	346	340	358
Day 2	386	354	347	344	356
Day 3	384	354	342	340	355
Day 4	384	355	340	339	354
Day 5	382	350	338	338	350
Day 6	381	351	338	336	353

In this example, although all redox numbers are still pretty close to the suggested best values, one can notice that over the course of 5 days all values have somewhat dropped. Look at all values taken at 7.00 am, or all values taken at 7.00 pm (19.00 hours), and see for yourself that they are slowly, but surely, going down.

This is an indication that the water quality is slowly deteriorating. Ever so slightly, but the discerning hobbyist will take that as a message that he or she better find out exactly what is happening "before" the situation really gets out of hand, and problems that are much harder to deal with start. Keeping records of what is happening becomes, therefore, even more important. Without records you will not know what the trend is.

We are not suggesting that you take five or more readings each day. Such is not practical for the majority of hobbyists anyway, but you can certainly record two or three. Usually one or two can be taken early in the morning, with one being a minimum. Two should be taken in the evening, one some time before the lights go out, and one after they have been out for about an hour to two hours. Such readings will give you enough material to work with and will tell you what the redox value's tendency is.

Looking at the trend obviously tells you whether you are in the recommended value range, but it tells you much more because you can see by the numbers whether your aquarium water is stable, or going up or down in quality, depending on how the redox potential values move.

When an action/ reaction on your part is necessary, it can be planned and taken care of sooner and before things really get out of shape completely. This can save your animals and the looks of your tank. For example, a dropping redox potential may be an early indication that a fish has died, and that you need to find it and remove it from your system before too much pollution is added to the water.

10.6.3 Aquarium with falling redox tendency

In such aquariums the redox falls continuously over a period of a few hours, and nothing seems to be able to make it rise again unless, of course, some type of action is initiated by the hobbyist. Which particular one is not relevant at this point. It will be any of the ones mentioned already, but more likely than not, a combination of several.

A falling redox potential may happen slowly, as in the following example of two days' readings :
Day 1   396 379 372 taken at 7.00 and 10.00 am, and 10.00 pm
Day 2   355 343 331 taken at the same hours one day later.

In each case the readings have fallen substantially from the previous day, a definite indication that something is wrong, and that some sort of action is required to counter-act this effect.

Or it may happen much faster. For example, if the readings taken on the first day, at the same times, showed redox potential values of respectively 326, 299, and 264 mv. Obviously, in this particular case trouble is already at hand, because the numbers are falling so rapidly.

10.7 Influencing the redox upwards

It should be fairly clear by now to you that increasing the redox is not just the result of one action. Redox potential values rise when a combination of factors favorably influence it. Most of the ones commonly used have been described either in this chapter, or in other parts of the book.

Follow the suggestions made and your tank will definitely improve in water quality and appearance in a matter of a few weeks or less. Plan on using a really efficient protein skimmer, with ozone, and low redox values will be a matter of the past.

Keep your maintenance and husbandry up and your redox will stay high. Do not overfeed and do not overcrowd the tank and you will not have to upgrade your filter, as long as it was correctly sized the first time around. Even when using an efficient skimmer, make sure that you change the air stones frequently. Loss of efficiency because of worn out air stones is very common, and can so easily be avoided.

Sand Filter for Fine Filtration

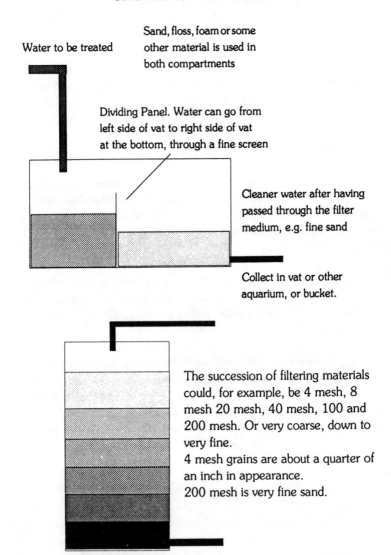

Water to be treated

Sand, floss, foam or some
other material is used in
both compartments

Dividing Panel. Water can go from
left side of vat to right side of vat
at the bottom, through a fine screen

Cleaner water after having
passed through the filter
medium, e.g. fine sand

Collect in vat or other
aquarium, or bucket.

The succession of filtering materials
could, for example, be 4 mesh, 8
mesh 20 mesh, 40 mesh, 100 and
200 mesh. Or very coarse, down to
very fine.
4 mesh grains are about a quarter of
an inch in appearance.
200 mesh is very fine sand.

Remark : fine filters such as these do not remove dissolved material, e.g.
phosphates and nitrates. To do this you will need a totally different filter,
described later in this section.

11. Heating and Cooling the Reef Aquarium

11.1 Heating

11.1.1 Introduction

The temperature of the tank's water determines the metabolic rate of all animals that are in it. When the temperature fluctuates too much and too rapidly, many lifeforms kept in the tank will suffer. Fish, in particular, adapt their body heat to the ambient heat, unlike humans. This reduces the span of temperatures that are life sustaining greatly. Whereas humans can take great temperature variations, fish and corals cannot, and will die if you do not adjust the temperature of your tank correctly.

Temperature changes of smaller magnitudes must be avoided as well. Parasitic disease outbreaks are not uncommon when the temperature is changed quickly, either upwards or downwards.

Many a hobbyist has experienced this already, often with loss of life forms because parasitic diseases are so hard to eradicate even in fish-only tanks, let alone in reef aquariums where copper or quinine based medications cannot be used.

Because the life forms kept in reef aquariums are quite sensitive, not as resilient as their fresh water counter parts, changes that the hobbyist considers minimal in a fresh water tank do not apply in reef aquariums. A variation of 2° Fahrenheit can be enough to cause problems. This must be kept in mind when, for instance, making water changes. Always make sure that the water you add is of the same temperature as the one already in the tank.

Around natural reefs the temperature never varies very much, and when it does it varies very very slowly. Keep that in mind as well. Do not make temperature changes rapidly. If your tank is now running at too high a temperature and you take steps to reduce it, which you should, make the changes slowly. Don't go from a present 82° to a new temperature of 76° in a matter of hours. You are guaranteed to have problems if you do.

Depending on where your animals came from, and more likely than not they will have come from Indonesia, Hawaii or the Philippines, they are accustomed to temperatures in the range of 75° to 77° degrees most of the time. For short periods of time these temperatures may be lower or slightly higher, for example as low as 73° and as high as 80°.

Short periods of time does, unfortunately, not mean days or continuously. Too high temperatures, maintained for too long, will damage the corals and will hurt other invertebrates as well.

11.1.2 Conversions

Frequently, references to temperature, in books, magazines and so on, are in degrees Celsius rather than Fahrenheit. One reason is that many books come from Europe, and another is that the scientific community uses Celsius or Kelvin rather than Fahrenheit.

Converting from one to the other is simple. You have probably seen the formulas often, or learned them many years ago in school. For those in need of them, here they are again :

(1) Degrees Celsius   = $\frac{5}{9}$ (degrees Fahrenheit minus 32)
(2) Degrees Fahrenheit = $\frac{9}{5}$ of Celsius, plus 32

Let's look at two examples : We want to convert 25 degrees Celsius to Fahrenheit, according to formula (2) the calculation is : $\frac{9}{5}$ of 25, plus 32 or after calculating 77.0° Fahrenheit. How much is 82° Fahrenheit in Celsius degrees ? Again, according to formula (1) this time : $\frac{5}{9}$ (82-32), or after calculating 27.77 Celsius degrees.

To allow you to quickly interpret Celsius and Fahrenheit de-grees, we are including a conversion chart of the temperature range that you may be dealing with when reading books on aquarium keeping. The chart allows you to go either way.

Celsius	Fahrenheit	Fahrenheit	Celsius
19	66.2	66	18.9
20	68.0	68	20.0
21	69.8	70	21.1
22	71.6	72	22.2
23	73.4	74	23.3
24	75.2	75	23.9
25	77.0	76	24.4
26	78.8	77	25.0
27	80.6	78	25.6
28	82.4	79	26.1
29	84.2	80	26.7
30	86.0	81	27.2
		82	27.8
		83	28.3
		84	28.9

Many aquariums are kept at too high temperatures, and many ani-mals are lost as a result. Often the hobbyist does not even want to admit this fact to himself or herself, and will try to make everything in the tank look good, even though the temperature is way out of control. Such is, I am afraid, not possible.

Calling manufacturers and asking many questions in an effort to make such tanks work is really a waste of your time, especially if you do not admit the fact that the temperature is far above what it should be. Of course, hobbyists realize that when they admit to such high temperatures the answer is simple : lower it first, and things will get back in control.

Some animals are even more sensitive than others, as some hob-byists may have found out about, for example, carpet anemones. If you cannot keep them alive, suspect the temperature.

11.1.3 Where does Heat come from ?

Excess heat in the aquarium can have several causes that the hobbyist can possibly eliminate without incurring great expenses, usu-ally buying a cooling unit.

A few that are easy to solve, or at least less expensive to solve than buying a cooler are :

➡ Determine whether the pumps you are using are the cause for the excessive heat. Submersible pumps are always suspect. Indeed, they cool down by transferring heat to the water. Power head pumps do the same. Too large a submersible pump, or too many power heads will raise the temperature several degrees, perhaps several too many. Use only pumps that run cool and do not exchange heat with the water. Blast cooled pumps are your best bet.

➡ Lights that are not equipped with internal fans, or that are placed too close to the water, will heat up the water, possibly by several degrees.

➡ Heat transfers to the water from the surrounding air. If the room in which the aquarium is placed is very hot, the tank's temperature will rise.

➡ Heat transfers to the water from the inside of the cabinet where you placed your trickle filter, or from the cellar if that is where yours is. Watch the ambient temperature in both of those areas.

If you cannot solve your temperature problem by changing pumps, or by installing fans in the lighting hoods, you may be in a quandary that only be resolved by installing a cooling unit.

Cooling units cost from $500.00 to several hundreds more, depending on size, and because they are compressor operated, consume a fair amount of electricity as well. Try to solve your problem otherwise if you can.

Changing pumps, or installing fans in your light hood is much cheaper than buying a chiller. Seriously considerit if you have to.

11.1.5 Heater types

Many hobbyists do not have a heat problem and need to provide supplemental heating to their tank. Such is easily done by installing one or more bayonet heaters in the sump of the trickle filter, depending on how much heat needs to be generated.

Because bayonet heaters can stick, meaning stay in the on position, I always recommend the use of several, rather than just one, especially if you need a fair amount of heating. For example, I would use three 50 watt heaters, rather than one 150 watt. Since it is unlikely that all three will fail at the same time, and since 50 watts cannot do as much damage as one 150 watt heater, I find such much safer.

Bayonet heaters, also called stick heaters, come in various finishes: plain glass tubes, glass covered with silicone, glass covered with a protective cover, ceramic, Teflon™, stainless steel, and so on. Your budget determines which one you get. I prefer the Teflon coated ones because they cannot break in the sump, but they cost a great deal more. So do the stainless steel ones.

If the heater you acquire does not have a built-in temperature on off regulator, you will have to install a separate one to allow you to adjust the set point. Temperature controllers, similar to the units existing for pH and redox, are also available from certain resellers and from the catalog companies already mentioned.

When it comes to heaters, accuracy in the on and off switching is key. Such is also the reason you should buy a sell known brand, not some cheap knock-off. You have too much at stake. Don't let an extra $20.00 for a good quality heater endanger the life of the animals in your tank. Believe me, cheap heaters will stick.

Besides using Teflon units, I also like the German Ebo-Jaeger units a lot because they are submersible, adjustable, accurate, and covered with a protective layer so the glass is not easily shattered.

Cable heating is yet another and a more stable form of heating and mainly so because it spreads the heat much more evenly throughout the tank. Unfortunately the cables rip easily because of rocks and bully fish, urchins and so on. At Thiel•Aqua•Tech we are working on the development of such a system that holds up better in reef and freshwater plant tanks. Unfortunately it is not ready, and no date for its introduction is available at this time.

11.1.6 Making an Inexpensive Cooler

Rather inexpensive coolers can be made using a small second hand freezer. Many hobbyists have tried it and they work fairly well. One can reduce the temperature about 4-5 degrees if the system is properly set up, and if metal type tubing is used to conduct the water in and out of the freezer.

You must run water very slowly through a small diameter tube that enters the freezer somewhere through a hole you have to drill through its side. A coil on the inside ensures that the water remains inside for a certain amount of time. The longer the coil, and the slower you flow the water, the better cooling effect you will get.

Another hole needs to be drilled through the side for the tube to exist again. water is pumped through the tube by means of a very small pump, maybe even a small power head pump. Alternatively, use water from a by-pass on the main water return line, the one going back to the aquarium. This will require that you glue a Tee-fitting in-line, and then bush it down to the size of the tube (hose) that you are using. After you have passed the coil through the holes you drilled, isolate the inside of the unit by applying a liberal amount of aquarium silicone around the holes, both inside and outside the freezer.

Because certain types of material inhibit heat exchanges, e.g. plastics, the best cooling effect is obtained with stainless steel tubing. You must use 316 SS, as other types will not resist salt water for very long. Copper can, of course, not be used. Another metal that is safe, but much more expensive, is titanium.

Since you are pushing warm water through the freezer unit all the time, it will run just about continuously. This is a major consideration in terms of electric consumption.

11.2 Cooling Units

The best way to cool the tank if the temperature is too high, is to use a chiller or cooling unit matched to the size of your tank, and the number of degrees you want to lower the water temperature.

Cooling units are fairly expensive by hobby standards, but if you absolutely need one few alternatives exist as we have already seen. Several companies now offer such equipment and advertise in magazines such as FAMA : Aquanetics, Aquarium Sales and Service and TAT. Call around before buying. Prices can vary quite a bit.

Investigate all other avenues open to you first, and if none bring the temperature down enough, consider getting a cooler if you are really interested in making your tank look much better, because it will make a big difference.

Whichever way you go, keeping the tank at the recommended temperature is yet another important aspect that you have to attend to. Trying to run the tank at far too high a temperature will not work, and will end up costing you more money in the long run anyway, not to speak of all the animals that will have been killed in the process.

12. Lighting the Reef Tank

12.1 Introduction

Lighting already was a most controversial subject when the first printing of this book hit the stores in early 1988. It still is, perhaps even more so, now that the seventh printing of this book is out. Whereas a few years ago the controversy was over whether to use metal halides, or metal halides combined with actinic lighting, it has now expanded to include many other forms of lighting offered for sale in hobby magazines such as, for instance, a number of specialized type fluorescent tubes that have been introduced in the early 1990's.

While I am certainly not saying that you cannot run a reef tank with fluorescent light, as long as you use the right ones and enough of them, in my opinion, everything that surrounds lighting the reef tank, is a matter of degree, more than a matter of controversy. It is similar to the performance of cars. Porche and racing cars do a hell of better job at it than others. Does that mean the others won't get you to point B ? Similarly, at least two types of lighing can do the job for you, as we shall see later, but each provide a different degree of efficiency and ease of use.

Heated arguments can be read in magazines as to what lighting is best, and why you should use only bulbs from such and such a company. What it really all comes down to, though, is **"do the corals in our tanks look healthy and large, and are they surviving for long periods of time, more than the usual 6 to 8 months that most hobbyists experience with the lights used"**.

Articles authored by other hobbyists gain fame because of some new twist they introduce, or some "experiment" they conducted that no one can verify. All very confusing to me, and to many hobbyists I am sure. Who are these "experts" anyway ? How much do they know about lighting and photosynthesis ? Or are they just looking at brightness, or appealling colors, or how one or two species of corals react ?

Sprung (1989), a marine biologist, makes a case "for" actinic lighting and a case "against" metal halides, but offers very little substantiation for his strong position. He has done so for about two years, when his name first appeared in magazines, working for a company that was heavily into selling actinic lighting. To be fair, his strong stand "against" was recently mollified (Sprung, 1990) and he now offers a more moderate approach stating that "certain" types of metal halides must be avoided. Such is, however, again skirting the issue; which metal halides and especially why ? Again, no information that can be easily related to. Or not technical information that one can verify in other books. Mind you, I respect Mr. Sprung's knowledge a lot and think he has done a great deal for the hobby, but in the lighting area he has not convinced me.

The only light that shines over natural reefs day in and day out, for months on end, and year after year, is the sun. The strongest light available in nature becomes corals fine, and allows them to build reefs and multiply unhindered. Granted, it is attenuated by clouds, refraction, water depth, turbidity, and so on, but it is still stronger, when measured with light measuring equipment, than whatever the hobbyist can possibly place over his aquarium, save perhaps Xenon arc light. And strength of light is important under the new photobiologic approach, as we shall see later.

Note: The explanation in this introduction may seem too technical to some, for which I apologize if you have no interest in how one arrives at the conclusion that I have arrived at myself, namely that metal halides are high on the list of lighting types to consider for your tank. It is the only way for me to try to convince the reader that there is merit to the claims I make. Without explaining, my position would do the reader a disservice, and would not give him, or her, a chance to evaluate what I stand for, and verify some statements in other literature.

The sun over the reef can at times develop 150.000 lux at sea level. Strength or intensity of light is important, but not the only factor that needs to be considered. Indeed, which type of light the corals receive from the sun, and which type they can absorb is an important factor too.

Because water filters out certain portions of the light spectrum, and because blue wavelength lighting passes through the water to greater depths, some have suggested that such blue light should be maximized for the corals to thrive, to the detriment of all other lighting they require, and to the detriment of what other corals may need.

Nothing is, in my own experience further from the truth. Providing too much actinic wavelength is harmful at best. Short wave light, defined as a narrow spectrum around 300 to 320 nanometers by those strongly advocating actinic light, is only a small part of the light energy that corals, and other animals in the tank, require and can utilize during photosynthesis. Providing a more complete spectrum by using a different light source, has always given me better results, and has allowed photosynthesis on a larger scale.

Philips, whose bulbs were touted by many an entrepreneurial so-called expert, were the first surprised to find out that such bulbs were used over aquariums. Granted, their nanometer range is important for photosynthesis' photosystem I, but so are the higher 670-680 nanometer ranges for photosystem II (see later and see references). Pho-tosynthesis is an extremely complicated matter, especially in aquatic en-vironments. Those wishing to read more on the subject are referred to a textbook on the subject by Kirk [2], or one of the many textbooks on algae, especially the sections dealing with photosynthesis.

There is no question that blue wavelength lighting has to be provided, but this can be done as part of a much more complete spectrum, for instance the one provided by metal halide lighting of the 5500 K type, but I am jumping ahead of myself.

In photobiology light energy is nowadays measured quite differently than it used to be. Rather than using lux, or foot candles, or lumens, the preferred unit of measurement is now the photon, or photon irra-

diance, a unit of measurement derived from Einstein's law of photoche-
mical equivalence[2]. These units are used to determine how much energy
a molecule can absorb from a certain type of light.

Einsteins are defined as the amount of energy absorbed by one
mole of a compound (mole = gram/molecule). Since different types of light
have different wavelengths, and since each wavelenght provides a certain amount of "energy", calculations can be made of how much "energy"
can be derived from whatever amount of a particular wavelength that,
for instance, algae, more specifically symbiotic algae absorb. More irradiance from a low energy type of light would give a higher total energy
level than less of a stronger energy type of light.

It is, moreover, a fact that photobiologists have greatly advanced
their knowledge of photosynthetic processes that take place in aquatic
environments, and that one of the great changes that has occurred *is the
stronger belief that photosynthetic processes depend more on the number
of photons of irradiance that reach a surface than than the energy content
of these photons*[1].

If such is indeed correct, which, not being a photobiologist I
have no reason to doubt, then, providing more intensity of each spectrum
type (blue but also many others) will achieve a far higher energy absorption level than just providing strong light skewed towards one particular
spectrum (actinic). Higher energy absorption means higher levels of photosynthesis, means higher rates of metabolism and reproduction, which
is to the benefit of corals and invertebrates that harbor symbiotic algae.

Likewise, because photosynthesis does not take place in just
one specific area of the spectrum, but over a much wider range[1], providing high intensities of light of various spectral lengths benefits the process and benefits the corals and invertebrates that harbor symbiotic algae,
because photosynthesis is what makes them, and the corals they live in,
thrive.

Photosynthetic algae contain pigments that assist in the uptake
of light energy, these pigments start and sustain the photosynthetic process. We should be strongly interested in promoting this process because

the corals and invertebrates kept in our tanks feed off the by-products of this process. This is, for example, the reason why many can survive without external food sources for extended periods of times.

The nanometer levels (wavelengths) at which this occurs vary, meaning the types of light at which this process occurs vary as well. Below are merely a few examples of nanometer ranges and the pigments involved (adapted from [1]):

Chlorophyll a	420 and 660 nanometers
Chlorophyll b	435 and 643 nanometers
Chlorophyll c	445 and 465 nanometers
Chlorophyll d	450 and 690 nanometers
Beta carotene	425, 450 and 480 nm
Alpha carotene	420, 440 and 470 nm
Luteol	425, 445 and 475 nm
Phycoerythrins	490, 546 and 576 nm
Phycocyanins	618 nm
Allophycocyanin	650 nm

As this table shows, photosynthesis involves many more absorption spectra than advanced by some who suggest that this only happens efficiently at 320 nm, and that actinic lighting is therefore needed in large amounts. And keep in mind too that this is only a partial list.

All what blue light and actinic light emitting bulbs do, in my evaluation of many texts on the subject, is provide one of the spectra necessary for photosynthesis on one hand, and "enhance" the color of certain corals, especially purple mushrooms, because of fluorescence associated with Actinic 03 bulbs, on the other.

If the latter is what you are after, then, by all means, use a little actinic light, and make your tank look less natural. Or use a lot of it, and make it look eerie and bizarre. But be aware of the risks, as after several months your Bubble, Flower, Elegance corals may be starved of nutrients, unless supplemental light is offered as well.

Suggested Reading on Lighting and Photosynthesis :

(1) Photosynthesis 4th Edition, D.O. Hall and K.K. Rao, New Studies in Biology, Institute of Biology, London, 1987

(2) Light and Photosynthesis in Aquatic Systems, John T.O. Kirk, Cambridge University Press, 1983

(3) The Biology of Marine Plants, M.J. Dring, Contemporary Biology, Edward Arnold, 1983

(4) Primary Productivity in Aquatic Environments, Charles R. Goldman, University of California Press, 1974

as well as many other book dealing with photosynthesis in macro and other type of algae.

12.2 Requirements

Premise 1 : *To provide lighting that is beneficial to **all** lifeforms kept in an aquarium, not just a few, we must provide more than a narrow spectral band of light, or light skewed towards a particular part of the spectrum.*

Using specialty lighting does not meet the above premise and is, as a result, not recommended. It is not the best type of light that the hobbyist can use over his, or her, tank. It may not do any harm as such, but the hobbyist can do better. As an analogy, it is a bit similar to taking only one type of vitamim when, in fact, you should be taking a multivitamin supplement.

Premise 2 : *If, as we have seen in the introduction, intensity is important because of the modern interpretation of light energy that quantity can be more important in photosynthesis than the type of light offered, lighting that can provide very high intensities seems very desirable, and fits the requirement.*

Specialty lighting, which includes actinic lighting, does not usually offer strong intensities and does not fit this premise either. Certain types of other lighting offered, e.g. regular fluorescent tubes does not fit the picture either, unless many bulbs are used. Because several types of fluorescent tubes can be obtained in an H.O. variety (high output), such bulbs can be used, as long as enough of them are placed over the tank, as in such a case they will fulfill premise 1. Newer aquarium light fixtures can now house mutltiple bulbs, are to be preferred.

Premise 3 : *If we are believers that, whatever works over a natural reef is what we should use over our own tanks, then certainly, day light type spectra should be strongly favored, as such is the spectrum of sunlight.*

The daylight spectrum is defined as a 5500 Kelvin degree spectrum. Many fluorescent tubes with daylight ratings exist, for example Vita Lites, Spectra-Lites and so on. Such bulbs are excellent for use over the reef tank.

Conclusion : Putting the three premises that I have suggested together, it becomes clear that what we need is a very high intensity of light, with a 5500 K rating. If a bulb meets these criteria it will include the blue and actinic spectrum as well, because day light does.

Such bulbs exist. They are of the metal halide type. They are the bulbs that I have been advocating for a long time. They are now finally available in North America from a U.S. manufacturer: Coralife. I suggest you seriously consider using them. Certain Osram Power Stars also fit the picture, but are presently not available in North America in the 5500 K rating.

Alternatively, use fluorescent tubes with a 5500 K rating, and use as many of them as you can, as the intensity premise needs to be fulfilled as well. This sometimes poses problems because of the limited amount of space available above a tank.

Using high output (H.O.) bulbs is certainly better because you will typically gain 25% to sometimes 50% more light. Unfortunately the V.H.O. bulbs (very high output) change their spectrum too rapidly, although they can be used for yet an additional gain in intensity. You must, however, replace them frequently to compensate for the spectrum loss. Usually every 4 to 5 months.

Two options are available as you can see. Pick the one that suits both your situation and your budget.

12.3 Remarks on Installing Lighting

Not all lifeforms kept in a reef tank need the light intensities that were discussed so far in this chapter. Some may need only moderate amounts, and others may be night type corals, requiring even less.

You must try to identify which ones you have placed in your tank. One easy way to do so is to look at your tank after the lights have been out for some time. Any coral that opens more, or wider, while the lights are out obviously does not require very strong lighting and should be placed in a protected area of the tank. Ledges can be built using pieces of rock, or coral, to accommodate such lifeforms. Leaving them in strong metal halide or fluorescent lighting will quickly damage them. As a result your tank must have a high and a moderate to low lighting zone.

To prevent strong lights from heating the aquarium water, you must ensure that hoods are equipped with fans, and that pendant lights are hung about 12 to 15 inches from the water level. Make sure too that all lighting equipment is firmly in place so it cannot fall in the water. Protect yourself, it happens, believe me, especially with children around the house.

Certain types of metal halides, e.g. halogen quartz iodine lights, may need to be protected by a U.V. filtering glass. If you do not place such a barrier between the light and the tank corals may be burned by the ultraviolet radiation. Osram Power Stars need such shields. Coralife's and Venture lighting bulbs do not.

You may have read in certain articles that metal halide lighting "burns" corals. This can only happen if you are using a bulb that needs a U.V. shield, and omit to install it. Other bulbs may result in some corals taking on a brownish color. This is not coral burn! It is a normal occurrence : symbiotic algae are growing inside your coral and giving it a browner color than it used to have.

Changing over from regular fluorescent lighting to the much stronger metal halide type should be done in steps. Do not switch from a low wattage set-up to a very strong one overnight. Acclimate the tank to more and more light progressively. Do so by restricting the number of hours the lights are on, and/or the amount of bulbs that are on at one time. Take several days to a week to complete the change over. As with all changes made to the reef tank, you must go slowly.

How many hours should your lights be on ? I recommend a total of 12-14 hours, depending on how much intensity you are providing. If yours is a tank with about 3 watts per gallon, leave the lights on a little longer, perhaps as much as 14 hours. If however you provide close to 5 watts per gallon, 12 hours will do.

Try to stagger the on and off of the lights, especially if you are using three or four of them. In a four light set up with the lights called A, B, C, D, the pattern would be as follows, (this is an example and you can substitute your own times) :

A   on at 9.00 am and off at 11.00 pm
B   on at 9.30 am and off at 10.30 pm
C   on at 10.00 am and off at 10.00 pm
D   on at 10.30 am and off at 9.30 pm

Of course, many variations exist, especially if you are using a different number of bulbs. Work out your own lighting schedule based on the number of bulbs and intensity used.

12.4 Conclusion

The last word on lighting has not been said. As time goes on more evidence pointing in the direction of 5500 K metal halides will become available, and make those skeptics out here believers, the way I am, and have been, after many years of using such lights, first European imports and then the U.S. Coralife ones. These bulbs are now available in 175 watt strenght from many dealers.

Perhaps stronger versions of 5500 K fluorescent tubes will become available too, making the lighting set up for the reef tank not quite as pricey, and easier to mangae for a lot of hobbyists. Metal halide lighting is not inexpensive, but as far as what is now available, it is the best.

I welcome calls from any hobbyist who wishes to discuss lighting more in detail, or ask questions about specific situations, and can be reached at Aardvark Press.

Lighting is, indeed, one of the more complicated areas that the hobbyist has to deal with, and is often misunderstood. Moreover, advertising is often skewed to make one particular feature very attractive, confusing the hobbyist even more.

13 Protein Skimmers and Ozone

13.1 Ozone

Ozone is one of the most misunderstood additives used around aquariums.This is mainly because few articles have been written about its function and use, and because even Pet Stores are not all that familiar with how to incorporate it safely in a salt water or reef system. Ozone is an allotropic and very unstable form of oxygen. Ozone does not exist on its own, it needs to be produced for you to be able to use it, therefore, hobbyists interested in injecting this gas, somehow, into their tank's water need an ozonizer. It cannot be bottled in pressurized canisters.

Because of its strong redox (2076 millivolt), much stronger than oxygen (1360 millivolt) ozone quickly oxidizes a great number of compounds, transforming them into compounds of a different chemical nature, often much less harmful than the original ones. This oxidizing ability is what underlies its use around marine tanks, and its injection into either protein skimmers or ozone pressurized reactors.

Ozone quickly breaks down because it is so unstable. Even in nature it cannot exist for any length of time, unless new quantities are produced continuously. You may have been exposed to ozone without knowing it if you have visited large waterfalls, coniferous forests, or in coastal areas during a massive die-off of seaweed. Ozone is also produced during large electrical storms. None of it can, however, be collected and stored. If you need ozone you will have to produce it right where you need it, and you will have to do so continuously to have an unending supply.

Excess ozone is harmful to all animals in the tank, to humans if too much is present in the air ($\frac{1}{10}$ mg per m^3). Ozone also damages all non-ozone resistant tubing and hose it comes in contact with, and is neutralized in the process. Practically, what this means for the hobbyist, is that unless you use ozone safe tubing you will lose a lot of the ozone you produce to the chemical reaction taking place with the tubing itself).

13.1.1 When should you use Ozone ?

If the water quality in your tank is low, which would be demonstrated by low redox potential levels and low dissolved oxygen levels, and a tank that does not really look in good shape, you may wish to consider using ozone to improve your water quality.

Tanks with these characteristics are usually in need of additional equipment to reduce the amount of organic material, alleviate the stress on all the filters because of the high load or poor water quality, and increase dissolved oxygen levels in the process.

Ozone will also keep parasitic disease in check. It may not cure the problem completely on its own, in a short period of time, but it will definitely kill off all free floating parasites that go through the skimmer and/or ozone reactor. Because free floating parasites are the ones that spread the parasites to other hosts, this is a plus.

Ozone also oxidizes nitrites, and can be used to cope with small amounts. Whenever you find nitrite you should, however, look for the real cause and deal with it, rather than using a patch solution such as ozone injection. Typically though, in tanks in which a fair amount of ozone is injected, no nitrites will be present, unless things get really out of hand. In such a case, major changes may have to be made to your system to bring it back in line.

13.1.2 How is Ozone Produced ?

Ozone is first produced by an ozonizer, or ozonator as it is sometimes called, and then mixed with water either in a protein skimmer, foam fractionator, or it is injected into an ozone reactor.

Two types of processes are used to produce ozone. Corona discharge units use very high voltage transformers (several thousands of volts) and transform some of the oxygen that is blown through a special tube inside the unit, into ozone. To do so efficaciously a good air pump is required. Wisa 200 and Wisa 300 pumps are, in my opinion the best suited for this process. Typically 1 percent of the oxygen passing through the tube will be converted to ozone, at 6000 volts.

Many factors affect the process, and generating ozone is not at all as simple as it sounds. Ozone generators can be very temperamental indeed. Moisture and dust in the air reduce the output of these type of units considerably. A loss of 50% or more is not unusual, especially since air around aquariums is usually extremely moist, over 90% is not uncommon. Dust inhibits the formation of ozone as well, which is the reason some hobbyist buy and install small in-line air filters.

A second process used, is to blow air over and by a specially constructed bulb that emits light in a specific nanometer range, and generates ozone while irradiating oxygen that passes through the unit as part of the air that is blown into it. These units too are rather touchy, as moisture, dust and temperature all affect the amount of ozone that will be generated, although to a lesser degree than in Corona discharge units. These units operate at regular house current voltages.

In both of these processes you must blow air through the unit itself, except if you have installed a venturi protein skimmer as the latter such in their own air, and do so through the ozonizer if you have installed one. In this respect, venturi skimmers can save you a good deal of money, as a strong air pump can cost quite a bit of money.

Several companies now offer a number of models to fit just about any situation you may be in. Small units from Sander producing 25 or 50 mg of ozone are available, and so are much larger units producing 250 mg, 500 mg, or even 1.0 gram from TAT. Regardless of which unit you buy, look for a long warranty because you may need it. Ozonizers can be very temperamental.

As indicated, moisture greatly reduces the amount of ozone your unit will produce. Adding an air dryer to your system is one solution, as it will pull moisture out the air that goes through before it enters your ozonizer. Problem is, air dryers need constant attention. The compound that absorbs the moisture needs to be dried itself just about every couple of days (and I do mean 2).

This is laborious, not as easy to do as you think, and many hobbyists quickly tire of it, and neglect the dryer. As a result, less ozone than is necessary is injected into their system.

The alternative is really simple. Buy a unit that produces about twice the amount you need, and do not use an air dryer. You will still end up with enough ozone and will not have to mess around with air dryers and the compounds in it, often calcium sulfate or silica gel.

Which unit is right for you depends on many factors. Mostly on the size of your tank, and the load you keep in it. Additionally the type of unit you need is determined also by whether or not you will be using an air dryer and an in-line air filter.

13.1.3 Injecting Ozone

Not much time needs to spend on this as most hobbyists know that this can be done in two ways : through a protein skimmer, or with a pressurized ozone reactor.

After ozone is generated the mixture coming out of your ozonizer contains both air and ozone. This mixture is pushed into the protein skimmer and escapes into the water from so-called air stones. Since protein skimming happens more efficiently when the bubbles are small, appropriate air stones should be used, and they should be changed as soon as the size of the bubbles starts to increase. You may want to make it part of your maintenance schedule to change your air stones one a month. Limewood and oak seem to work best. The latter requires a stronger air pump than the former, because they offer more resistance to the air, however they make much smaller bubbles.

Some hobbyists want to use two small units rather than one, usually because they already have them. The correct way to hook them

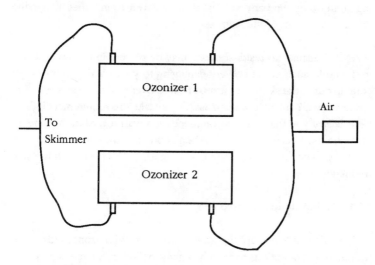

up is in parallel, not in series. The above diagram shows the correct method of hooking up 2 ozonizers.

When ozone is injected into a reactor, often just a plain acrylic cylinder filled with a medium to disperse the water, the process can be made efficient by raising the internal pressure of the cylinder. As the partial pressure of ozone is increased, it is forced more strongly into the water and a higher efficiency rate is achieved. What this means in simple terms, is that you get more oxidation from the amount of ozone used.

You will remember that earlier in the book my premise was that it does not really matter how much ozone you use, as long as none can be found in the water in the tank itself. This must, of course, be somewhat qualified ! My recommendation is that you size the ozonizer you acquire to deliver 2 mg per gallon water in your system, and that you do not use it with an air dyer, and preferably install a redox potential controller.

Two milligrams per gallon in your system, rounded off to the nearest available size of ozonizer available, may seem high. It is not in my many years of experience with ozonizers. I personally use a 500 mg unit on a 135 gallon tank, but because of all the water in the sump and pipes, the true volume is really around 200 gallons. Even with that 500 mg unit I do not find any residual ozone in my system, other than in the water coming out of the skimmer.

Because no residual ozone may be present in the water that is in the tank -such could be very damaging to your corals- all the water coming out of the skimmer must be flowed over activated carbon before it remixes with the main water mass. Do not take this requirement lightly, especially if you follow my recommendation with regard to the amount of ozone used. As the activated carbon neutralizes the ozone, it exhausts its ability to do so. Change the carbon regularly. Once a month is a safe frequency.

13.1.4 Using Redox Controllers

As you "clean up" the water in your tank with ozone, and reduce the amount of pollution, especially organic pollution, the redox potential will go up. If you now adhere to sound feeding and stocking practices, it will take less ozone to maintain the water at that quality level, than it took to get it there in the first place.

This may seem like a dilemma. It is really not. If you operate a redox controller on your tank, the unit will shut your ozonizer on and off whenever the redox goes over or below the set point. Because of this automation no changes have to be made to your system, and you can let the ozonizer operate exactly the way it has done before.

If you do not use a redox potential controller you must use a different method, but you must use a redox potential meter, a device that will cost you between $50.00 and $100.00 depending on its quality. Buy one, or borrow one, or rent one from a pet store. You can rent such units from TAT as well. A one week rental will cost you $20.00, plus a refundable deposit of $30.00. The rental can even be applied towards the purchase price (price applied at the time of this writing, check with them for current pricing).

Proceed as follows, do not switch the ozonizer off :

• Obtain a redox potential meter.

• Measure the redox potential in the morning and make a note.

• Measure the redox potential in the evening twice, once before the lights go out, and once after they have been out for about 2 hours. Make notes.

• If the three readings you obtained are well below the values suggested in this book, your water quality is not nearly where it should be and you should leave the ozonizer on all the time. First clean up the water conditions and start the procedure again when the redox is over 350 mv. If it is, proceed with then next steps.

• Measure again the following morning and again twice that evening.

• Do so again on the third day.

• You now have three days of morning and evening values, and you will have a fairly good idea of how your system evolves redox potential wise.

• On the fourth day take only a morning reading, and write it down.

• In the evening take your first reading. Write it down, switch your ozonizer off for 15 minutes and then on for 15 minutes and off again for 15, and on again for 15. Use an inexpensive digital timer with 1 minute on and off cycling time to do so. You can buy these timers at Radio Shack.

• After about 3 such cycles, take a reading of what your redox is when the meter is on, and a little later after it has gone off but is about to come back on. This will give you a high number and a low number. Measure again just before the ozonizer goes off again. This will give you another high reading.

• If the high reading you obtained after the cycling is just about the same as the one you had when the ozonizer was running continuously, a 15 minute cycling time will be all right for your system to stay around the same redox potential.

• If it is not, reduce the cycling to 10 minutes and conduct the same tests.

• Do so until you have found the correct switching time for your system.

Although this exercise may be somewhat time consuming, and although you may have to repeat it several times, it certainly is less expensive than acquiring a redox potential controller of good quality.

Not only will it allow you to operate your ozonizer more efficiently, but it will, in addition, give you a better understanding of what is going on with your tank, which in itself is a plus.

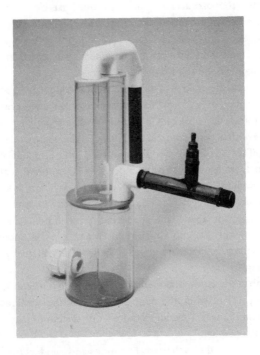

Venturi Operated Protein Skimmer as sold by Thiel•Aqua•Tech.
Super efficient Unit. Can be operated with Ozone.
Does not require air pump. Does not require air stones.
Also sold incorporated in Platinum Series Trickle Filter.

13.1.5 Conclusion

Whether you like it or not, the use of ozone will greatly improve the quality of the water in your system. Used as explained in this chapter, ozone's mystique is no longer a problem, and it can safely be used, even by a novice.

Used in the amounts suggested it will bring the quality of your water up to levels where it has not been before. Both the animals and the appearance of your tank will reflect it and the overall result will be a much more vibrant looking aquarium.

Read up on ozone in other books if you still feel uncomfortable with it. Talk to others who have used it for a long a time, or call us at Aardvark Press. We will gladly help you.

13.2 Protein Skimmers

13.2.1 Introduction

Whether you use a protein skimmer of the columnar or of the venturi type, and whether you use it with or without ozone, is a matter of how much you want to improve your water quality. My experience has taught me that you must use one, if you want to improve that water quality. There is no way around it, except running a largely understocked tank with an oversized filter.

Although the use of protein skimming has greatly increased in the last year or two, many hobbyists still feel that such a filtration may not really be required, or that they can get away with a real small unit. Such is not my experience, and such is also not the experience of recognized German authors such as G. Hueckstedt, P. Wilkens, Sander and Lemkemeyer.

Protein skimmers work on the principle that if small air bubbles are chased forcefully through a column of water, they will pick up organic and other material as they rise, and create a strong foam that contains all the matter they have picked up. Removing that foam removes the matter, and since it is no longer part of the system, it cannot break down and stress the filtration and the animals in the tank. Just looking at what comes out of a well operated skimmer should convince even the skeptics.

13.2.2 Types of Skimmers

Two types are commonly available in the hobby: columnar skimmers and venturi skimmers (also called power skimmers). Columnar skimmers are more widespread and therefore more familiar. They are less expensive to make, especially when certain of the parts are molded, as is the case in some of Route 4 Marine Technology's units, and of the of Sander ones.

Foam fractionation, as it is called in industry where such filters emanated from, has been around for decades and is nothing new or fancy, just an efficient way to remove certain compounds from water.

The problem the hobbyist must deal with when deciding on the purchase of a skimmer is not only which type (columnar or venturi), but the size and the quality of the unit. This is especially so if ozone is to be used.

The photograph show both a columnar and a venturi skimmer. If should be obvious that venturi skimmers are much smaller and can, therefore, be placed underneath the aquarium, in the cabinet.

Venturi skimmers operate on exactly the same principle as columnar ones, but differ in the manner in which the air is mixed with the water. Rather than using a rather crude wooden air diffuser approach, specially made valves, manufactured manually or molded, are used to generate extremely small bubbles very forcefully, much more forcefully, and in larger quantities,s than is possible with air stones. Because of this improvement in bubble size, bubble quantity and mixing, the units can be much smaller. And since space underneath a tank is always at a premium...

Being able to hide the skimmer from view is one advantage of venturi skimmers, but the additional efficiency is much more appealing.

Better efficiency means better water quality, means a better looking aquarium. TAT builds venturi skimmers into all their trickle filters, making that filter perhaps the best buy on the market, because you get not only one of the best filters, but for the same price you get a venturi skimmer as well. And since stand alone venturi skimmers can cost $500, you may want to think about this carefully if you are in the market for a filter.

Whereas columnar skimmers require a fair amount of adjustment, venturi skimmers usually do not. You set them up and regulate the water flow and the foam height, and you are skimming without having to re-adjust the levels ever so often. This, too, is an advantage to consider and factor into your decision.

Venturi skimmers with molded venturi valves are more efficient than venturi skimmers with manually made ventures, but your system may not need the higher efficiency of the molded venturi if it is only stocked at medium level and operated with a good trickle filter. Talk to the manufacturer and then decide which one is better for you. The difference in price is worth the time.

With any skimmer, but especially with venturi skimmers, make sure that you can operate them with a great deal of ozone if that is what you have in mind for you system. Not all can.

13.2.3 Operating the skimmer

After installing your unit, operate it with a pump, or a by-pass from the main water return line, and adjust the flow rate to equal about 1 to 1.5 times the amount of water in your system. If you do not have a flow meter you will have to gauge this somewhat. The amount of water you push through the skimmer is not extremely critical, but enough must go through for all the water to be skimmed in a regular fashion. Many hobbyists flow greater amounts of water through their simmers and report better results. Experiment a little until you have it set right.

In fact, if you own a redox potential controller or meter you can measure the redox of the outflowing water at various speeds and decide on which one is best. That would obviously be the setting you would want to select.

Venturi skimmers typically require more water flow because of the venturi valve. The more forcefully you push water through the valve assembly,the more forcefully you will draw in air, and the better skimming levels you will attain. On the venturi skimmer in the photograph 600 gallons per hour is a minimum, but what an effect.

Because ozone changes the consistency of the foam that develops at the top of the skimmer, levels and foam must be adjusted each time you make a change in the amount of ozone that is injected. This applies to all skimmers. Observe the levels when you make the change and re-adjust if necessary. Sometimes changes in water and foam levels take time to become apparent. Do not walk away from a skimmer unless you are sure that the level is not changing. This may take 10 to 15 minutes to be visible.

Air stones wear out quickly, especially if used with a lot of ozone, and the bubbles they produce will rapidly increase in size. This reduces the efficiency of the skimming process a great deal. Your air stone(s) need to be replaced when this happens. Make it a point to do so. There is no sense spending money on a skimmer and then not operating it the way it should be operated.

If ozone is injected into the skimmer, use ozone resistant tubing to connect the output of the ozonizer to the air/ozone mix input on the skimmer. Not doing so reduces the amount of ozone that is actually available for the skimming process. Norprene™ is the recommended tubing. Silicone tubing will last for s while, and polysulfone is the best but also the most expensive, fetching as much as $8.00 a foot retail for the very high grade quality.

If ozone can be smelled in the room where the skimmer is placed, suspect that it is coming out of the top of your columnar skimmer, or that you have a leak in the ozone line. The former is more often than not the explanation though. To prevent this from continuing, install an ozone cap on the top of your skimmer. This is a round cup, of the same diameter as the top of the skimmer, with a perforated bottom, and filled with activated carbon. All air/ozone coming out of the skimming column must now go through the carbon before it can escape into the free air. Since carbon neutralizes ozone your problem should be solved.

Clean the top cup of your skimmer regularly. This will allow you to better determine where the foam level is and it will also reduce odors that may otherwise emanate from the scum that collects in the cup. Alternatively, make a connection with a small diameter hose from the skimmer cup, to a larger container with a lid, placed on the floor. Scum will now flow from the top to that container, and the lid will prevent odors from getting into the surrounding air. You will have to make a small hole through the lid to pass the hose through. Make it tight. Some companies, for example, Route 4 Marine Technology and Marine Technical Concepts, offer special containers to do just that.

Certain additives can make your skimmer foam much more forcefully than normal, usually because they contain binders or colloids, or both. To prevent the skimmer from overflowing, test a small amount of any new additive you plan to use and make sure it does not affect the way your skimmer operates. Be especially careful of KH generating compounds, some vitamins, some nutrient elements, and a number of others. This does not mean that you cannot use them, but you must add them only in very small quantities. In the case of KH generators this is not practical, and I suggest you get yourself one that does not affect your skimmer.

Skimmers are meant to run 24 hours a day. I see no reason why you shouldn't. When a time comes that little is to be removed from the water, the skimmer will not produce as much foam. That's all. When later on, e.g. after feeding, or when algae die, and they do all the time, more organic matter will be present in the water, and the skimmer will start removing it again. Do not be misled, a skimmer that has been running for a while may not have anything to remove from the water, so it won't. Such does not mean that your skimmer is not working properly. It probably is.

Once you have adjusted your protein skimmerproperly, leave it alone. The more you adjust, the more re-adjusting you will have to do, and the more unnecessary work you are creating for yourself. Note that this applies to both columnar and venturi skimmers.

Small Reef Aquarium Basics, and a few issues of Marine Reef, the newsletter we publish go into even more detail on skimmers and outline a chart on how to size your protein skimmer accurately. You may wish to refer to them if you need still more information.

Two volumes of back issues of Marine Reef now exist. Volume one, Year one includes issues 1 through 17, and Volume two, Year two includes all issues from 18 through 34. Both are available form Aardvark Press for $30.00 each, or for $50.00 if you order both of them. To keep yourself up-to-date on what is happening in the hobby, and to learn more about the requirements of the animals you keep, consider subscribing to the newsletter. It will be a worthwhile investment.

14. Pressurized and Non-pressurized Reactors

14.1 Introduction

In an effort to further sophisticate their systems, German hobbyists innovated the hobby in 1986 and started building and selling pressurized acrylic cylinders that could be used for the purpose of introducing air and ozone, air on its own, or carbon dioxide, in a manner that had not been tried before, but seemed to give good results after a period of testing and adjusting the design: under pressure.

The first reactors to appear in stores were oxygen reactors, soon to be followed by ozone and carbon dioxide ones. Hobbyists responded enthusiastically and soon such reactors became part of the normal equipment used by the more advanced hobbyist, both in Germany and other European Countries.

During a 1986 visit to Germany I saw these reactors at Nollman Aquaristik, in Bielefeld, and decided to import some of them into the United States, convinced that they were a important addition to the reef tank, and that the reef tank would benefit from their use.

Since that time we have gone from importing, to building them, after having changed the original design and added gauges to some of them. Testing determined that water distribution was more important than had been originally taught, and that pressures of 0.1 bar (about 1.5 PSI) did not give as good results as higher ones. After all modifications were made, my company made them part of the wide range of products we offer, and that are mostly used on reef aquarims and some also on freshwater plant aquariums

We subsequently also introduced a series of more advanced reactors to automatically adjust the carbonate hardness, add calcium carbonate, and offer the hobbyist the ease of using chemical filtering media, and nitrate removing compounds, in a canister format that could be run in conjunction with the main water supply.

All these reactors are described in this section. Many are available from specialized companies such as Marine Technical Concepts and Route 4, and all can be ordered from my own company.

Because of the unique nature of some of them, not every hobbyist may have a need for each of these reactors though. Study your system, determine what you are trying to achieve, take a close look at your water chemistry parameters, evaluate whether the equipment that you are now using can do the job for you, and if not, decide on which one(s) you may want to add to your water management system.

When going beyond the basic four filtration methods discussed so far, plus pretreating the water used to fill and top off the aquarium, the word filtration does not seem to accurately describe what the hobbyist does, anymore. I therefore prefer to use the terminology "water management system".

Important note on pressurized reactors : to operate such a reactor efficiently the air, or the mix of air and ozone, or the CO_2, must be replaced continuously. If such were not the case, the amount of oxygen, respectively ozone and carbon dioxide, would soon be exhausted. All what would then happen is that you have a reactor that operates at a higher pressure than normal, but no more transfer of the desired gasses occurs, and the reactor is not achieving anything for you.

Reactors that are properly adjusted, therefore, always show a stream of both water and bubbles coming out and mixing with the area where you return the effluent. If this is not the case you must further adjust your reactor. Because such can be noisy, it is best to submerse the hose attached to the "out" side of the reactor. This will greatly reduce the noise, if not eliminate it altogether.

If all the reactors you use, or at least most of them, can be fitted into the trickle filter that you operate, you will have a more streamlined system that requires considerably less space. This is a plus because space underneath the aquarium is limited. Such is possible with all Platinum Series Trickle Filters.

14.2 Oxygen Reactor

A reactor used to inject oxygen under pressure into the water, called an oxygen reactor, is nothing more than a cylinder, usually of acrylic material, filled with a medium that disperses the water efficiently, in which air is blown at the same time as water is forced in.

Providing your air pump is strong enough, and providing your water pump can handle the back pressure, one can increase the internal pressure by adjusting both at the same time, and using a gauge to determine what, in fact, the pressure inside the reactor is.

Because of the over-pressure inside the cylinder, air -which contains 21% oxygen- is made to give up more of its oxygen to the water (the partial pressure of oxygen now being higher). This increases the dissolved oxygen levels of the water, and benefits the system overall.

The recommended over-pressure is 3 PSI, but I run my own system at 6 PSI and obtain better results. Approximately 75 gallons of water per hour flow through the reactor. You must determine what is best for yours by experimenting with various pressures, making sure that the reactor you are using can handle them. If not, it will blow out and a seam will "give" somewhere, creating a potential leakage situation.

14.3 Ozone Reactor

An ozone reactor operates on exactly the same principle as an oxygen reactor. Setting one up, and adjusting it is done in the same manner as well. Make sure though that the reactor you are using is certified for ozone use. Remember, ozone is a very strong oxidizer. Pay attention to the medium inside, and to the small fittings that are used to hook the air/ozone mix up to.

Instead of running such reactors at 3 or more PSI, I have found them to operate efficiently at 2 to 3 PSI, and run mine at that level. Again about 75 gallons per hour are flowed through the reactor. Experiment with yours, both the pressure and the amount of water you flow through, until you are satisfied with the result. Remember that ozone must be neutralized with activated carbon.

14.4 Carbon Dioxide Reactor

Because, to some extent, the amount of carbon dioxide that is required by your system is determined by the efficiency of the injection system itself, ensuring that such is done in an optimal fashion will save you many trips to the welding supply place to refill your CO_2 canister.

CO₂ reactors are not pressurized reactors in the same sense as the previous ones, except for the short periods of time when carbon dioxide is actually being released and mixed with the water. As a result, all they require is hooking up. Water needs to be brought to them, either by means of a by-pass in the main water line, or by means of a small power head pump.

Because the water going through the reactor will itself create some back pressure on the carbon dioxide supply system, you will need to adjust the pressure reducer valve on your CO₂ gauges to enable them to overcome that back pressure. In my experience 5 to 6 PSI is usually enough, but you will have to determine what works for you yourself.

Each time CO₂ is injected into the reactor, the water level will diminish, and water mixed with CO₂ will escape from the "out" side.

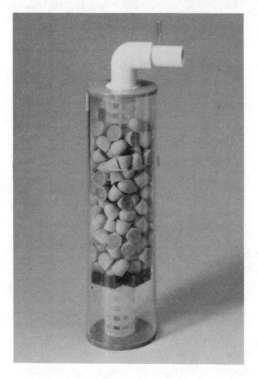

When the CO_2 supply stops, the reactor will fill itself with water again. Some hobbyists wonder whether such is the correct way for those units to operate. It is.

14.5 Molecular Absorption Reactor

Molecular absorption discs are chemical filtering media developed by Poly Bio Marine Inc. and sold by TAT under license, for use in this particular reactor. You can, of course, buy these discs from all of Poly Bio Marine's dealers, but without the special TAT reactor. Poly Bio Marine

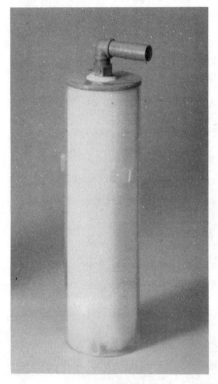

Inc. do sell another type of housing in which 12 or more discs can be placed, and that can be piped in-line with the main water flow. The modular TAT reactor fits into a compartment in the Platinum Series filter.

This highly efficient medium, also sold by Poly Bio Marine in the Poly Filter® form which is probably known to most of you, is so efficient that I can not conceptualize a system that is running without them. If you are truly interested in maximizing the efficiency of your water management system, you must include these discs, or the Poly Filers, in your chemical filtration set up.

Poly Filters and molecular absorption discs do not leach any compounds they have absorbed back into the system, and progressively change color as they exhaust their absorption capability. This gives the hobbyist a clear signal when time has come to replace them. To prevent the discs, or pads, from acting as a mechanical filter as well, it is good practice to pre-filter the water that goes to the molecular absorption reactor.

14.6 Carbon Reactor for Air

A small acrylic cylinder, filled with activated carbon, that is used to clean up the air of impurities, before it is blown inside the biological chamber of the trickle filter, where the bacteria use some of the oxygen it contains, and where some of that oxygen transfers to your water, raising its dissolved oxygen content.

All airborne pollution that would otherwise end up in your system, and transfer to the water, is removed in this fashion. An alternative way is to fill the reactor with molecular absorption discs, or cut up Poly Filter pads. Because both of the latter do not remove gasses, for example oxygen, such is, in my opinion, a better way to go.

The correct way to use this type of reactor is to blow the air coming out of your air pump into the reactor first, and then from the reactor into the trickle filter's biological chamber. You can also use these reactors to improve the quality of the air going into your ozonizer. The hook-up procedure is the same as the one just described.

14.7 Carbon Reactor for Water

What many hobbyists used to do with canister filters can be done with a specialized reactor filled with activated carbon. Water is flowed in through one end and emerges from the other, and is then mixed with the water in the sump of the trickle filter, or guided back directly to the tank. Because the need for using large amounts of activated carbon is greatly reduced when you use M.A. discs or Poly Filters, evaluate whether your system needs this type of a reactor carefully.

14.8 X-Nitrate Reactor

This reactor is similar to the one just described, but is filled with a nitrate removing compound called X-nitrate which is sold by TAT. This efficient medium requires that a fair amount be used for each 50 gallons of water in your system. As a result, traditional canister filters may be too small to handle that amount of material. If you need more than such a canister can handle, and if you do not have spaces provided for its use in your trickle filter or elsewhere in the system, this reactor will solve your problem.

14.9 Carbonate Hardness Reactor

Although similar in its size and operation to a carbon dioxide reactor, the carbonate hardness reactor serves a totally different purpose. Both water and carbon dioxide are flowed through it, and the contact made between the calcareous material inside the reactor, and the acidified water (because of the CO_2) results in some carbonate and bicarbonate material going into solution. This raises the carbonate hardness of the whole system in a more automated fashion.

Flow water slowly through these reactors and monitor your carbonate hardness frequently because this is a highly efficient system and your KH level may rise quickly over a period of a few days to a few weeks. After you have attained the desired KH level, you will have to adjust the amount of CO_2 going into the reactor by means of either pH control, or by means of a timer.

This will require that you experiment with CO_2 flow rates a little to determine how many hours a day the reactor needs to be provided with carbon dioxide for your carbonate hardness to remain at the level where you want it to be. Trial and error may seem laborious, but it will probably only take you a day or two to figure out exactly how to operate this highly efficient unit.

14.10 Kalkwasser Reactor

Kalkwasser reactors are used to increase the amount of dissolved calcium carbonate in your system in a more uniform manner. Calcium carbonate is very much required by all corals with hard exoskeletons, as has been pointed out repeatedly by for example P. Wilkens and A. Thiel.

2 nd Generation Plastic Media for Biological Filters : Super•Techs.
Promote greater Oxygenation while offering all the surface area you need.

These are the types of corals that most hobbyists keep or want
to keep, by their common names they are known as : Sunflower, Elegance (Elegant), Bubble, and so on.

Because it can do so very efficiently, this is one of the most inte-
resting reactors to install. It should be filled with pure calcium carbonate
rock, and very small amounts of CO_2 should be injected into the reactor.
This is easily done with a manual carbon dioxide injection system, or with
a bypass from the main automated system

Filling it with any other material than calcium carbonate rocks
will not do an efficient job for you, and may result in too large an increase
in your carbonate hardness if left unattended for too long. This unit is
meant to add calcium carbonate only, not other hardness factors. It is

operated independently of any other CO_2 driven reactor, and should not be confused with them.

Pure calcium carbonate rock must be obtained from a chemical supply house, and you must specify that you want the highest purity grade. Do not use calcium carbonate powder, in bags, because the powder will quickly escape, and mix with the water without dissolving. Such will create a real mess and it will be hard to remove the powder from your system. Additionally your pH may rise rapidly and in a way that you will find hard to control

An alternative to the reactor itself, is to mix some calcium carbonate rocks in the mix that is already in your CO_2 reactor. If you do so, mix only 4 or 5 of them and determine what the effect is, by using a calcium hardness test (LaMotte Chemicals). if the calcium hardness rises too rapidly remove the rocks and resort to the alternate method suggested below.

Alternatively, if you decide on not using this type of a reactor, add Kalkwasser bought commercially from one of the companies that specializes in reef products, and add it on a regular basis, preferably continuously by means of a drip method, as suggested by Wilkens, and re-explained by Thiel in several articles in the Marine Reef newsletter.

14.11 Conclusion

The use of reactors to improve the water management system is new. Many hobbyists and many pet store owners are unfamiliar with them and may not fully understand what they can do for your tank, and for the stability of its environment. They all benefit the water quality, but whether you want to install them or not is a personal decision. Talk to manufacturers and let them explain some of the benefits, as they see them, to you, and then make a determination.

As the hobby evolves newer techniques always come about, but it sometimes takes a long time for the hobbyist to adjust to them. Reef tanks are only now really catching on, and they have been around in Europe for about 10 years, and in the States for 5.

15. The Algae

15.1 Introduction

Algae is such an all encompassing word, that it means different things to different people, especially to hobbyists. As a general rule hobbyists classify all algae they do not like in the micro-algae category, all other green algae in the macro-algae category, and then have separate classifications for red, and slimy red, an so on. Frequently not very conducive to clearly understanding which type of algae, in fact, the hobbyist is talking about. Some even pronounce the name with a hard g (as in good), and some with a soft g (as in George).

Algae share a lot in common with plants, but they are unique, and often difficult to classify, even when a microscope is used. Some algae are, in fact, very close to bacteria (Cyanobacteria or blue-green algae). Literally thousands upon thousands of species and varieties exist, making it very hard for anyone to identify them easily, except for a few dozen macro-algae types that are commonly kept in aquariums.

Algae can be aquatic or terrestrial. They can exist in fresh and salt water, even in environments with salinities as high as three times what our aquariums are kept at. The diversity of their habitats is just phenomenal, and such is not an exaggeration either. They adapt quickly to a different milieu and can go in a dormant state, only to reappear when conditions are right again. They are extremely resilient, flexible in their requirements, and can be very hard to remove from the aquarium if types that you do not want happen to grow there and do well.

Surprisingly though, the varieties that hobbyists do not care for are, more often than not, associated with lesser water quality conditions.

Such should be an indication that improving the water quality by equipping your tank with an efficient water management system, will in most cases rid the tank of the undesirable varieties.

Algae can be suspended (planktonic), attached (bentic), live on the surface of the water (neustonic), attached to other algae (epiphitic) and many other in between. They grown particularly well attached to rocks and glass (or acrylic) as just about every hobbyist has found out.

Epilitic algae live on stones, Epipelic on mud and in sand, Epiphytic on plants and other algae, and Episoic algae are attached to other animals. Yes even that. It should be obvious that algae can grow just about anywhere, and that when conditions are propitious they will do so, often to the dismay of the hobbyist. As should be clear by now, algae are extremely opportunistic.

Algae have been around for billions of years, and range from the infinitesimally small to the very large 180 foot tall Kelp varieties. Some algae grow extremely slowly, while others grow so fast that one gets the impression that you can watch them grow (for example the red slime algae that infest many tanks, are cyanobacteria, and hard to eradicate). Some algae require great amounts of light, while others do much better in low or medium light conditions.

As you may have surmised, because of the infinite number of auspicious conditions, you will have many types of algae in your tank whether you like it or not. The key then will be to maintain the water quality in such a manner that only minimal amounts of undesirable algae are present, and that the ones you want to grow, do so, perhaps even profusely, because of their beneficial qualities. Indeed macro-algae not only clean up the water by removing many toxins, compounds that are harmful in larger quantities, but they also strongly oxygenate the water.

To try and shed some light on the various names you will encounter when reading about algae, a listing is offered for those interested. It is not complete, and it is only one of several classifications that are still used :

Cyanophyta	Blue-green Algae
Prochlorophyta	Blue-green Algae
Chlorophyta	Green Algae
Charophyta	Stoneworts
Euglenophyta	Euglenoids
Phaephyta	Brown Algae
Chrysophyta	Golden Yellow-green algae
Pyrrhophyta	Dinoflagellates
Cryptophyta	Cryptonomads
Rhodophyta	Red Algae

Representatives of all can appear in reef aquariums, especially aquariums stocked with many types of so-called live rock from different areas of the world. Frequently though, the ones that are more common are the green, the blue-green (unfortunately) and the red. Some brown algae varieties appear as well in tanks with low levels of lighting. Macro-algae (by the hobbyist's definition) are part of the Chlorophyta group, a name derived from the fact that they all contain chlorophyll, the very important component necessary for photosynthesis.

The study of algae is called Phycology, and treatises have been written about their ecology, biology, and any other scientific approach than can be taken. unless you are a true algaephile, they are all very dry and no fun to read. Some works however stand out by having brought algae closer to the lay observer.

If you have a more definite interest in algae, you may wish to refer to the following books for more details and information that you can use in your tank's management :

♦ Introduction to the Algae : Harold C. Bold, Michael J. Wynne, Second Edition, Prentice Hall, 1985.
♦ Micro-Algal Biotechnology : Michael A. and Lesley J. Borowitska, Cambridge University Press, 1988.
♦ A Textbook on Algae : H.D. and H.N. Kumar, Macmillan Tropical Biology Series, Macmillan Press, 2nd Edition, 1979.
♦ Experimental Phycology : Christopher S. Lobban, David J. Chapman, Bruno P. Kramer, Cambridge University Press, 1988.

◆ Introductory Phycology : F. R. Trainor, John Wiley and Sons, 1978.

◆ Marine Algae of the Northeastern Coast of North America, Prof. William R. Taylor, The University of Michigan Press, Second Printing of the Second Edition, 1962.

◆ Marine Algae of the Eastern Tropical and Sub-tropical Coasts of the Americas, Prof. William R. Taylor, The University of Michigan Press, 1960.

15.2 Micro-Algae

As already pointed out, "micro-algae" is an all encompassing term used by hobbyists to describe algae they do not want in their tanks but that, unfortunately, are so common and difficult to deal with, that untold hours are devoted to ridding aquariums of them. They have become the focus of a great deal of controversy as many authors and many hobbyists tout their particular way of killing them off, as the one all other hobbyists should be using. Unfortunately, many of these methods either do not work, or do not provide long term protection.

The problem is so wide-spread, and the algae so difficult to eradicate, that more than an undue amount of time is devoted to this problem by just about every hobbyist at some time or another. This is not unwarranted as it is, indeed, a plague in many ways, able to ruin an otherwise good looking aquarium in a matter of days. Often too, books will totally avoid the subject, except for making some very general remarks that are usually of no use to the hobbyist who already has the problem, except to point it out, something they are already aware of.

Micro-algae are present in the tank as spores that come in with rocks, fish, other algae, food, invertebrates, corals, the water, the salt, or are airborne. They are present whether you like it or not. If the water conditions are not conducive to their growth they will, however, never appear in amounts that become problematic; but if conditions are right, their will proliferate very quickly and will overtake the aquarium in a matter of weeks or sometimes days.

Most micro-algae outbreaks can be attributed to excess amounts of two types of compounds that are normally present in tanks as by-products of organic breakdown and mineralization : **nitrates and**

phosphates. As we have already seen, nitrates and phosphates build up in tanks that are not well maintained, or in tanks were phosphates and nitrates are introduced through the use of water and salt that contain them, and activated carbon that leaches it into the water.

We indicated earlier that micro-algae grow in tanks where water quality conditions are right for them to do so. If, as we have just seen, this means tanks with high levels of nitrates and phosphates, it would be sense to keep these levels as low as we possibly can. Most hobbyists understand this and agree with this statement, but two problems exist :

• Keeping levels low requires testing and knowing what low means in each case. Not all hobbyists are aware of how low, low really is. Not all hobbyists test, at least not on a frequent enough basis.

• Not all hobbyists are willing to go to the extent of changing some of the products they are using, or test them for nitrates and phosphates, because they currently do not have micro-algae problem.

If micro-algae are to remain under control, the hobbyist needs to take some definite steps and be prepared to do whatever is necessary to make conditions unfavorable for their growth. Besides testing the tank water, the products and water used, this is really boils down to regular and good husbandry techniques, such as changing water, not over feeding, not over crowding, and making sure that no nitrates and phosphates are introduced into the tank in any way that can easily be avoided.

The maintenance and husbandry schedule was discussed throughout this book, and outlined in a special chapter. Adhere to it, set up the right kind of filtration, and you will not be plagued by micro-algae.

If everything else fails, two companies now offer products that can help in ridding the tank of micro-algae : Micro-algae Controller from Coralife, and Ridalgex from Thiel•Aqua•Tech. If you are interested in more information on these products call the respective companies for more details. More of these products may appear on the market as time goes on, so check the ads in the magazines.

A short list of possible actions that you may wish to take looks as follows :

❑ Adhere to a strict regimen of husbandry and maintenance.
❑ Test for nitrates and phosphates regularly and take corrective action immediately if it proves to be necessary.
❑ Do not let nitrates exceed 5 ppm of NO_3.
❑ Do not let phosphates exceed 0.05 ppm of PO_4.
❑ Don't use water additives that contain phosphates and/or nitrates.
❑ Ensure that whatever water source you use does not either.
❑ Plant the tank with macro-algae, as they too feed on nitrates and phosphates, and lower their levels in the process.
❑ Introducing food competition "will" reduce the amount of micro-algae problems.
❑ Maintain your tank at the redox levels recommended in this book.
❑ If this requires the installation of a better protein skimmer, do so.
❑ If you must use ozone, do so too.
❑ Whenever you see algae growths of the type you do not want, remove them from the tank immediately. This applies especially to red slime algae (often cyanobacteria).
❑ Place more grazers, or algae eating fish, in the tank.
❑ Reduce the amount you feed, or change food brand.
❑ Check the type of lighting you are using. Light with too much red in the spectrum promotes the growth of many forms of undesirable algae. Such light has a low Kelvin degree rating, often in the 3000 to 3500 level. Use 5500 K type instead.

If you now have micro-algae problems, don't expect immediate results. It may take several weeks of hard work for you to rid yourself of this bane. G. Bepko (1987) reports that it took him about 6 weeks of maintaining his redox at a high level before he could finally see the light at the end of the tunnel.

Besides nitrates and phosphates, silica, usually in the form of silicic acid can be the cause of another problem : the appearance of diatoms. Silica tests are available from, for example, LaMotte Chemicals and can be used to determine at what level your tank runs. To reduce the silica level many authors, including myself, recommend the use of treated water for top-offs. Use distilled, deionized or reverse osmosis water. You will see an improvement in a week to 10 days.

Although silicic acid has been identified as a problem compound, more research is still necessary until definite recommendations can be made. At this stage such is too early to do.

15.3 Macro-Algae

Just as there are great numbers of micro-algae, the variety and profusion of macro- algae types that can be kept in aquariums can be disconcerting. To give just one example, Caulerpa, one of the favorite marine algae, already has more than 75 classified types.

Most of the algae types that hobbyists wish to grow are of the Chlorophyta type, -the green algae- because they are easily obtained and grow rather easily, putting only moderate requirements on nutrient levels and water quality. Just about the only factors that most green algae do not deal with easily, is changes in salinity, pH, and too high temperatures.

All green algae of the Caulerpa type require high amounts of light and do best under daylight type bulbs. Since these are the same bulbs we recommended for corals, installing such light will not only benefit the corals and invertebrates, but will also promote algal growth. The intensities recommended earlier apply as well.

Green algae thrive because they are able to photosynthesize, meaning use light energy to produce the compounds they need for their growth, but such are not the only compounds needed. Algae also need iron and a carbon source. Recommended levels of iron go from a low of 0.05 ppm to a high of 1.5 ppm, with a mean of 1.0 ppm. Recommended carbon dioxide levels are 3 to 4 mg/l. Use accurate tests to determine the level of both in your own tank if you use these additives. In the case of iron you can rely on a qualitative test, as long as it has been salt water adjusted by the manufacturer. I do not recommend fertilizers that contain non-chelated iron , because the iron will not stay in solution at the high pH of a reef tank. It will precipitate quickly and will not be available to the algae you are trying to grow.

Use Liquid Gold from TAT, perhaps the most complete supplement for Reef Tanks

Iron is provided in the form of a fertilizer that contains iron, preferably in a chelated form to make sure that it will stay in solution, and a number of other compounds known to be beneficial. What these compounds are, is often not divulged by manufacturers because of competitive reasons, but manganese, for example, is one of them. A good marine fertilizer should, in light of what we have said earlier about micro-algae, not contain nitrates and phosphates. Although macro-algae need both, they are always available in a large enough supply in the aquarium.

Carbon is provided in the form of carbon dioxide by using manual or automated injection systems. Macro-algae are able to utilize carbon dioxide very efficiently during the photosynthetic process. Even though many authors do not recommend its addition, all agree that it is necessary. Because testing highlights that it is frequently in short supply, and because it can be added safely as long as the hobbyist understand the principles underlying it, my recommendation is that it be used. Not only because macro-algae require it, but because it assists in the stability of the pH of the tank, as we have seen elsewhere in this book.

Excessive amounts of macro-algae growth in reef tanks, should be trimmed. Algae send out runners, at least many do, and spread quickly across rocks. This may impede on the space required by corals and other invertebrates, and result in the latter losing out in a battle for the small amount of area available in tanks. Always keep in mind that around real reefs algae do not grown amongst the corals, but usually in areas removed from them. Too many algae will harm the corals, and although it may not kill them, it will certainly affect their appearance in a negative way.

When trimming algal growth one always breaks some of them off and causes the fluids inside the algae to leach into the water. Performing a water change is often recommended to counteract whatever noxious compounds may have gotten into the water as a result. The more algae you remove, the larger the amount of water you change should be.

Algae are adversely affected by many changes that the tank water undergoes, either naturally or because of an intervention by the hobbyist. Salinity and pH are two. Temperature is another one. If these changes are too brusque, and/or too large, an algal die- off may occur.

Should this happen to you, quickly remove all dead algae before they can pollute the water, and cause stress on all other life forms. This may be a time consuming task, but it is a necessary one.

More advanced hobbyists sometimes use the fact that macro-algae clean up the water by removing nitrates and phosphates, to their advantage. This is done by setting up so-called algae filters. These filters are discussed in my other books and also in the Marine Reef Newsletter. If you have an interest in these filters check them for more details.

Calcareous algae, e.g. Halimeda and Penicillus, require sandy substrates and high amount of light. They are more difficult to keep than Caulerpa species and are not recommended for the beginning hobbyist. Get as many details of what they require to stay alive and grow from the supplier that you buy these algae from. They should be able to give you this information and help you out. two stores that I have found to be particularly helpful in this respect is World Class Aquarium in Brooklyn, New York, and Aquatic Specialists in Knoxville, Tennessee. Ask for respectively Robert and John.

Keeping macro-algae in reef and marine tanks is such a complex matter, that a book could easily be written on the subject. I had hoped to be able to do so soon, but more pressing issues have made me decide on writing other books first.

15.5 Symbiotic Algae

The algae that live inside corals and invertebrates, and even inside the lips (mantle) of many clams, are called symbiotic algae. Although they never receive much recognition in reef tank literature, they are of utmost importance to us, because our corals and invertebrates would not survive for very long without them.

Symbiotic Algae, or Zooxanthellae, live in an harmonious relationship with their host, and provide the host with nutrients in the form of the algae's metabolic processes. The relationship between the host and the symbiont is both chemical and biological, allowing both to cope with the rather low nutrient level around natural reefs.

Zooxanthellae microadriatica, the most commonly found symbiotic algae is a photosynthesizing algae that requires strong light to do so. Because we know from the lighting chapter that this can be done with 5500 K degree metal halide lighting, no hobbyist should have problems keeping Zooxanthellae thriving, and their corresponding corals in healthy looking shape. Light however is not the only factor to be considered. Granted, Zooxanthellae will do fine, but corals also uptake nutrients directly from the water. Providing these extra nutrients is, as a result. an additional requirement and task.

You are probably already aware of the need to use a trace element mixture to supplement the water with nutrients that are depleted by many processes taking place in the tank. There are a few others that need to be added as well : micro nutrients and specialized supplements such as strontium, molybdenum and iodine. These supplements can be obtained from companies marketing reef aquarium products that were developed for the Reef, and not for the fish-only tank. Two such companies are Coralife and Thiel•Aqua•Tech. You may wonder why the same company names keep being repeated in this book. The reasons are obvious : those companies make products that are designed for the reef, were brought to market after reef tanks had become a reality, and are of very good to excellent quality. If these companies made the effort to develop products for the totally different type of tank that the reef tank is, they deserve to be brought to your attention, not only because of the effort they made, but because you should be aware where you can get the products you will need to keep your reef tank in healthy condition.

Although a great number of invertebrates can survive for extended periods of time without symbiotic algae, corals cannot because they are not able to derive enough nutrients from the water, especially in a tank. Providing the tank with both the required amount of light and the necessary nutrients is therefore very important part of keeping the tank. Keeping a reef aquarium involves a lot more than just going to a pet shop, buying corals and placing them in the tank. You must care for them for as long as you have them, and the better you care for them the longer you "will" have them. Compare the work required to what you would do to a new car that you want to keep in top shape : you not only put in gas, change oil, change air filters, oil filters, add water, wash it, polish it, but you also change transmission fluid, brake fluid, windshield wiper fluid, inflate the tires, change tires, change brake pads, etc. Similarly, all the maintenance tasks outlined for the reef tank are necessary as well, if you plan on keeping the animals you have for a long time.

Depending on the type of pigments a particular alga harbors, its exterior coloration will be vary greatly, as many hobbyists will have observed. Some of these pigments are due to the algae and some are part of the host. The colorations of symbiotic algae containing animals can, as a result, vary considerably. For the corals and invertebrates to keep their colors, all required nutrients must be provided on a regular basis, and light needs to be commensurate with their requirements. Some corals will turn brownish when exposed to strong light. Such is normal because Zooxanthellae are reacting to that light by multiplying and deepening the coloration of the animal. Because algal cells can vary greatly in numbers in relationship to coral cells, the coloration of such animals can go from rather drab to multicolored. Darley (1982) suggest 1 to 300 as the span of this ratio.

15.6 Conclusion

Algae are important to the tank in many ways. Macro-algae clean up the water by removing mineralized compounds and releasing oxygen. Symbiotic algae ensure the survival and growth of your corals and invertebrates.

As such algae deserve a much larger part of your attention, and should be cared for by providing them with the nutrients they, too, require.

Micro-algae can be a problem. Follow the steps recommended in this book and you should not have to cope with this hard to eliminate variety. Remember, in the case of micro-algae prevention is the easiest route. A good water management system should, however, spare you from their appearance.

A last Word ...

I hope you have enjoyed this 7 th completely re-written edition of the Marine Fish and Invert Reef Aquarium.

This book has been extremely successful, having sold over 50.000 copies already, and it is still going strong.

Many hobbyists have called to tell us they liked the content of the first printings a lot, mainly because the book cleared up a lot of mistunderstanding surrounding reef aquariums. We thank them for the time they took to let us know.

Hopefully this new edition will also have greatly reduced the number of typographical errors that had slipped into the previous ones. We apologize to those holding such copies.

Albert J. Thiel
Trumbull, Connecticut
March 1990

Many thanks to Sarah for her understanding during the re-writing of this manuscript.♥

Request for a free Catalog

Name : ....

Address : ....

....

....

....

City : .... **State :**........... **Zip :** ....

Please fill in this form and return it to Thiel•Aqua•Tech, 575 Broad Street, Bridgeport, CT 06604, or call (203) 368 2111

Marine Reef Subscription Form
Special Offer

To subscribe to Marine Reef, fill out the information below,
in caps please, and send a check or money order to :
Aardvark Press, 575 Broad Street, Bridgeport, CT 06604

Yes, please enter a 1 year subscription, equal to 17 issues,
at the special price of $31.50, and send the newsletters to :

Name : ....

Address : ....

....

....

....

City : .... **State :**........... **Zip :** ....

Allow up to 4 weeks for the first issue to arrive.

Special Offer for Required Supplements

**You must use this form to receive the special offer.
No phone calls. Pre-paid only. No cash. Check or money order.
Allow up to 2 weeks for receipt of merchandise.
No P.O. Boxes unless UPS will devliver to them.
Your order will be delayed if you give us an address
UPS cannot deliver to.**

Yes, please send me 1 gallon of Kalkwasser, 1 gallon of Reef KH,
4 oz of Vitamins, 4 oz of Reef Elements, 4 oz of KSM, 16 oz
of Liquid Gold, and 2 oz of Tech•Iodine for the special price
of $ 75.00 (a $117.00 value), including shipping.

Name : ....

Address : ....

....

....

....

City : .... **State :**............ **Zip :** ....

**Mail this coupon, or a copy of it,
together with your payment to :
Thiel•Aqua•Tech
575 Broad Street
Bridgeport, CT 06604**

Stores : Please call for store pricing.

Table Of Contents :

Foreword	5
Introduction	11
The Basics	15
The Aquarium	15
Sizing the Aquarium	18
The stand	21
Aquarium Substrates	22
Other requirements	25
Artificial Sea Salts	25
Raw or treated water	31
Filtration Techniques	35
Biological Filtration	37
Traditional Methods	43
Newer Methods	46
Canister Filters	46
Box or Outside Filters	53
Corner Overflow Filters	55
Trickle Filters General	57
The filter itself	62
Advanced Trickle Filters	69
Trickle Filter Biological Media	70
Aeration of the Media	75
Dripe Plate Fabrication	76
Space for other media	78
Built-in Protein Skimmer	79
Min. Biological Surface area	81
Calculating size of chamber	88
Denitriying Filters	92
Denitrators	93
Compounds to lower nitrates	97
Instrumentation for the Reef	101
pH meters and controllers	104
Electrodes	109
Calibrating Electrodes	111
Redox Meters and Electrodes	116
Conductivity controllers	117
Combination Controllers	118
Temperature Controllers	118
Dissolved Oxygen Meters	120
Carbon Dioxide Diffusion	121
Manual CO2 Diffusion	122
Automated CO2 Diffusion	127
Dosing Pumps	129
Water Changes	133
Manual Water Changes	136
Automatic Water Changes	138
Water Quality Parameters	143
Alkalinity	147
Arsenic	151
Boron	152
Chlorine	153
Copper	154
Cyanide	156
Mercury	157
Phenol	157
Phtalate Esters	158
Lead	158
Pesticides	158
Airborne Pollution	159
Carbon Dioxide	160
Nicotine	161
Iron	162
Permanganates	162
Hydrogen Sulfide	163
Nitrates	165
Phosphates	169
Water Flow in the Reef Tank	171
Designing the water flow	176
Fittings and Valves	183
Testing the Water	195
Suggested Values	196
Carbon dioxide	198
Phosphates	200
Ozone and Ozonizers	202
Copper	207
Carbonate hardness	208
Dissolved Oygen	210
Ammonia	213

Nitrite	214	Lighting Requirements	276
Nitrate and Nitrogen nitrate	215	Remarks on installation	278
Salinity, Specific gravity	218	Conclusion	279
Pre-treating the water	219	Ozone	281
Reverse Osmosis	221	When should you use it	282
Deionizers	223	How is it produced	282
Activated Carbon	225	Injecting Ozone	284
Tangential flow filters	226	Using Redox controllers	286
Laboratory Water tests	228	Conclusion on ozone	289
Maintenance and Husbandry	231	Protein Skimmers	289
Redox Potential	241	Types of skimmers	290
Definition	241	Operating the skimmer	291
Redox Equipment types	243	Reactors	295
Measuring Redox Potential	247	Oxygen Reactor	297
What lowers the redox	250	Ozone Reactor	298
Increasing the redox	252	Carbon dioxide reactor	298
Protein Skimmers	252	Molecular absorption reactor	300
Permanganates	254	Carbon reactor for air	301
Ozone	255	Carbon rector for water	301
Iodine	255	X-nitrate reactor	301
Suggested redox levels	256	KH-reactor	302
Redox Chart	257	Kalkwasser reactor	302
Working with redox levels	258	The Algae	305
Influencing the redox	261	Micro-Algae	308
Heating and Cooling the tank	263	Macro-Algae	311
Where does heat come from	266	Symbiotic Algae	313
Heater Types	267	A last word	316
Cooling Units	269	Free catalog	317
Lighting over the Reef Tank	271	Marine Reef subscription	317
Introduction	271	Supplements order form	318